"As a Christian educator, I have witnessed the unrelenting demands of curriculum and standardization. Patrick Manning invites us into a necessary countercultural rhythm—a scholarly retreat into the proposed 'desert' of the classroom. With the precision of a theologian and the pedagogical acuity of a seasoned instructor, Manning synthesizes centuries of monastic insight with contemporary research on contemplative learning, demonstrating that true epistemic growth flourishes in those intentional pauses of reflection. His work charts a clear course for integrating ancient practices of *lectio divina*, prayerful silence, and communal stillness within modern classrooms, thereby cultivating not only intellectual rigor but spiritual wisdom. *Be Still and Know* is indispensable reading for any educator who believes that formation of the whole person—mind, heart, and spirit—must be at the heart of our academic enterprise."

—Greg Bottaro
CatholicPsych Institute

"Who among us doesn't yearn for wisdom, peace, order, and love? Patrick Manning's *Be Still and Know* offers a practical framework for reimagining and gently restructuring our frenzied days to reap those things. He offers sustainable practices that help readers lean into creating lives that are richly full, but never frantically busy. Reading this book the first time was a soothing, robust conversation with great hearts, minds, and spirits from many centuries and regions, presented in humane, manageable segments of time. I will be revisiting this book often, striving to become a modern contemplative and practicing until I get it right."

—Karen Eifler
Collegium

"Our capacity to learn depends on our ability to attend to what puzzles and perplexes us. That is why distraction's diminishment of attention is so disastrous for education. In this timely book, Manning reintroduces us to pedagogical treasures buried in ancient disciplines of contemplation. At once visionary and concrete, this book does something remarkable: it speaks to an urgent need by inviting us to non-anxious rest as the fount of learning."

—James K. A. Smith
Calvin University

"Patrick Manning's *Be Still and Know: Contemplative Practices for Christian Schools and Educators* fills an important gap in literature related to contemplation and education. Drawing from the richness of Christian tradition, Manning presents a holistic vision of contemplative life as related to the very places and spaces of the educational setting: from classroom to various departmental meetings. Manning's presentation is accompanied by exercises intended to facilitate appropriation of a contemplative disposition into one's teaching. This book would be a great read for any educator, from primary to collegiate, interested in leading a contemplative revolution in the school."

—Timothy P. O'Malley
University of Notre Dame

"Drawing from the wisdom of the Christian tradition, Patrick Manning reminds us of the one thing needful in education—the love of God. He offers simple practices, gestures, and habits by which to cull distraction and attend instead to God and our learning community. I recommend this book as essential reading for faculty and teachers at the beginning of the school year."

—Jessica Hooten Wilson
Pepperdine University

Be Still and Know

Contemplative Practices for Christian Schools and Educators

Patrick R. Manning

WILLIAM B. EERDMANS PUBLISHING COMPANY
GRAND RAPIDS, MICHIGAN

Wm. B. Eerdmans Publishing Co.
2006 44th Street SE, Grand Rapids, MI 49508
www.eerdmans.com

Published 2025
Printed in the United States of America

31 30 29 28 27 26 25 1 2 3 4 5 6 7

ISBN 978-0-8028-8512-8

Library of Congress Cataloging-in-Publication Data

A catalog record for this book is available from the Library of Congress.

The images in this book are courtesy of Seton Hall University. Photographs are by Brian Kutner.

Unless otherwise noted, Scripture quotations are taken from the New Revised Standard Version of the Bible.

For the Contemplative Pedagogy Fellows
at Seton Hall University:

Paula Alexander
Kelly Goedert
Kate Hinic
Angela Klaus
Grace May
Meryl Picard
Jon Radwan
Lisa Rose-Wiles
Kelly Shea
Bonnie Sturm
Chad Thralls
Ruth Tsuria
Deb Zinicola

In gratitude for your dedication, openness, and generosity of spirit. Our time together has taught me the meaning of learning community and shown me how beautiful and transformative such a community can be.

Contents

Foreword

I've been trying for years now to create at least some learning tasks in every education course that generate a sensation something like the experience of striding off the end of a moving walkway in an airport, the brisk forward glide suddenly arrested, the center of gravity shifted, the legs momentarily less certain that they know how to walk. One of those tasks simply involves assigning a thoughtful, evocative reading (lately I have used a chapter from Parker Palmer's writings about teaching) in the third week of the semester, and then assigning the same chapter in the ninth week of the semester. I ask students to read it again and journal about the experience.

Students' responses have been fascinating. Some find profound ways of reengaging with the material. Some seem nonplussed by the exercise. *I already have notes on the main points from last time*, they comment. *What could I be finding out this time if there is no new information?* That is an excellent question. *I found myself speeding up and skim-reading*, others confess. *I used to love reading*, one reflected, *but the forced quantity of text assigned to me during a college semester has eroded that in favor of just getting the task done.*

As we talk through their responses in class, I tell them that the assigned chapter is one that I have read quite a few times, yet one that I still find worth reading again. I reread it not because I hope the words have changed, but because I am not sure whether I have changed.

There are truths in the chapter that I am not sure I have quite learned how to obey in my own daily work of teaching. I come back to the text not for more news but in a fresh attempt to let it teach me.

It is my impression having done this a few times now that those who are not quite sure what to do with the rereading exercise include a good share of high-achieving students. Some will confess that what they have internalized from their education is a drive toward the kind of success beloved of life hacks gurus, a maximizing of efficiency and productivity that slays each task to make space for the next in a determined ascent of the mountain of continuous achievement. They have rarely if ever been asked to return to a past reading. The explicit request to slow down and reflect causes a stutter step, an off-balance moment that tells us something about our formation and invites us to reflect on why reflection would so unbalance us.

Patrick Manning offers us here a valuable guide to such moments. Rather than surfing the latest findings, he digs deep into the Christian past, drawing upon a long and rich tradition of reflection and experiment in the realm of contemplation and its place in our devotion and our formation. He invites us to draw from the Christian heritage not just beliefs to debate, but postures to inhabit and disciplines to test. He invites us to change our stride.

Such a move risks triggering initial anxiety among teachers, who are themselves well trained to move at a determined pace, to cover ground, to take every minute hostage. Does risking a sideways glance at the contemplative tradition imply canceling the curriculum, skipping required content, shirking necessary learning goals, and trying to turn the classroom into a monastery? Like someone complaining they can't eat salads because they are too full after finishing the burger and fries, many of us will immediately wonder if any concession to contemplative practices is at all compatible with our activist drive and demanding professional obligations.

Manning takes the wise path here, not asking us to tear it all down and start new schools in the desert, but inviting us to reflect in concrete, practical ways on how specific, modest changes might change the tone and texture of schooling, leaving the regular learning goals in place but seeking a mode of engagement that is healthier for students' (and teachers'!) minds and spirits and perhaps a little closer to peace, hope, and joy. I recommend reading it, and then choosing a chapter and rereading it, riding out the momentary lurch, settling into a gait that might prove more comfortable after all, and exploring fresh pathways to fruitful learning.

David I. Smith
Calvin University

Prologue

Two thousand years ago a diverse group of people in Palestine encountered something or rather Someone who utterly transformed their lives. We see a trace of this encounter in these words from the First Letter of John:

> We declare to you what was from the beginning,
> what we have heard,
> what we have seen with our eyes,
> what we have looked at and touched with our hands,
> concerning the word of life—
> this life was revealed,
> and we have seen it and testify to it,
> and declare to you the eternal life that was with the
> Father and was revealed to us—
> we declare to you what we have seen and heard
> so that you also may have fellowship with us;
> and truly our fellowship is with the Father and with his
> Son Jesus Christ.
> We are writing these things so that our joy may be
> complete.
>
> (1 John 1:1–4)

These people encountered—saw, heard, touched—a man they were convinced was the very Word of God become flesh. In his presence, they experienced eternal life within earthly time. That encounter gave their lives new meaning and depth as well as an abiding sense of peace and joy that persisted even in the face of suffering. The Christian faith, insofar as it is a living reality and not merely an ossified institution, is the reverberation of that human encounter with the incarnate Word around the world and down through the centuries. It is the possibility of new encounters with this Mystery whenever persons open themselves up to God's presence in their lives.

Like the first Christians, we have experienced something that has transformed our lives. When I say "we," I refer to a community of educators who are endeavoring to go about our work in such a way that we intentionally remain open to the presence of the Mystery in our schools, our students, and ourselves. What I write in the following pages reflects not only my own thoughts and experiences but also those of this wider community of which I have been blessed to be a part. I have drawn together the collective wisdom of this community in this book because we feel compelled to share what we have experienced. As a result of approaching our work in a more contemplative manner, we have become better teachers and human beings, more connected to our students and to each other, less anxious and more grateful, peaceful, and joyful. And we want to share our joy with you.

It is my hope that you, dear reader, will experience something of what we have experienced, perhaps on account of what you find in these pages. Indeed, I have written these things with the explicit intention of facilitating such an experience, of creating opportunities for others to see, hear, and feel what it is like to live and work with an abiding awareness of God's presence. But words are only ever signs pointing to a fuller, ultimately indescribable and mysterious reality. Each of us must encounter this reality for ourselves. So I encourage you to enter into this book with eyes, mind, and heart open and to be alert to the presence of the Mystery behind these words.

Our encounter with this Mystery has changed everything. I invite you now to come and see for yourself.

Introduction

The Challenges and Promise of Christian Education Today

"You are worried and distracted by many things; there is need of only one thing" (Luke 10:41–42). Might these words, initially spoken to an overburdened hostess two thousand years ago, hold wisdom for Christian educators today?

As teachers, professors, school leaders, and administrators, we are worried and distracted by many things. We worry about our students—students like Justin, who missed the first two weeks of my freshman year core course and did not respond to the many emails I sent trying to find out what was going on. He finally showed up at class with none of the required materials and no assignments completed. Through several conversations, it became apparent that Justin was dealing with significant challenges in his home life and with his mental health. After several weeks of trying to catch up, he decided (prudently) to drop the course. The hole he had dug was too deep to climb out of. Sadly, even picking up the signed course withdrawal form proved too daunting a task, even though failing to do so cost Justin $2,000.

We are worried for our schools. Hundreds of Christian elementary and high schools have closed in recent decades. More than two dozen Christian colleges have shut their doors since 2016. Many of those schools, like Findlandia University, in Hancock, Michigan, had storied histories. Findlandia was founded in 1896 by the Finnish Evangelical Lutheran Church of America to serve Finnish immigrants laboring in local copper and lumber industries. Like many other religiously affiliated institutions, it had watched its enrollment slipping for several years. When the pandemic struck, it did not have the financial resources to ride out the storm. Even though the pandemic has subsided, many schools are not out of the woods yet. With the demographic cliff now upon us, many more closures are almost certainly over the horizon.

Beyond the schools we serve, we are worried for the faith traditions that have been for us a source of meaning, hope, and community. The declining enrollment in our schools parallels declining participation in our church communities. Today it is rare that I talk with a parent whose grown children are all practicing the faith. Choking back tears and battling with feelings of shame, they talk about everything they did to raise their children in the faith—praying together, attending worship together, sacrificing to send them to Christian schools—and the various paths these young people have taken walking away from the church. These conversations are haunted by lurking fears that our faith traditions will not survive the coming generation and that the young people we love will wander through life like vagabonds in search of a home they will never find.

All of this takes a toll on teachers and school leaders. We are constantly asked to do more to support our students—more accommodations, more emotional support, more communication with parents—and seldom provided with more resources to support this additional work. There never seems to be enough time in the day to do everything that needs to be done. Having witnessed widespread layoffs, shrinking budgets, and school closings, many of us worry for our jobs. We have seen colleagues reach their breaking point and leave their positions at the school. We may have thought about leaving ourselves. We are fatigued, stressed out, and desperate for relief.

What Matters Most

The challenges we face in Christian schools are serious and many. There is no denying that. However, we always have abundant cause for hope. What would you say if I told you that there are largely untapped resources in our Christian tradition that can help us address our students' current challenges with learning and mental health? Or if I told you that utilizing these resources will also lead your students into deeper relationships with God and with other people? If people knew that the students in your school were thriving academically, mentally, socially, and spiritually, don't you think enrollment would be less of a concern? Well, these resources do in fact exist. That is the reason I have written this book.

But before getting into the specifics of this wisdom from our Christian tradition, we need to get clear on one thing. There is a problem even more fundamental than any of the challenges mentioned above. The greatest present danger for Christian schools is being distracted by these many challenges and losing sight of the one necessary thing. Disoriented by the storm of concerns swirling around us, we can lose sight of who we are and what our purpose is. How we answer these questions about identity and purpose (or fail to do so) determines the state of our schools and the quality of the education we give our students. It is crucial that Christian educators get clear on these two matters, which will be at the heart of our explorations in this book.

So, who are we? And why do our Christian schools exist? The answer to these two questions is the same. Love.

It is upon this truth that all the rest hinges. "God is love" (1 John 1), and, as beings formed in God's image and likeness, we too are created to be love. God desires that we share in the same life of abundance enjoyed by the Trinity (John 10:10). In the words of Irenaeus, "The glory of God is man fully alive."[1] To become the person God wants us to be is to activate our human (and potentially divine) capacities to the fullest possible degree. The saints, past and present, are proof of this. People such as Saint Benedict of Nursia, Saint Ignatius of Loyola,

1. Irenaeus of Lyons, *Against Heresies* 4.20.7, in *Ante-Nicene Fathers*, vol. 1, ed. Alexander Roberts, James Donaldson, and A. Cleveland Coxe (Buffalo: Christian Literature Publishing Co., 1885). Here I use the translation of John Paul II.

and Thomas Merton, who are among the guides we will meet in this book, encountered and abided in the divine presence within and all around them, thereby tapping into an inexhaustible wellspring of energy, peace, joy, and gratitude. To be fully human is to live in love, and there is no more desirable condition than this.[2]

Unfortunately, we modern people do not know ourselves. We live in an age of many distractions. Enraptured with the pleasures and entertainment afforded by contemporary culture, we dart off in pursuit of these things, confusing the quick dopamine hit they offer for real happiness. Over time we internalize a lie constantly insinuated in advertisements, music lyrics, and social interactions that our value and happiness as human beings depend on what we acquire and achieve. Having forgotten who we truly are, we carry the constant burden of constructing our own identity and creating meaning and purpose for our own lives. This burden and the deception behind it have everything to do with the historic levels of anxiety, depression, and loneliness that we are currently experiencing, especially by our young people. We have forsaken our true identity and with it our birthright to peace, belonging, and beatitude.

Finding Our Way Again

Is there a way for us contemporary people to rediscover ourselves and reclaim the lives of abundance that God wants for us? We may find a hint if we stick with Irenaeus a little longer. "The glory of God is man fully alive and," he adds, "the life of man consists in beholding God." The fullness of life is not attained through human efforts but rather by resting in God, not by achieving something but rather by receiving

2. Besides being enjoyable for its own sake, enjoying loving, supportive relationships contributes to better health and higher levels of happiness. See Robert Waldinger and Marc Schulz, *The Good Life: Lessons from the World's Longest Scientific Study of Happiness* (New York: Simon & Schuster, 2023); Lisa Miller, *The Awakened Brain: The New Science of Spirituality and Our Quest for an Inspired Life* (New York: Random House, 2021).

Someone. The Christian tradition has a word for this receptivity to God's self-gift, and that word is "contemplation."

Contemplation means something different in the Christian tradition than it does in popular usage, where it commonly denotes thinking deeply about something. In the traditional Christian sense (as in the writings of Teresa of Ávila, John of the Cross, and others), it signifies a passive form of prayer that transcends active speaking and thinking. It is God's gift of God's self and therefore cannot be reduced to a certain technique. Contemplation is simply resting in God's loving presence. Thomas Merton, perhaps the most famous of contemporary contemplatives, describes contemplation as the highest expression of a human being's intellectual and spiritual life. "It is that life itself, fully awake, fully active, fully aware that it is alive."[3] It is wonder at the sacredness of life and of all being and awareness of the reality at the source of it all.

Although the word "contemplation" may smack of something ethereal, its effects are quite concrete. Once we find ourselves enveloped in God's unsurpassing love, it transforms all the rest of life (although the transformation may be gradual). In the words of a poem attributed to Father Pedro Arrupe:

> It will decide
> what will get you out of bed in the morning,
> what you do with your evenings,
> how you spend your weekends,
> what you read, whom you know,
> what breaks your heart,
> and what amazes you with joy and gratitude.[4]

3. Thomas Merton, *New Seeds of Contemplation* (New York: New Directions, 2007), 1.

4. Attributed to Fr. Pedro Arrupe, SJ, quoted in *Finding God in All Things: A Marquette Prayer Book* (Milwaukee: Marquette University Press, 2009). Used with kind permission from Marquette University, ©2009.

It will even decide how we go about our work and social lives. On this note, Rowan Williams, the former archbishop of Canterbury, argues that nothing is more necessary for the world today:

> Contemplation is very far from being just one kind of thing that Christians do: it is the key to prayer, liturgy, art and ethics, the key to the essence of a renewed humanity that is capable of seeing the world and other subjects in the world with freedom—freedom from self-oriented, acquisitive habits and the distorted understanding that comes from them. To put it boldly, contemplation is the only ultimate answer to the unreal and insane world that our financial systems and our advertising culture and our chaotic and unexamined emotions encourage us to inhabit. To learn contemplative practice is to learn what we need so as to live truthfully and honestly and lovingly.[5]

If Williams is right to assert that contemplation is the key to a renewed humanity and society, as I believe he is, that is because to enter into contemplation is to return to our deepest selves. When we turn to the presence of Mystery within ourselves, we encounter the true Source of our being and identity. Coming to know ourselves in the God who sustains us, we are freed from the burden of creating an identity and meaning for ourselves and from all the anxiety that comes with that impossible task. Different people have different capacities for contemplative prayer. Nevertheless, we all share the same vocation to contemplation. To enter heaven is to enter into a state of perpetual contemplation, otherwise known as the beatific vision. All of life—including Christian education—should be a preparation for this. After all, if love is the key to our fulfillment as human beings, should not growth in love be at the heart of the educational enterprise? What is more crucial to a human being's formation than this?

5. Rowan Williams, "Address to the Roman Synod of Bishops," Vatican City, October 11, 2012, https://tinyurl.com/4wyetnzk.

A Vision for Thriving Christian Schools

I have been hinting that the Christian contemplative tradition has something important to say about the work of education. Indeed, how we understand ourselves as human beings determines our educational aims and methods. As long as human beings have been engaged in the work of education, an understanding of humans' spiritual nature has undergirded that endeavor. As Mark Schwehn observes, "Whether we look to the Platonic Academy or to the teachers of ancient Israel or to St. Augustine at Cassiciacum or to the medieval University . . . we find learning flourishes in communities formed by the conscious practice of spiritual virtues."[6] However, a change has taken place in the world (and the schools) around us. Enraptured with the power of modern technology and the comforts and entertainment of modern culture, we have grown inattentive to the spiritual dimension of our being and our hearts' deepest desires. This shift is evident in our educational systems. Rather than nurturing students in the fullness of their humanity, our modern schools train them for something much narrower and less fulfilling, namely, for fulfilling their role as producers and consumers in society. We are educating people to be less rather than more human.

Christian schools are called to something more. For the better part of two thousand years, Christian schools have been sites of cultural renewal and human transformation. Even though many are struggling at present, we have the resources at our disposal to reclaim this heritage. Our schools can be places where young people not only gain skills and credentials for their future careers but also, and more importantly, grow into people who live out of a sense of connectedness with their Creator and all of creation; who nurture loving, compassionate relationships with others; who speak and act with wisdom; who confidently and graciously put their gifts at the service of their

6. Mark R. Schwehn, *Exiles from Eden: Religion and the Academic Vocation in America* (New York: Oxford University Press, 1993), 45.

communities; and who bring peace into the situations in which they find themselves. In short, our schools can be places where future generations grow into beings who are fully alive. If we are true to this vision and calling, we will be less tempted to follow secular cultural and educational trends and more emboldened to provide schools where the curriculum, environment, and personal interactions help students to recognize and receive God's love, awaken them to their full human potential, and prepare them to live into their divine calling. We have the resources within our Christian tradition to realize this vision. We need only remember and recommit to them.

My hope is that this book will help us to remember. In these pages, I make the case for recovering our heritage of contemplation in our Christian schools. The time is ripe. Teachers are burned out and desperate for support. Students are hungry for meaning, depth, and peace of mind. School leaders are looking for ways to strengthen their schools' identity and distinctiveness. Ironically, many secular educators, students, researchers, and mental health professionals have recently discovered the numerous benefits of contemplative educational practices for student learning, mental and physical health, and interpersonal relating. These are powerful, proven means for addressing some of the biggest educational challenges of our day.

The fact that non-Christians are discovering and using them does not make Christian contemplative practices any less Christian. These practices have the potential to bring us back to our deepest Christian identity when we understand and practice them as did our predecessors in faith. While the focus of this book is Christian contemplative practices, I will also consider practices that are not explicitly Christian but are nevertheless consistent with Christian faith (for example, napping and eating mindfully). I write out of my own Roman Catholic tradition, in which practices of contemplation have been particularly well developed (if not always widely practiced), but I do so in dialogue with Protestant and Orthodox sources, and I write for educators of all Christian traditions. While my focus in this book is the Christian school context, Christian educators in other contexts (public schools, congregations, etc.) will likely also find much that is of interest.

I shall expound upon the benefits of contemplative practices in due course, and I expect that seeing these benefits will alleviate readers' concerns that taking a more contemplative approach in our schools will make the education there less rigorous. However, this book is not primarily about the benefits these practices offer for learning and mental health. For us as Christians, these benefits are of secondary importance. What is primary is nurturing human persons in their inner depths wherefrom they are constantly generated by the Mystery who abides within them. This hidden Source is the secret to the effectiveness of Christian contemplative practices for learning, well-being, and relating. We Christian educators should be the first to recognize this. Even if we have been slow to recognize it up to this point, the yearnings of our students and the work of our secular colleagues are pointing us back to it now.

I am convinced that if Christian schools are faithful to their purpose of forming people in love, so many of the challenges currently facing them will work themselves out. Why am I so confident? Because Jesus said, "Strive first for the kingdom of God and his righteousness, and all these things will be given to you as well" (Matt. 6:33). The true purpose of our Christian schools is to address the deepest yearnings of the human heart. This is the power of Christianity. This is what has drawn people back to the faith over and over again despite all the scandals and vicissitudes in the history of the church, and the moment is ripe for it to happen again. The needs of our students are calling us back to our roots, identity, and charisms, beckoning us to reach into the storeroom of the Christian tradition and bring forth gifts for those who are eager for something good and life-giving.

And so I invite you, dear reader, to come and see what life can be like in our schools when we live into this promise. In the following chapters, we will walk through a day in the life of a school wherein we experience time, space, people, objects, and activities in a different way. Our journey will take us into the classroom (chapter 3), the conference room (chapter 4), the study hall (chapter 5), and the places where we recreate and rest (chapter 6). In each place we will find ourselves in the presence of our loving God and explore practices and wisdom for engaging each aspect of our work and rest in our schools in a more contemplative manner. I emphasize that this will be an experience, not merely an intellectual examination of these contemplative practices. We do not understand these things by being told; we understand by entering into them.

We are also helped by following guides who have walked this path before us. Jesus invited his disciples to "come and see" (John 1:39). His disciples invited others to do likewise, and so on through the ages until the present. Therefore, before we enter these different spaces of the school, we will first walk down the ancient paths trod by our predecessors in faith so we can learn from them what contemplation is and what it has to do with the work of education.[7]

7. Readers who are eager to get to the practical details may wish to skip chapter 1 and jump directly to chapter 2.

1

The Roots

Christianity's Contemplative Tradition

The prophet Jeremiah once announced to the people of Israel:

> Thus says the LORD:
> Stand at the crossroads, and look,
> and ask for the ancient paths,
> where the good way lies; and walk in it,
> and find rest for your souls. (Jer. 6:16)

Like them, we stand at a crossroads today. We face important decisions, not only about the future of our country, the environment, and technology, but also about our religious traditions. Arriving at this spiritual crossroads with many possible paths open to them, young people are abandoning the Way that generations of their ancestors walked in before them. Christian educators, too, stand at a crossroads. Confronted with declining enrollments, pervasive (and often invasive) technology, and new student needs, we must discern which path will lead to the best future for our schools. Should we imitate the methods of secular schools in order to compete for students, or should we recommit to the traditional way of doing things? Should we embrace the new technology in our schools or attempt to protect a different kind of space? Is it all too much? Should we simply shut our doors? The challenges are great, and the complexity of our situation can be overwhelming. How can we know the best way forward?

Rediscovering the Ancient Paths

The words of Jeremiah quoted above have spoken wisdom to the people of God for generations and, I believe, speak wisdom to us today. We who stand at these crossroads and face these challenges are not without help. Our ancestors in faith confronted challenges not so different from those we confront today. Guided by the Holy Spirit, they responded to these challenges and passed on their wisdom, which now comes to us in the form of a two-thousand-year-old tradition that transcends our personal experience and capacities and even educational "best practices." We do not have to go it alone. We can learn from those who have gone before us. We can once again walk in these ancient paths and find rest for our souls.

Although contemporary research largely confirms the wisdom of what Christians have done for centuries, we ought to be grounded in something deeper than current research, which, though valuable, has yet to pass the test of time. I will engage this research in neuroscience, psychology, education, and contemplative practices in later chapters, but we will begin our explorations by considering the wisdom and history of the Christian contemplative tradition. To be clear, this book is not a work of history. I delve into Christian history here for the very particular purpose of excavating a piece of our Christian heritage that many have forgotten but which holds great potential for contemporary Christian schools. In so doing I hope to accomplish two things: first, to demonstrate that contemplative practices have deep roots in Christianity and are not merely imports from Eastern religions, and, second, to show how these practices have nurtured life and wholeness in Christians throughout history and stand to do the same for us today.

Although many contemporary Christians know little about Christianity's contemplative tradition, it is no more peripheral to Christianity than it is to our humanity. In a sense, contemplation is the heart and wellspring of the Christian tradition.[1] Christianity is vibrant, living tradition to the extent that its teachings, practices, and community flow from a participation in the inner life of the Trinity. Contemplation is the name Christianity gives to this participation. Included among these teachings, practices, and community is the church's work of education. This work of education grew out of Christians' desire to know God more deeply and to abide in the divine Mystery.

If Christian schools and Christianity in general have hemorrhaged members in recent years, it is largely because we have lost contact with this vital source. Cut off from the vine and the wellspring, the branches have withered. We need to find our way back to the wellspring, to rediscover the old ways. So, without further ado, let us now direct our feet down these ancient paths.

The One Necessary Thing

We have all had moments—too few and too fleeting—when we felt truly alive, when we glimpsed how good life can be. These are the moments we live for. Recalling these experiences in our own lives, we have some sense of what it was like for those men and women who encountered Jesus of Nazareth two thousand years ago. There must have been something irresistibly attractive about this man, so much so that these people left behind their families, homes, and occupations to follow after him. The story of the postresurrection encounter on the road to Emmaus captures the effect Jesus had on people. "Were not our hearts burning within us while he was talking to us on the road?" say

1. I maintain that abiding in God's love (i.e., contemplation) is the heart of the Christian life while acknowledging that specific contemplative practices and writings have historically been a more significant part of Catholic and Orthodox traditions than they have in Protestantism. While I will draw most heavily upon Catholic and Orthodox sources in this chapter, my intention is to present this contemplative tradition as the common heritage of all Christians.

the two disciples (Luke 24:32). Those who encountered Jesus sensed in him the thing they had always been seeking, the thing we all seek—fullness of life (John 10:10). What did he teach them about the fullness of life? Apparently so many things that all the books in the world could not contain them (John 21:25). For our purposes here, we will focus on just a few of the most essential, beginning with *the* most essential.

We all seek happiness, and we seek it in many different things—in pleasure, in career success, in the esteem of others, in nice cars, homes, and vacations. However, Jesus tells us that there is only one thing necessary for fullness of life. He shared this secret once when he and his disciples were gathered in the home of his friends Mary and Martha. Martha was trying to be a good host and was probably a bit overwhelmed by the crowd. Meanwhile her sister Mary was sitting at Jesus's feet listening to him. Eventually Martha erupted and demanded that Jesus tell Mary to help her. Jesus responded, "Martha, Martha, you are worried and distracted by many things; there is need of only one thing. Mary has chosen the better part, which will not be taken away from her" (Luke 10:41–42). Mary had found what most of us spend our whole lives seeking. Many go to their graves without ever finding it. What did she figure out? How do we achieve fullness of life? What this story suggests is that it is not something we can achieve at all. Jesus pointed Martha, who is full of activity, to her sister Mary, who seems to be doing nothing. She is simply sitting. Listening. Resting with Jesus.

Elusive though it seems, what Mary found is available to us at all times. Jesus taught his disciples how to access it:

> "Whenever you pray, go into your [inner] room and shut the door and pray to your Father who is in secret; and your Father who sees in secret will reward you. When you are praying, do not heap up empty phrases as the Gentiles do; for they think that they will be heard because of their many words. Do not be like them, for your Father knows what you need before you ask him." (Matt. 6:6–8)

When we take these instructions in context with Jesus's other teachings, it seems Jesus meant to tell us something more than the best location for prayer. Aphrahat the Persian, a fourth-century Christian, interprets Jesus's teaching this way: The inner room is the heart. The door is the mouth. If we want to rest in Christ and his peace, we should be quiet and seek him in our hearts.[2]

We see Jesus himself doing this constantly in the Gospels, more often than not retreating to solitary, wild places (see Mark 1:35; Matt. 14:23; Luke 5:16; 6:12). This time Jesus spent in his own "inner room" abiding with his Father sustained him in his ministry. This constant union was the source of his peace, joy, authority, and power, as is particularly evident during his temptation in the wilderness (Matt. 4:1–11; Mark 1:12–13; Luke 4:1–13). When repeatedly assaulted by Satan, Jesus remains united with the Father, repelling the devil's attacks with God's words in Scripture. He has nothing to fear because he is secure in the Father's love. Even later, when he is at the height of his passion, Jesus is able to entrust himself into the Father's hands (Luke 23:46).

As mortal creatures, ours is an inherently vulnerable existence, and our anxiety for our existence has been on full display from the very beginning (see Gen. 3). When Jesus tells his disciples, "Do not be afraid" (Matt. 10:31; Luke 12:32) or "Do not worry" (Matt. 6:25; John 14:27), he speaks as one who knows full well the anxieties of being human. He assures us that, even in the midst of the trials and tribulations of life, we can find peace by abiding in prayer with our Father from whom we receive our very life. God is present to us at all times. When Jesus ascended to heaven, he promised his disciples that he would be with them always (Matt. 28:20) and, in fact, that it was better for them that he should go (John 16:7). How can that be? Saint

2. Aphrahat, "Demonstration IV, on Prayer," in *The Syriac Fathers on Prayer and the Spiritual Life*, trans. Sebastian Brock (Kalamazoo, MI: Cistercian Publications, 1987), 14.

Augustine suggests that Jesus departed from our sight that we might seek him and find him in our hearts where he always awaits us.[3]

Jesus had revealed the key to abiding in God's love everywhere and at all times. The foundation for Christian spirituality had been laid. Now the task for Jesus's followers was to build their lives upon this firm foundation, this one necessary thing.

Seeking Peace in the Desert

The mountaintop experience never lasts long. It didn't for Peter, James, and John when Jesus was transfigured before them. Once the vision has faded, we tend to settle back into what is easy and comfortable. We can even begin to doubt that the mountaintop experience ever happened. Jesus warned his disciples about this in the parable of the sower. When the seed of faith does not land in good soil, it lacks deep roots and withers.

Such was the threat to the fledgling Christian religion in the fourth century. For the first several centuries the followers of Jesus were a persecuted minority. In these circumstances, converting to Christianity was not a decision to be taken lightly. Christians had to believe their faith was worth dying for. However, the winds changed in 313 when the emperor Constantine legalized Christianity. This turn of events was certainly good for Christians, who no longer needed to fear for their lives, but it also created ulterior motives for professing to be Christian. Since Constantine himself identified as a Christian, being Christian suddenly became socially and politically advantageous. Christianity appeared to flourish, but there were many weeds among the wheat.

Today in the United States and Europe, many people are abandoning religious institutions they feel have been corrupted or otherwise fail to meet their spiritual needs. Not finding the fullness of life

3. Augustine, *Confessions* 4.12, trans. Henry Chadwick (Oxford: Oxford University Press, 1998).

they desire in the church, they seek it in alternative communities and spiritual practices and in nature. Something similar happened with the Christians of the third and fourth centuries. They had grown disenchanted with a Christianity that had become too comfortable and too easily aligned with political interests and agendas. Some of these Christians, rather than abandoning Christianity, sought to practice it in a purer form. Anthony of Egypt (ca. 250–355) was one such person. Around 270 AD Anthony was struck to the heart by a sermon on Matthew 19:21: "If you want to be perfect, go, sell what you have and give to the poor, and you will have treasures in heaven." In short order, Anthony sold all his possessions and left the city for the desert, where he would spend the rest of his days.[4]

Others soon followed him. A new expression of Christianity coalesced around Anthony in the Egyptian desert as well as in the regions of Syria and Palestine. Shortly after Anthony's death, one of his biographers, Saint Athanasius, wrote that the "desert had become a city."[5] Clearly something powerful was drawing these early Christians into the desert. They sought a peace and freedom that was hindered by the culture of the Roman Empire and the inauthentic versions of Christianity they experienced there. They found the noise of society stifling, so they left it behind in order to find God in the stillness of the desert. Once they arrived, however, they realized they could not escape noise and distraction simply by leaving the city. As the writings of the desert fathers and mothers attest, they continued to experience much noise and agitation within themselves. We moderns experience the same today. In the rare moments that we escape from the noise of the streets, our offices, and our schools and unplug from our devices, we find that our heads nevertheless remain full of noise.

4. Anthony made his retreat to the desert during a lull in Christian persecutions. Persecution would resume under Diocletian in 303 and end with the Edict of Milan in 313.

5. John Chryssavgis, *In the Heart of the Desert: The Spirituality of the Desert Fathers and Mothers*, rev. ed. (Bloomington, IN: World Wisdom, 2008), 15.

This inner noise can be even more agitating than the noise outside, so we tend to stay plugged in. The desert fathers, however, recognized that they could not achieve true peace by distracting themselves. Instead they strove for freedom from this inner turbulence (*apatheia*, as they called it) resulting in an interior stillness (or *hēsychia*).[6] They found their model for this inner work in Jesus's temptation in the wilderness. As contemplative author Father Martin Laird explains, "Jesus' own battle with thoughts becomes, then, the Christian foundation of the practice of contemplation: the quiet repetition of a scriptural phrase in order to keep the attention focused."[7] This spiritual practice became the heartbeat of the lives of the early desert fathers and mothers.

Clearly something was working because people continued to flood into the desert, drawn by the reputations of holy figures like Anthony, his student Macarius (ca. 300–ca. 391), and his student Evagrius (345–399). People would come to them begging, "Give me a word, Father," hoping for a ray of wisdom that would help them achieve something like the peacefulness and holiness of these elders.[8] When Evagrius made such a request of Macarius, for example, he received the following response:

> Secure the anchor rope to the rock and by the grace of God the ship will ride the devilish waves of this beguiling island sea. . . . The ship is your heart; keep guard over it. The rope is your mind; secure it to our Lord Jesus Christ, who is the rock. . . . Say with each breath, "Our Lord Jesus, have mercy on me."[9]

6. Evagrius Ponticus, one of the desert fathers, writes, "The [one who possesses] apatheia [dispassion] lives in tranquility without any fear of evil [tempting-thoughts]." Evagrius, *Scholia on Proverbs*, trans. Luke Dysinger, accessed November 1, 2024, https://tinyurl.com/k95y495u.

7. Martin Laird, *A Sunlit Absence: Silence, Awareness, and Contemplation* (Oxford: Oxford University Press, 2011), 13.

8. For examples, see Thomas Merton, *The Wisdom of the Desert: Sayings from the Desert Fathers of the Fourth Century* (Boston: Shambhala Publications, 2004).

9. Antoine Guillaumont, "The Jesus Prayer among the Monks of Egypt,"

This is one of the earliest recorded instances of a practice that eventually became known as the "Jesus Prayer" or the "prayer of the heart," which has now been in practice for over 1,600 years.

This practice of the "prayer of the heart" passed from Evagrius to Gregory of Nyssa (ca. 335–ca. 394), John Climacus (ca. 579–ca. 649), Maximus the Confessor (ca. 580–662), Symeon the New Theologian (ca. 949–1022), and others.[10] At the heart of this practice was the conviction that achieving interior freedom and union with Christ required guarding one's heart and remaining watchful of one's interior thoughts and feelings.[11] Take, for example, Symeon the New Theologian, who writes, "for someone who desires spiritual rebirth, the first step towards the light is to curtail the passions, that is to say, to guard the heart." He adds, "God asks only this of us, that our heart be purified through watchfulness."[12] In the eighteenth century, Nicodemus the Hagiorite and Macarius of Corinth compiled the written wisdom of these "hesychasts" into a volume known as the *Philokalia*, which eventually became the primary spiritual text for Eastern Orthodox churches, second in influence only to the Bible.

As more and more people moved to the desert and sought instruction from holy anchorites, this teaching and spiritual practice

---

Eastern Churches Review 6 (1974): 66–71, at 67. Note also the connection between breathing and prayer. Although Christians often assume that breathing techniques come from Eastern religions, this is one of many texts in which early Christians give attention to breathing as part of prayer. See Martin Laird, *Into the Silent Land: A Guide to the Christian Practice of Contemplation* (Oxford: Oxford University Press, 2006), 36–42, for examples.

10. Another classic albeit more recent literary embodiment of this tradition in Russia is *The Way of the Pilgrim*, which is available online at https://tinyurl.com/28tzpfv9.

11. Modern readers might be struck here by the similarity between this practice and contemporary mindfulness. For a discussion of how the two compare and differ, see Gregory Bottaro, *The Mindful Catholic: Finding God One Moment at a Time* (North Palm Beach, FL: Beacon Publishing, 2018).

12. Symeon the New Theologian, "The Three Methods of Prayer," in *The Philokalia: The Complete Text*, trans. G. E. H. Palmer, Philip Sherrard, and Kallistos Ware (London: Faber & Faber, 1998), 4:74–75.

became more formalized.[13] Students studied Scripture, the teachings of desert fathers and mothers, and sometimes philosophical writings. They learned skills of reading, interpretation, and shaping memory to support their spiritual work. In order to accommodate the growing crowds, Pachomius the Great (ca. 290–346), a student of Anthony's, began to organize houses where anchorites could live together. He also installed an *abba* (father) and *amma* (mother) to oversee each community and developed a "rule" to govern the life of these communities that included regulations regarding discipline, obedience, manual labor, silence, fasting, and set periods of prayer. The desert had become not only a city but also a school.

Contemplation Takes Root in the Monastery

Eventually the waves of people flooding to the deserts slowed to a trickle, but the impulse for stillness, rest, and intimacy with God remained an undercurrent in Christian history. It continued to emerge in new forms, like an underground reservoir bubbling up in unexpected places. It has been said that every time there is a renewal in the church, the desert is there. One such period of renewal occurred early in the sixth century. Much had changed in the world since Anthony and his followers fled Roman society for the desert. Rome had been sacked by the Visigoths in 410 and again by the Vandals in 455. The Roman Empire collapsed completely in 476. Society was in moral decay. John Henry Newman records that among the people of the time there was a common sense that "the world was too bad to mend, and . . . destruction was close upon it."[14] It was not so much that society

13. The Russian tradition of poustinia, retreating to a solitary cabin (or *pustyn*) to be alone with God in prayer, is another part of the legacy of desert monasticism in the East. More recently this practice was popularized in the West by Catherine Doherty's book *Poustinia: Encountering God in Silence, Solitude, and Prayer* (Combermere, ON: Madonna House Publications, 2000).

14. John Henry Newman, "The Benedictine Schools," in *A Benedictine Education*, ed. Christopher Fisher (Providence: Cluny Media, 2020), 61.

was ordered toward something anti-Christian as it was that all order had broken down.

This was the world of Benedict of Nursia (ca. 480–547), who in time would be recognized as the father of Western monasticism. Confronted with a society in total disarray and disappointed with his academic studies, Benedict retreated into the mountains east of Rome around the year 500. As had happened with Anthony, his reputation for holiness grew and many would-be disciples sought him out. After an initial failure in which one community of monks tried to poison him, Benedict founded thirteen monasteries and developed his famous rule to govern them.[15] In so doing, Benedict followed the model established by Pachomius's rule and the example of the desert fathers as it came to him through the writings of John Cassian (ca. 360–ca. 435).[16]

According to the rule Benedict set down, monastic life was ordered into set times for private and communal prayer, manual labor, spiritual reading, and rest. Writing about Benedict and his followers, Newman says, "Their object was rest and peace . . . their occupation was some work that was simple."[17] This simple work commonly consisted of cultivating the land and copying manuscripts. The peacefulness and orderliness of the Benedictines' lives proved highly attractive for the people of their time. Perhaps this is why the Rule of Benedict has emerged as the single most influential rule in the history of Western monasticism. The rule and the Benedictine way of life continue to attract many people today, who, like Benedict, are seeking peace and order in a time when these things are lacking in the wider society.[18]

15. An online version of the Rule of Benedict can be accessed here: https://tinyurl.com/yc7p48nr.

16. Cassian spent over a decade living among various desert fathers and reproduced his conversations with them in his book *The Conferences*, trans. Boniface Ramsey, OP (Mahwah, NJ: Paulist, 1997).

17. John Henry Newman, "The Mission of Saint Benedict," in Fisher, *A Benedictine Education*, 12.

18. This ongoing attraction is evident in the significant numbers of Christians who practice this way of life as Benedictine oblates.

Study was and is an important element in the Benedictine way of life. Like the desert fathers before him, Benedict recognized meditation on Scripture as an indispensable means of setting our hearts on God. However, where the desert monastics achieved this aim by memorizing lines of Scripture, Benedict emphasized meditation on the written Word of God. This Benedictine approach to reading Scripture came to be known as *lectio divina* (divine reading). As opposed to a more analytical approach, the purpose of *lectio divina* is to take the Scriptures into our hearts and be transformed from within by the inspired Word of God.[19] More important than reading a certain amount of text is listening attentively to God's voice in Scripture whenever we hear it. When we are seized by a particular word or phrase, we stop reading and dwell upon that word or phrase in our heart. The Carthusian monk Guigo II (1114–1193) later formalized the practice in four steps—*lectio* (slowly reading the text), *meditatio* (meditating upon a word or phrase), *oratio* (speaking with God about the text), and *contemplatio* (effortless resting in the Lord).[20]

Because Benedict's rule required all monks to study Scripture, those who could not read needed to be taught. So it was that primitive schools grew within the early Benedictine monasteries, as had happened in the desert communities of Egypt and Syria. As the Benedictine monasteries continued to attract more people, including children, the curriculum developed to include writing, singing (for Mass and the Divine Office), grammar, poetics, and rhetoric as well as reading of Scripture, church fathers like Saint Augustine, and philosophical and rhetorical texts.[21] This curriculum was the precur-

19. For more on the history and practice of *lectio divina*, see Michael Casey, *Sacred Reading: The Ancient Art of Lectio Divina* (Liguori, MO: Liguori/Triumph, 1996). We will explore educational uses of *lectio* in chapters 3 and 5.

20. Guigo II, *The Ladder of Monks: A Letter on the Contemplative Life and Twelve Meditations*, trans. Edmund Colledge and James Walsh (Kalamazoo, MI: Cistercian Publications, 1981). Available online at https://tinyurl.com/4fesyth6.

21. For a detailed examination of the medieval Benedictine curriculum and

sor of the curriculum later taught in the great medieval universities. Motivating the whole of the monastic curriculum, like monastic life in general, was the monks' "love of learning and the desire for God," to use Jean Leclercq's famous phrase.[22] This desire for God, the one necessary thing, was the passion and driving force in the lives of medieval monks. All the practices and learning of the monastery flowed from and aimed at that singular goal.

A Flowering of Religious Orders

For contemporary Christian educators trying to rediscover their roots, understanding the role of the Benedictines in the history of Christian education and in the contemplative tradition is vital. When the world of their time was crumbling around them, the Benedictines turned within to search for God, and in so doing discovered spiritual and intellectual resources that enabled them to preserve the learning of the past for future generations. The universities in which we study and the monasteries that keep the flame of prayer burning today are tributes to this Benedictine legacy.

Still, as important as the story of the Benedictines is, it is not the only story. The cast of the "theodrama" of salvation history is large. No one character dominates (aside from Jesus Christ, of course). Throughout history, God has raised up diverse saints and communities to meet the particular challenges and opportunities of each age. It is instructive to learn about these different religious communities, their charisms, and their approaches to education as we work to discern what is needed and what gifts we each bring to our Christian schools today. Although the contemplative tradition has come down

how it facilitated the ascent of the mind and heart to God, see Abbot Thomas Frerking's interpretative essay "Saint John Henry Newman on Benedictine Life and on Benedictine Schools," in Fisher, *A Benedictine Education*, 175–210.

22. Jean Leclercq, *The Love of Learning and the Desire for God: A Study of Monastic Culture*, trans. Catharine Misrahi (New York: Fordham University Press, 1961).

to us via numerous streams, I will focus here on two—the Dominicans and the Jesuits—whose distinctive styles of contemplation have shaped their respective approaches to education.[23]

By the time Dominic of Guzman was born in 1170, society had rebounded from the fall of the Roman Empire. The cities' populations were rapidly growing, and new economic systems were emerging. Cognizant of these social changes, Dominic saw the need for a new kind of religious order that would have greater mobility and flexibility than monastic orders like the Benedictines and Carthusians. This new order would have to keep pace with the active lives of contemporary people and engage them in more familiar terms, including preaching in the vernacular. The reemergence of bustling society also meant new distractions. Desiring to draw people back to what was true and good, Dominic founded his new order, the Order of Preachers (OP), dedicated to the salvation of souls. Because they needed to understand thoroughly what they were to preach, Dominic strongly emphasized study in the formation of his Dominicans. He sent them to the great universities of the day in Paris, Bologna, Palencia, Montpellier, and Oxford, where they established priories focused on study and preaching. Once again the imperative to study arose in support of the spiritual work of a religious order.

The Dominican approach to study is shaped by this spiritual and pastoral impetus in significant ways. For all their learnedness and intellectual rigor, Dominicans are quick to point out that the fullness of truth (*veritas*) is found in a person rather than in books or syllogisms. Jesus is "the way, and the truth, and the life" (John 14:6), and we cannot know the full truth apart from him. In this sense, contemplation—abiding in the Mystery of God—is the most important means of

23. The astute reader might note my omission of the Carmelites, a religious order with a strong emphasis on contemplation. This is not an oversight. I pass over the Carmelites here for the sake of focusing on religious orders that bring contemplation to bear on education more directly. Nonetheless, the insights of Carmelites like Teresa of Ávila and John of the Cross will appear throughout later chapters.

attaining to the truth. Dominicans thus conceive of their teaching and preaching as *contemplata aliis tradere* (sharing the fruits of contemplation with others).[24] Bound up with this way of thinking about teaching is an understanding of learning as a communal activity. Indeed, Dominicans regard the community itself as the primary source of teaching. This emphasis becomes concrete in the practice of *disputatio*, in which interlocutors engage in discussion and debate around difficult questions and issues, exploring multiple perspectives in the pursuit of truth. Dominicans find the inspiration for this practice in the story of when Dominic once stayed up all night conversing with and ultimately converting an innkeeper who had been confused by heretical Cathar teachings. This method of *disputatio* would later be enshrined in the writings of the most famous Dominican, Saint Thomas Aquinas.[25]

Not unlike the Benedictines, the Dominicans recognize the benefit of a balance of active labor (in this case, teaching and preaching), study, and prayer. The Dominicans, however, place a stronger emphasis on the active work of sharing the fruits of contemplation. As scholar Paul Philibert notes, when Dominicans think about contemplation, they are thinking more in terms of "complete self-investment in a way of living that is circumscribed by the word of God" than of certain acts of the mind.[26] This emphasis, deriving from Dominic's response to the needs of his time, accounts for the energy Dominicans subsequently demonstrated in founding schools around the world and producing an impressive body of scholarly work spanning many disciplines.[27]

24. Thomas Aquinas, *Summa Theologiae* II-II qu. 188, a. 6., Fathers of the English Dominican Province, trans., online edition (New Advent, 2017), https://tinyurl.com/3t6bsrb5.

25. Other notable Dominicans include Albertus Magnus, Meister Eckhart, Catherine of Siena, Yves Congar, and Gustavo Gutiérrez.

26. Paul Philibert, "Roman Catholic Prayer: The *Novum modi orandi sancti Dominici*," in *Contemplative Literature: A Comparative Sourcebook on Meditation and Contemplative Prayer*, ed. Louis Komjathy (Albany: SUNY Press, 2015), 526.

27. For a contemporary articulation of the gifts and principles of Domini-

Several centuries later, Saint Ignatius of Loyola (1491–1556) would respond to changing social and ecclesial needs in a similar manner, though the circumstances were quite different. Ignatius and his contemporaries lived through a period of breathtaking change. He was born the year before Christopher Columbus landed in North America and lived through the "age of discovery," during which time seafarers representing the European powers were opening up the New World. Their discoveries changed dramatically people's image of the world they lived in. Around the same time, the Reformation and Counter-Reformation were upending the Christian world. It is not overstating the matter to say that never in human history did so much change so dramatically and so fast—never, perhaps, until our own time.

As happened with Dominic, Ignatius became convinced that a new kind of religious order was needed. His military background influenced how he conceived the Society of Jesus, or the Jesuits, as they are more commonly known. Given the rapid pace of change in the world of his time, Ignatius saw a need for a religious order that could respond swiftly to papal directives. Practically, this meant that members of the Society of Jesus needed some degree of freedom from the encumbrances of "the cowl, the cloister, and the choir," that is, of ritual requirements and a formal rule.[28] Nevertheless, Ignatius recognized that it would be all the more important for his Jesuits to be anchored in Christ in the midst of their apostolic activity. That anchor was the Spiritual Exercises, a thirty-day retreat intended to help retreatants discern God's will in their lives.[29] All Jesuits undergo the full Spiritual Exercises two times during their formation, but they strive to remain "contemplative in the midst of action"[30] by more regular means as well. Every year they return to the Spiritual Exercises in

can education, see "A Vision in Service of Truth," accessed November 1, 2024, https://tinyurl.com/c46jav7z.

28. Newman, "The Mission of Saint Benedict," 197.

29. For more information on the Spiritual Exercises, see https://tinyurl.com/3fm6bf3f.

30. This phrase was coined by Jerónimo Nadal, one of Saint Ignatius's first companions.

an abridged form during an eight-day retreat. Every day Jesuits pray the "examen," a sort of examination of conscience (or consciousness) through which they review their day in order to be more aware of where God was present and where they may have failed to love.[31]

In addition to their missionary activity, the Jesuits have devoted tremendous energy to the work of education. Currently they maintain 28 colleges and universities in the United States and 189 around the world, in addition to many secondary schools. Through their schools, the Jesuits form students in key aspects of Ignatian spirituality such as "seeing God in all things," doing all things *ad majorem Dei gloriam* (for the greater glory of God), and being "men and women for others." The examen is commonly incorporated into the daily routine at Jesuit high schools, and students at Jesuit institutions often have the opportunity to undertake an adapted form of the Spiritual Exercises.

Peering back into the stories of the Benedictines, Dominicans, and Jesuits, we see three living streams through which the Christian contemplative tradition has come down through the ages and shaped the work of Christian schools. Abbot Thomas Frerking, OSB, summarizes the distinctive character of each order in this way: The Benedictines taught the contemplative life, the Dominicans taught "the active life of handing on to others the things contemplated," and the Jesuits taught the active life of being contemplative in the midst of action.[32] Each approach has yielded its distinctive gifts and fruits and comes with its particular challenges. As we will see in later chapters, these gifts have much to offer Christian schools today.

Losing Sight of the One Necessary Thing

The deepest identity of Christian education and the legacy bequeathed to us by these religious orders is learning grounded in

31. For more information on the examen, see "The Spiritual Exercises," Ignatian Spirituality, accessed November 1, 2024, https://tinyurl.com/3fm6bf3f.

32. Frerking, "Saint John Henry Newman," 199.

prayer, that is, learning as a form of contemplation. For the desert fathers, the early Benedictines, the Dominicans, and the Jesuits, learning was one piece of a whole way of life directed at deepening their knowledge and love of God. The knowledge they aspired to was not a purely theoretical or academic knowledge but rather the intimate knowledge that grows in the context of a relationship. They sought to know a Person, not merely information.

We heirs of this tradition must ask ourselves if we can say the same today. I think that, if we are being honest with ourselves, many of us cannot. In many cases, the Christian schools in which we work today bear only the faintest resemblance to the schools that the Benedictines, Dominicans, and Jesuits founded. Prayer in our schools, far from being central, is frequently a perfunctory matter like taking attendance or saying the Pledge of Allegiance. Where our ancestors in faith pursued communion with God with a determined single-mindedness, we are more often focused on meeting educational standards or increasing enrollment.

At this crucial moment in the history of Christian education, we need to pause and take stock: Is this who we want to be? Are we prioritizing the right things? If we acknowledge that we have gotten off track, we must ask ourselves how this happened. Extending our trip through Christian history might help to answer some of these questions.

From the beginning, the Christian church has always been a bit of a blessed mess—holy and guided by the Holy Spirit and yet undeniably marked by the sins and errors of its human members. The same is true of the denominations, religious orders, movements, and faith communities that constitute the universal church. Therefore, we should not be surprised to find occasions throughout history when even the contemplative orders became distracted and veered from their single-minded pursuit of divine communion.

Take the Benedictines, for example. The flexibility of the Rule of Benedict has made it applicable to many contexts over many centuries, but at times flexibility devolved into laxity. Such was the charge of Abbot Robert of Molesme and his supporters (thereafter known as Cistercians), who broke off from the Benedictines in 1098 in order to recover the rigor and simplicity of the rule. Similar stories exist in the history of the Dominicans. The scholastic methods the Dominicans championed helped to advance learning in the great medieval universities by making possible greater intellectual precision, but at times this pursuit of clarity and precision reduced God to an abstract idea devoid of any intimacy.[33] This intellectualized approach to study prevailed as cathedral schools and universities eventually replaced monastery schools. Discovery of new knowledge, rather than initiation into a wisdom tradition, became the central work of the university.[34] Looking back at such historical developments, we can wonder if Christian educators have at times gotten caught up in educational and cultural trends when they would have done better to stand by tradition. The Jesuits have sometimes been the targets of such criticisms, their critics alleging that they conceded too much to the wider culture in their efforts to enculturate the gospel and "meet people where they are."

In identifying these shortcomings, I do not intend to undermine all the good the Benedictines, Dominicans, and Jesuits have done nor to lay the blame for Christian schools' current woes at their feet. We would find similar missteps in the story of any religious order or community we investigated. Each group was dealing with complicated social challenges and usually doing the best it could. When confronting such complexity, it can be easy to lose sight of that one necessary thing.[35]

33. For a discussion of how abstract theology and apologetics inadvertently paved the way for secularization, see Charles Taylor, *A Secular Age* (Cambridge, MA: Belknap Press of Harvard University Press, 2007), 225–28.

34. As we will see in later chapters, this model has largely shaped common ideas about the purpose and value of the modern university, often with negative consequences for how we approach teaching, learning, and research.

35. There have even been times when church authorities suppressed contemplative prayer. For a brief history of how contemplative prayer was mar-

It is no different for Christian educators today.[36] We strive to draw our students into a tradition and a relationship with Mystery in the context of a particular time and place marked by its own challenges and opportunities. Like the early Benedictine monasteries, our schools operate within a milieu of moral decline. How exactly we should respond as Christian educators is far from clear. Should our schools function as bunkers sheltering our students from the maelstrom outside, or more as centers of cultural renewal, or as some combination of the two? Today we teach in an academic environment in which positivistic, analytical thinking dominates. Do we as Christian educators possess the confidence and the grounding in tradition to balance rigorous thinking with humility before the incomprehensible Mystery of God, as the Dominicans have typically striven to do? Like the early Jesuits, we are living in a time of rapid social, technological, and religious change. How can our schools prepare our students adequately for life in the modern world without losing sight of the timeless wisdom of the Christian tradition?

These are complicated questions, and the solutions are often imperfect. The key question is: According to what criterion of discernment do we seek solutions and make decisions? Saint Paul offers us wisdom in this regard when he writes, "Do not be conformed to this world, but be transformed by the renewing of your minds, so that you may discern what is the will of God—what is good and acceptable and perfect" (Rom. 12:2). The details will vary with the situation, but there is always a constant in God's will for us. This is the one necessary thing

---

ginalized in the modern era, see Thomas Keating, *Open Mind, Open Heart*, twentieth anniversary ed. (New York: Bloomsbury, 2006), 140–52.

36. For discussions of more recent developments and challenges in Christian education, see Mark R. Schwehn, *Exiles from Eden: Religion and the Academic Vocation in America* (New York: Oxford University Press, 1993); George Marsden, *The Soul of the American University: From Protestant Establishment to Established Nonbelief* (Oxford: Oxford University Press, 1994); Robert Benne, *Quality with Soul: How Six Premier Colleges and Universities Keep Faith with Their Religious Traditions* (Grand Rapids: Eerdmans, 2001).

of which Jesus spoke to Martha when she became distracted by her anxieties, namely, loving him and receiving his love. This love was the North Star that guided Anthony the Great, Saint Benedict, Saint Dominic, and Saint Ignatius as they navigated the challenges of their day. It can guide us still today. Indeed, if we press on a bit further into recent history, we will see numerous contemplative figures and communities who reflect that eternal light onto our contemporary landscape.

Contemporary Contemplatives

There has been much handwringing in recent years about the secularization of Western culture and the growing segment of the population who no longer identifies with any religious tradition (the "nones"). Yet at the same time that so many people—especially young people—have grown disenchanted with dogmatism and institutional religion, we have seen a profound renewal of interest in spirituality. This interest is reflected in the immense popularity of modern contemplative figures such as Thomas Merton (1915–1968). Merton was a Trappist monk who lived in the Abbey of Gethsemani outside of Louisville, Kentucky. As a Trappist, Merton traced his spiritual lineage back through the Cistercians to the Benedictines. His writings also evidence how profoundly influenced he was by the desert fathers.[37] Though deeply grounded in his relationship with Christ, Merton took an interest in Confucianism, Taoism, Hinduism, Sikhism, Jainism, Sufism, and Buddhism (especially Zen Buddhism) and formed friendships across religious boundaries with people like the Dalai Lama, Thich Nhat Hanh, and Zen scholar D. T. Suzuki.[38]

A gifted writer, Merton was able to convey the insights of the Christian contemplative tradition to a wide audience through books

37. For example, see Merton's book *The Wisdom of the Desert.*

38. Far from contaminating his Christian faith, Merton felt that his study of these Eastern religions helped him to understand his Christian tradition better and unite him more deeply to Christ.

such as *New Seeds of Contemplation* (1962) and *Contemplative Prayer* (1969). With over sixty books and hundreds of poems and articles to his name, Merton is arguably the most influential American Catholic author of the twentieth century. When Pope Francis visited the United States in 2015, Merton was one of three American Christians he singled out, praising him as "above all a man of prayer, a thinker who . . . opened new horizons for souls and for the Church."[39]

Merton was a frontrunner of a contemporary spiritual renewal in the Catholic Church and in the larger Christian community. In 1965, near the end of Merton's life, the bishops at the Second Vatican Council in Rome recognized the spiritual priesthood of the laity and the need for their ongoing spiritual formation.[40] In several documents the council fathers made clear that a deep life of prayer, worship, and service is not restricted to priests, monks, and nuns but rather is open to (even expected of) the laity. The reforms of Vatican II in general had the effect of promoting a new springtime for spirituality (especially among the laity) in the Catholic Church and beyond. They created new and diverse opportunities for laypeople to grow in their spirituality, including different ways of praying, renewed interest in secular third orders, and new ecclesial movements (for example, Sant'Egidio, Opus Dei, Focolare, the NeoCatechumenal Way, Communion and Liberation, the charismatic movement). As these new spiritual communities were emerging within the Catholic Church, a "new monasticism," constituted mostly by laypeople, was being born out of Protestant communities and gathering energy among people from diverse faith traditions. These new monastics were seeking a common life oriented to prayer and service while remaining highly engaged with the social issues of their day.[41]

39. Francis, "Visit to the Joint Session of the United States Congress," September 24, 2015, https://tinyurl.com/5y4jnbr4.

40. Paul VI, *Apostolic Actuositatem*, Vatican, 1965, https://tinyurl.com/3unmhpfx.

41. See the Rutba House, ed., *School(s) for Conversion: 12 Marks of a New Monasticism* (Eugene, OR: Cascade, 2005).

One person who took the invitation of Vatican II seriously was Father Thomas Keating (1923–2018), another Trappist monk. Keating lived most of his life in an area of Massachusetts crowded with retreat centers run by different religious groups, and he encountered many people whose search for deeper experiences of spirituality had led them to Eastern practices. Many of these were former Catholics who knew nothing of the contemplative traditions within Christianity. Keating, along with fellow Trappists William Meninger and M. Basil Pennington, developed an approach to contemplative prayer intended to be more accessible to contemporary people.[42] Their teaching, writing, and retreats in the 1970s and '80s were the beginning of what became known as the centering prayer movement.[43] In 1984 Contemplative Outreach was created to support this movement with retreats, resources, workshops, small communities, and online meditation chapels. Contemplative Outreach has continued to grow and today supports over forty thousand people and ninety chapters in thirty-nine countries.[44]

Merton and Keating, as well as other contemporary Christian contemplatives such as Howard Thurman and John Main, were teaching and writing with an awareness of the relationship between Christian contemplation and similar forms of prayer and meditation in other religious traditions. They recognized that contemplative prac-

42. This approach has not been without criticism. In 1989, the Congregation for the Doctrine of the Faith issued "Letter to the Bishops of the Catholic Church on Some Aspects of Christian Meditation," warning against the influence of Eastern forms of prayer and New Age spirituality on Christian prayer. Although neither Keating nor centering prayer are explicitly mentioned, some have alleged that this document was a rebuke of Keating's approach.

43. The term "centering prayer" derives from the writings of Thomas Merton, who says, "Monastic prayer begins . . . with a 'return to the heart,' finding one's deepest center, awakening the profound depths of our being in the presence of God." *Contemplative Prayer* (New York: Image Books, 1996), 5–6.

44. "About Us," Contemplative Outreach, accessed November 1, 2024, https://tinyurl.com/nha9zvja.

tice remains highly attractive for modern people who have rejected many other aspects of organized religion. If anything, this trend has only gained momentum in recent years. Contemplative writer Father Richard Rohr has attracted a huge following, while authors such as A. J. Sherrill are bringing more attention to contemplative prayer in Protestant communities. Scholars and practitioners such as Jon Kabbat Zinn have helped to bring the Buddhism-inspired practice of mindfulness into mainstream culture. Books, podcasts, YouTube videos, and phone apps on mindfulness now abound. Interest in contemplative practices has taken hold in the education world as well. Numerous universities—including Brown, Dartmouth, Emory, University of Virginia, University of Michigan, and University of Southern California—now offer academic programs in contemplative studies. These institutions and others have embraced contemplative pedagogy as a valuable set of resources for enhancing teaching and learning. These programs and practices are supported by a large and growing body of research on their uses and benefits, which we will examine in the coming chapters.[45]

Oddly, Christian schools have been slower to embrace contemplative practices as this contemporary movement continues to gain steam. This reluctance seems to be driven by a mixture of suspicion of Eastern spiritual practices and ignorance of the Christian contemplative tradition. Most contemporary people, including many Christians, associate meditation and contemplative practices with Buddhism and other Eastern religions. They are generally unaware of the desert fathers' methods of cultivating inner watchfulness, the practice of *lectio divina*, the Dominican tradition of teaching as sharing the fruits of contemplation, the Ignatian practices of contemplation in action, not to mention the profound probing of the interior life by Christian mystics like Teresa of Ávila and John of the Cross.

45. For a helpful introduction to this research, see Daniel P. Barbezat and Mirabai Bush, *Contemplative Practices in Higher Education: Powerful Methods to Transform Teaching and Learning* (San Francisco: Jossey-Bass, 2014).

Ignorance of these spiritual gifts from the Christian tradition commonly contributes to two kinds of reactions. On the one hand, there are Christians (including Christian educators) who in their quest for spiritual growth or improved mental health turn to Eastern spiritual practices or secular mindfulness techniques because they are not aware of any alternative. On the other hand, there are those Christians who reject any form of prayer involving attention to breath or mantra-like repetition because they assume these are corruptions of Eastern or New Age influence.

Such reactions are unfortunate because, in overlooking or dismissing these practices, we miss out on beautiful, authentically Christian resources for promoting intellectual, emotional, relational, and spiritual growth. Of course, corruptions do occur. Syncretism is always a danger, especially in the present cultural milieu. However, I hope that by now I have demonstrated clearly that there are authentically Christian contemplative practices that we can trace back to the earliest days of the church and to Jesus himself.[46] Although Christian contemplative practices bear some resemblance to Eastern meditation practices, there are some key differences: Where Buddhist and mindfulness meditation aim at emptying the mind, Christian contemplation aims at union with God. Where the former strive to dispel the "illusion" of the self, in the latter we discover our true selves in Christ, who abides within us.[47]

Having undertaken this recovery, I will endeavor in the remainder of the book to show how Christian schools can reappropriate the gifts of the Christian contemplative tradition for the good of teachers, stu-

46. I am by no means the first to do this work of recovery. See, for example, Laird, *Into the Silent Land*; Bottaro, *The Mindful Catholic*; and Chad Thralls, *Deep Calls to Deep: Mysticism, Scripture, and Contemplation* (Maryknoll, NY: Orbis Books, 2020).

47. For more detailed discussions on the difference between Christian contemplation and Eastern meditation and mindfulness, see Bottaro, *The Mindful Catholic*, 175–86, and A. J. Sherrill, *Being with God: The Absurdity, Necessity, and Neurology of Contemplative Prayer* (Grand Rapids: Brazos, 2021), 31–32.

dents, and all members of their school communities. We will soon see that, besides serving as a powerful means of growing in communion with God (the one necessary thing), these practices promote learning, well-being, and our relationships with one another.

The Story Continues Today

It is my hope that, in reading these stories of our Christian forebearers, readers will hear resonances with their own story and circumstances. We can see ourselves in the desert fathers and mothers who sought refuge from the noisy society of their time and, even once they had left, struggled with the noise inside their heads. We can take heart knowing that they discovered spiritual practices that gave them peace and that these practices might do the same for us. We can see ourselves in the early Benedictines, who sought order, peace, and beauty when the world around them was falling to pieces. We have received from them precious gifts in a rule of life and an approach to study (namely, *lectio divina*) that can help us remain focused on what truly matters and stay connected with the deepest part of ourselves. We can relate to the early Dominicans and Jesuits, who sought to anchor themselves in something deep and lasting when their world was undergoing rapid change and confusion abounded. From them we inherit practices such as the examen that keep us grounded in Christ in the midst of all the distractions of our busy lives. These examples are a small sample of the riches of the Christian contemplative tradition that will continue to open up before us in the chapters ahead.

The story I have told here is not the whole story. I have traced a few of the streams of the Christian contemplative tradition that have nourished me and others I know and that I believe offer something particularly helpful to Christian educators today. Notwithstanding, I hope I have made my case sufficiently well to pique your interest and entice you to explore further what it might look like to appropriate these traditions in our Christian schools today. These contemplative practices and wisdom have transformed communities throughout history and are attracting interest today because they arise from and point us to the thing we yearn for most deeply, the one truly necessary thing. This is why they have proven transformative generation after generation, time and time again. It seems clear to me that so many of the signs of the times—our deteriorating mental health and shrinking attention spans, the breakdown in our communities, the spiritual seeking of younger generations—are leading us back to this ancient path.

At the same time, we cannot simply turn back the clock. We do well to heed Jesus's warning about putting new wine in old wineskins (Matt. 9:16–17). In telling this parable, Jesus was by no means rejecting tradition. Rather he was pointing out the truth that things change and that slavish repetition of old customs, rituals, and teachings is seldom adequate to meet the needs of new circumstances. This maxim certainly holds true for contemplative practices. The Benedictines, Dominicans, and Jesuits all adapted the contemplative tradition they inherited as needed for their particular time and place. While honoring the tradition bequeathed to them, they also made it their own. Indeed, adapting and developing the gifts we receive is an important way we honor the tradition.

We are the bearers of this tradition today. God is calling us to a task and an opportunity that is unique in salvation history. The way before us will surely be something more than a slavish observance of the rule Benedict wrote in the sixth century or of the exact method of *lectio divina* Guigo II developed in the twelfth. It is unlikely that converting our schools into medieval monasteries is the thing that will save them.[48] We can learn much from our predecessors in faith, but we are not obliged to take the same path they did. What is necessary is that our response to the current challenges flows from a practice of

48. Although I am not the only one to suggest that it might not be a bad idea for schools to be more like monasteries. See Molly Worthen's article "Why Universities Should Be More like Monasteries," *New York Times*, May 25, 2023, https://tinyurl.com/59yjht48.

abiding in God's love. This was the guiding light for Benedict, Dominic, and Ignatius when they developed their distinctive spiritual practices and educational approaches, and it is what we ought to strive for as we discern how to adapt these practices for our own time.

I aspire to such faithful adaptation in this book. As we move into the next chapter and the chapters following, we will move from the past into the present. Bearing this legacy of contemplation in mind, we will reflect on life in our schools as we experience it today and consider how these contemplative practices and wisdom might transform our experience. Contemplative Christians like Anthony of Egypt discovered wisdom and a way of life so attractive that people flocked to the desert by the thousands to learn from them. Might our schools become the desert of our time? I invite you to read on and begin to envision with me a new day for Christian education.

2

Beginning

Living and Learning on God's Time

"In the beginning was the Word, and the Word was with God, and the Word was God. . . . All things came into being through him. . . . What has come into being in him was life, and the life was the light of all people" (John 1:1, 3–4). In these majestic words, John the Evangelist describes the beginning of the world, so full of life and promise. In a sense, we relive the moment of creation every time we awaken. Each new day holds infinite potential and promise. How nice it would be to begin the school day with this sense of hope and expectation, and yet, if we are being honest, we rarely experience it this way.

Tell me if this description of my typical morning sounds familiar. From the moment I wake up, I sense the clock ticking. I could really use some more sleep, but there is no time. I drag myself out of bed and into the bathroom. I shower quickly, hoping that I finish before our youngest child wakes up. I pull my clothes on and rush to the kitchen to prepare breakfast. My wife is already there packing lunches. We exchange a quick "Good morning," but there is no time to talk. We need to get the kids up and moving. The next forty-five minutes are a flurry of activity—feeding, dressing, brushing teeth, combing hair, packing bags, and loading the kids into the car.

Once everyone is out the door, I finish getting myself ready. I am in the car and pulling out of the driveway when I realize I have forgotten my lunch. Angrily, I shift the car back into park, run into the house, grab my lunch, and run back out. I start backing out too fast and have to slam on the brakes to avoid the garbage truck turning around the corner. I let the truck pass and pull out onto the street. There I am immediately blocked by the school drop-off traffic. Just as a gap in the traffic appears in one direction, a long line of cars comes from the other.

It feels like I hit every red light between home and campus. As I sit at yet another light, I feel my body tensing. I stare ahead like a NASCAR driver waiting for the flag to drop. My car is stationary, but my mind is racing: *Did I finish my lesson plan for this morning? Yes. Did I print off everything I need yesterday? No. I will have to do that when I get there. That crummy printer better be working today. I wish they would just replace that thing. But finances are not good right now. What are we talking about at the Faculty Welfare and Compensation meeting today? Oh, right, the new salary study. Did I have to do something to prep that meeting? Shoot! Bernadette sent a long email and there were a couple of attachments. I don't know when I'm going to be able to do that. What else am I forgetting? There was another email. . . . Shoot! Damien sent something about his presentation for class today and I never got back to him. I'll have to email him as soon as I get into the office.* The refrain in this onslaught of thoughts is, *I don't have enough time, I don't have enough time. . . .*

Suddenly I am on campus. I was not even aware of arriving. I pull into the parking garage and start scanning, but every space in the first section is taken. I swing around to the back section and finally find a spot. After a brief struggle getting my bags out of the passenger seat, I slam the car door shut and speed-walk across the parking garage. I enter my building and blow past the reception desk, shouting a halfhearted "Mornin'" over my shoulder. After another brief struggle with my key, I am in my office and firing up my computer. It takes forever to turn on. As I stare at the screen, frustrated and helpless, I start mentally reviewing my schedule for the day. Every minute is accounted for. I have back-to-back meetings after class and not enough time to prep for tomorrow's class. I will have to eat lunch at my desk while catching up on emails. The day has barely begun, and already I feel exhausted.

Why Is There Never Enough Time?

We are all too busy—teachers, students, parents, all of us. We need to confront this reality right at the outset of this book because one of the most common reasons people dismiss a contemplative approach to education is that they feel they cannot spare the "extra" time. But before we give up so easily, we should ask why we feel we never have time to spare. This experience seems ubiquitous (at least in the United States). If we ask someone how things are going, we can pretty well count on them saying something about how busy they are. No one seems happy about it, yet we feel helpless to change the situation. In fact, it seems that we are only getting busier as time goes by. A century ago economists were highly optimistic that technological innovations would enable us to work less and enjoy more leisure time. Most famously, John Maynard Keynes predicted that by 2030 people would work no more than fifteen hours a week.[1] The year 2030 is just around the corner, and the future Keynes foresaw seems more remote than ever. The trend over the past fifty years has been toward longer work hours, not shorter.[2] What happened?

Clearly technology has not helped us as we hoped it would. For this we only have ourselves to blame. Dishwashers and washing machines undoubtedly save us time washing dishes and clothes. Cell phones and email have made communication quicker and more efficient than when we depended on snail mail and interoffice memos. But what have we done with the time we gained? We have filled it

1. John Maynard Keynes, "Economic Possibilities for Our Grandchildren," in *Essays in Persuasion* (New York: Norton, 1963), 358–73, https://tinyurl.com/26ntmwcx.

2. However, there are some indications that this trend may finally be changing, at least for some workers. See Derek Thompson, "America's Fever of Workaholism Is Finally Breaking," *Atlantic*, January 31, 2023, https://tinyurl.com/yeyjr8f2.

with more work.[3] Portable technologies have given us the capability to work anywhere and anytime, and many employers expect that their employees will do just that. The boundaries between work and home have eroded. In the United States, this problem is compounded by a culture of workaholism.[4] We complain about how busy we are, but we also take pride in it and even feel self-conscious about not being busy enough.[5] Subtle social expectations exert pressure on us to maintain the appearance of busyness lest others think us unimportant or unmotivated.

To say that we live and die by the clock is more than a figure of speech. Busyness creates stress, prolonged exposure to which inhibits the functioning of the immune system, digestion, and growth processes and puts us at higher risk for many health problems.[6] Medical professionals have warned us that our students' overpacked schedules are contributing to their increased levels of mental distress.[7] This warning comes as no surprise. Most of us know intuitively that our

3. Researcher Jonathan Gershuny has observed that greater efficiency in the workplace leads to greater productivity, which provides more for consumption, which in turn occupies more of our free time. See Jonathan Gershuny, "Busyness as the Badge of Honor for the New Superordinate Working Class," *Social Research* 72 (2005–2009), https://doi.org/10.1353/sor.2005.0018.

4. US workers work 442 more hours per year than German workers, 294 more hours per year than United Kingdom workers, 301 more hours per year than French workers. See "Average Annual Hours Actually Worked Per Worker," OECD Data Explorer, last updated September 18, 2024, https://tinyurl.com/yfmrjhbx.

5. Our attitudes toward work and leisure are largely the products of cultural norms. According to Gershuny's historical research, in 1900 busyness was a trait of the working class and leisure of the wealthy, but by 2000 the upper class was working longer hours, making busyness a mark of distinction and importance.

6. These include anxiety, depression, digestive problems, heart disease, heart attack, high blood pressure and stroke, sleep problems, weight gain, and problems with memory and focus. "Chronic Stress Puts Your Health at Risk," Mayo Clinic, accessed October 30, 2024, https://tinyurl.com/4j9bt77n.

7. "Is Your Child Overscheduled? Kids Need 'Down Time,'" Cleveland Clinic, July 16, 2018, https://tinyurl.com/52p5u35t.

overly busy lifestyles and the attendant stress are not good for us. Nevertheless, we make a devil's bargain, sacrificing our health for increased productivity, earnings, and career advancement. Unfortunately, that bargain turns out to be a raw deal. While working long hours may help some people to get ahead in the short term, research shows that in the long term sacrificing rest can actually diminish productivity and cause a host of professional and personal problems.[8]

We long for a less hurried life. We just do not see how it is possible. We watch time racing by and feel powerless to slow it. But we need not be so resigned. Even if we cannot stop the passage of time, what matters practically is our experience of time, and over this we have considerable control. Rather than accepting our accustomed routines as a *fait accompli*, we should ask ourselves if these routines are serving us well. We might ask, What would it look like to organize time in ways better suited to our human needs? What ways of inhabiting time are consistent with the life to which God calls us? A first step in this direction is to understand the factors that shape our experience of time. Let us enter the classroom with this question in mind.

How We Experience Time in School

Our perception of time is generated not only according to internal time markers (e.g., circadian rhythms) but also according to external ones (e.g., sunlight, clocks, and other people).[9] This fact implies that the ways we shape our environments affect how we experience time. Consider one important feature of the temporal architecture of a school: clocks. Although we typically pay them little conscious attention, on some level we are always aware of the clocks mounted

8. Alex Soojung-Kim Pang, *Rest: Why You Get More Done When You Work Less* (New York: Basic Books, 2018), 163.

9. For an in-depth exploration of human time perception, see Alan Burdick's *Why Time Flies: A Mostly Scientific Investigation* (New York: Simon & Schuster, 2017).

on every classroom wall and shining up at us from our watches and devices. It seems almost impossible to imagine a school without clocks. Obviously, they serve a practical and necessary function, namely, keeping us "on schedule" and synchronized with the rest of the school. When the clock hits a certain time, one class period ends and another begins. Because the clock dictates the flow of the school day, everyone's attention is constantly oriented to the clock.

What is less obvious is how this constant attention to the clock shapes our perception of time and our general mind-set. Like lab rats who receive electric shocks on a predictable schedule, we are constantly conditioned to anticipate the next bell and class period. The academic calendar conditions us in the same way, extending our expectations into the days and weeks ahead. We constantly anticipate the next assignment, test, weekend, and holiday. When our primary temporal markers all orient us to what happens next, our perception of time is shaped in a very particular way. Always anticipating a point in the future, we often experience time as either rapidly running out or dragging on. We worry about as-yet-uncompleted tasks, which creates a mental tension within us that manifests in feelings of anxiety and being overwhelmed. We rarely exist in the present moment because the present is filled with thoughts about the future.

No one enjoys such feelings of anxiety and hurry, and we need not resign ourselves to this condition. When we recognize that our sense of busyness is conditioned by our environment, we give ourselves the power to alter the environment and thereby our experience of time. As educator Felicia Wu Song observes, our problem is usually not that we do not have enough time but rather that we are not managing our attention to time well.[10] All our schedules, plans, and timekeeping devices are artifacts of human beings' ideas about time and decisions about how to organize it. We are the ones who set our schools up this way, and we can choose to do otherwise. Some schools already

10. Felicia Wu Song, *Restless Devices: Recovering Personhood, Presence, and Place in the Digital Age* (Downers Grove, IL: IVP Academic, 2021), 159.

have. Those of us teaching in Christian schools should be taking our cues not from the wider culture, which has a decidedly unhealthy relationship with time, but rather from the One who is Lord of time. If we are experiencing so much time-related stress, perhaps this is a sign that we are not using time the way God intends us to use it.[11] As we will see presently, it is possible to live life on God's time.

Living on God's Time

Our experience of time depends in part on the meaning we give it. Unfortunately, that meaning is often negative. Time is always "running out," and we are perpetually racing "against the clock." We perceive time limits as threats to our plans, our projects, our health, and our very life. We ruminate over past events that we cannot change and worry about things that have not yet happened. We are thus distended in several directions and live in a state of tension.[12]

As Christians, we are invited to understand time differently. For us, time is a gift rather than a threat because we trust that God turns all things for the good of those who love him (Rom. 8:28), even the hands of the clock. For a Christian, all time is God's time. God created time and endowed us with the ability to perceive the passage of time and order our lives within time. Reflecting on why God did this helps us to live in God's time (*kairos* time in the New Testament Greek) rather than in worldly time (or *chronos* time). Author and spiritual guide Father Wilfrid Stinissen suggests that the purpose of time—like the purpose of life in general—is to enter into the Trinitarian community of love. How does time facilitate this? Because the time we receive is limited, we must choose what to do with it. How we use our time reflects what is important to us, what we love. Like the servants in the parable of the talents, we can cling possessively to the time the Mas-

11. See Wilfrid Stinissen, *Eternity in the Midst of Time*, trans. Sister Clare Marie (San Francisco: Ignatius, 2018), 85.

12. Such was Saint Augustine's observation in *Confessions* 11.19.

ter has given us, or we can use it in a way that will be pleasing to our Master. In this way, we have the opportunity to give God something in return for the gift God has bestowed upon us. Living in time also gives us chances to grow. If we fail to love at one time in our lives, we have the opportunity to do better at another time (at least up to a point).

Understanding time in this way, we recognize that it is in our best interest to seek God's will in how we make use of our time because, as Stinissen says, God's time is always the right time.[13] We should not presume to know better how to use our time. All we need to know, says the Jesuit priest Jean-Pierre de Caussade, is that in every moment God calls us to an appointed task.[14] Once we abandon ourselves to God in this way, much of our anxiety about time dissipates. We always have enough time for what needs doing when we are doing God's will because God creates the time we need to do it.[15] By the same token, no time spent in God's service is ever wasted (even time spent fixing a jammed printer!). What Jesus promises in the parable of the wheat applies here. God can make every moment of our lives bear spiritual fruit one-hundredfold, even if we do not recognize the fruit immediately. But for this to happen, we need to surrender control over time to God's loving care and mastery. If we do, Caussade assures us, we can pass through life "light as a feather, fluid as water, innocent as a child," responsive to the lightest touches of grace in each moment.[16]

As we have seen, our attitudes toward time are shaped not only by our ideas about time but also by the concrete features of our environments and schedules. Christians in ages past recognized this fact. Over the centuries monastic communities have fine-tuned their *horarium* (the daily monastic schedule) to help them live on God's time. A typical monastic *horarium* looks something like this:

13. Stinissen, *Eternity in the Midst of Time*, 42.

14. Jean-Pierre de Caussade, *The Sacrament of the Present Moment*, trans. Kitty Muggeridge (San Francisco: Harper & Row, 1989), 1.

15. Stinissen, *Eternity in the Midst of Time*, 85.

16. Caussade, *The Sacrament of the Present Moment*, 22.

5:30 a.m.	Vigils and Lauds
6:30 a.m.	Breakfast
7:00 a.m.	Holy Reading
7:30 a.m.	Mass
8:30 a.m.	Work
12:00 p.m.	Midday Prayer and Lunch
1:00 p.m.	Work
5:00 p.m.	Vespers
5:30 p.m.	Holy Reading
6:00 p.m.	Supper
6:30 p.m.	Community Recreation
7:00 p.m.	Compline
7:30 p.m.	Recreation, Study, and Leisure
9:30 p.m.	The Great Silence

In the monastic *horarium*, "there is a time for every matter" (Eccles. 3:1)—for prayer, for work, for study, for rest. No one activity is permitted to crowd out another.[17] Each has its time and purpose that flows from an understanding of the kind of life God wills for us. It is a life in which we have purposeful work to do (Gen. 2:15), and yet it is a life that protects time for rest, which respects our human needs, and time for prayer, which honors God's sovereignty over life (Gen. 2:3). It is a way of life that honors our vocation for loving communion and reconstitutes the community daily by bringing its members together for worship, nourishment, and recreation. The members of the community thereby strive to live in sync with God and one another. It is a life that is "always full but never busy," as the Benedictines say.

17. Contemporary research affirms the wisdom of such a schedule that is highly structured but not overly packed. For example, such a schedule aligns well with what Gloria Mark's research reveals about the natural rhythms of human attention throughout the day. See *Attention Span: A Groundbreaking Way to Restore Balance, Happiness. and Productivity* (Toronto: Hanover Square Press, 2023), 275. See also Pang, *Rest*, for examples of how high-achieving scientists, political figures, writers, and entrepreneurs structure their days in ways that are not dissimilar from the monastic *horarium*.

It is thus possible to live life on God's time. It is possible to experience eternity in the midst of time, as Stinissen says. Christian monastics have done it for centuries. But to do it in our Christian schools today will require a concerted effort to push back against cultural and institutional pressures. Under the influence of these pressures, lessons, assignments, and extracurriculars have filled our school days and crowded out other forms of activity (and inactivity) that are equally important aspects of a full life, including time for prayer, community, and rest. We have become so accustomed to a work-centric schedule that it seems immutable, but it was not always so. In fact, the modern school schedule is a relatively recent innovation. Now I am not suggesting that we turn our schools into medieval monasteries. There is no turning back the clock, and it is not practical to simply demolish our current school schedules. Nevertheless, it is worth pondering what it might look like for our schools to be more like monasteries in which we move through the day with a sense of purpose but not anxiety or hurry.

We have taken an important first step toward entering God's time by identifying some of the conditions that shape our experience of time. The next step is to actually experience time differently so that we can know what possibilities exist for our schools. It is my hope that the following meditation will facilitate such an experience, however fleeting. I invite you now to step with me into God's time.

A Meditation on Time

Much is baked into our ways of thinking about time. In school settings we talk a lot about "time management." Such language can be a sign of an unhealthy and unrealistic desire to control time. We are forever trying to squeeze more into every hour and every minute. We act as if we could slow down the clock by looking at it compulsively. Of course, good time management is a necessity for teachers. Certain things must get done, and this requires good planning and execution. At the same time, even the most efficient teacher must acknowledge that he or she does not exercise total mastery over time. Yes, we should make good use of the time God has gifted us, but we should hold this gift loosely. We ought to have the humility to acknowledge that we can never predict with certainty the results of our efforts. We must have faith that our time at work will yield greater fruit if we surrender to what God is asking of us in this very moment.

One concrete way of training ourselves in this attitude is by keeping time as monastics have done for centuries. Monks have to be at definite places at definite times and, in many cases, face consequences for failing to be on time.[18] For most of the history of monasticism, monks did not have clocks, and they certainly did not have cell phones on which to check the time. How did they know when it was time for prayer or lunch or work? Bells. When the bell rang, everyone dropped immediately whatever they were doing and moved to the next task. Saint Benedict went so far as to say the monk should put down his pen without crossing his *t* or dotting his *i*. This simple but powerful ascetic practice helps the monk to cultivate a spirit of healthy detachment from work and responsiveness to God's call. The obedient monk does not sneak in a few more minutes of work before running to the chapel for prayer because he hears in the bell God's own summons. Promptly heeding the bell is a concrete way of entrusting time into God's hands.

I invite you to try this practice now. We will begin with some auricular stretching, habituating ourselves to listening better and more patiently. Listen to a recording of monastery bells rung by monks of the Benedictine Abbey of Calcat (https://www.youtube.com/watch?v=_WFkqJQBtgM).

Listen carefully, noting the different tones and cadences. At the end, try to follow the sound of the bell as long as you can before it fades into silence. For some, simply listening to the bells for the full three and a half minutes will stretch their patience. Conclude by taking in the sound of silence for a moment.

18. Chapter 43 of the Rule of Benedict specifies punishments for monks who are late for prayer.

Moving to the second stage of the exercise, try using bells to keep time for the next hour or two rather than the clock on your phone, computer, or wall. You can use a smart phone app like Mindfulness Bell[19] or set the timer on your phone for however long you want to devote to each activity in this next hour. Alternatively, you might set the timer to ring every twenty-five minutes.[20] When the bell rings, pause what you are doing and say a brief prayer or simply recall that you are in God's loving presence. These pauses are also good opportunities to take a deep breath and stretch.

After completing this exercise, reflect on the following:

- Did you experience time differently during this hour? How so?
- Did you experience your work differently? How so?
- Did you find it hard not to look at the clock or know the exact time? If so, why do you think that is? How do you feel about your reaction?

Beginning Well

Entering into a Christian sense of time can have profound implications for the way we live and work, and we will explore many of these throughout this book. Here we will focus on three foundational aspects of entering into God's time: beginning well, being fully present in the moment, and transitioning well between activities.

One piece of Benedictine wisdom passed down through the ages is the importance of beginning well. "Always we begin again," wrote Saint Benedict. From a psychological perspective, beginnings and endings exert an outsized impact on our thinking about things.[21] How

19. The app is available at https://tinyurl.com/52tvr5us.

20. Read more here about the benefits of the "Pomodoro Technique" of breaking up work time in twenty-five-minute intervals: Sanjana Gupta, "What Is the Pomodoro Technique?," Very Well Mind, December 18, 2022, https://tinyurl.com/mv9u5ct2.

21. This is what psychologists refer to as the "primacy effect" and "recency effect."

we begin sets the stage for everything that follows and sometimes has lasting effects regardless of how well we work afterward.[22] Our schedules reveal our priorities, and we tend to address first the things we consider the most important. It is therefore highly significant that the first thing in the daily monastic *horarium* is prayer. Before monks do any work or even take nourishment, they give the firstfruits of the day to the Lord. If communion with God is truly the one necessary thing, then it makes sense that every day should begin this way.

It is common enough in Christian schools for the day to begin with prayer, but how much heart and intentionality do we put into it? In many cases, the principal or a reluctant student offers morning prayer in a perfunctory manner, and then everyone is off to the races as if nothing had happened. It is a very different story at Saint Benedict's Prep High School in Newark, New Jersey.[23] Every day begins with convocation, during which members of the school community gather to pray, sing (and sometimes dance), communicate information, celebrate achievements, and affirm their love and support for one another. Officially convocation is scheduled for thirty minutes, but the school's leadership believes so much in its importance that they allow convocation to go as long as it takes and adjust the schedule for the rest of the day as needed.

Even if a school's administration is not willing to be this flexible with the schedule (and most probably are not), there is something here that every Christian educator can take to heart. It is important to begin the day well. We are often in a rush to get to school in the morning, and, with so much to do, the natural impulse is to immediately charge ahead. However, when we begin this way we are likely to miss graced opportunities and the subtle ways God is calling us to do God's work this day. Listening for God's voice at the beginning of the

22. For an overview of research on the impact of positive and negative beginnings and the significance of when we begin something, see chapter 3 of Daniel Pink's book *When: The Scientific Secrets of Perfect Timing* (New York: Riverhead Books, 2018).

23. The school's website can be accessed at https://www.sbp.org/.

day need not take the form of a thirty-minute all-school convocation. A few minutes of prayer in each classroom or over the intercom may suffice if it is done with intentionality. That prayer might be a reflection on the daily Gospel or, following the Ignatian tradition, an exercise in "preparing the day"[24] by visualizing the hours ahead and setting an intention to do everything for the greater glory of God.[25]

That being said, on at least some occasions the school community should make a grander gesture to rededicate itself to God's priorities. The beginning of the school year presents a propitious opportunity. Many schools begin the academic year with a Mass of the Holy Spirit at which the school community invokes the Holy Spirit to bless their undertakings for the year. At Swarthmore College in Pennsylvania, the new year officially commences at First Collection during orientation week.[26] An expression of Swarthmore's Quaker heritage, the First Collection gathers all first-year students in the school's outdoor amphitheater to hear addresses by the college's president, a member of the faculty, and a member of the senior class, followed by candle-lighting and hand-shaking rituals. These rituals of beginning set the stage for everything that will follow and remind community members why they are there. Even after the academic year is well under way, the changing of the liturgical seasons (Advent, Lent, etc.) provides opportunities to begin anew and rededicate ourselves with renewed vigor to our work in the Lord's service.[27]

Regardless of whether or not the school as a whole observes such rituals, teachers can make their own gestures of beginning the year well with their classes. Concrete gestures might include learning stu-

24. For more guidance with this practice, see "Morning Examen," God in All Things, accessed November 4, 2024, https://tinyurl.com/4xxh4ms6.

25. Research suggests that visualizing goals for the day makes people feel more productive and engaged at work. See Mark, *Attention Span*, 279.

26. You can read more about this tradition and view speeches from past First Collections at "Watch: First Collection and Community Gathering," Swarthmore, September 3, 2019, https://tinyurl.com/2r642uhb.

27. Stinissen, *Eternity in the Midst of Time*, 68.

dents' names and helping students to learn each other's names, team-building exercises, and discussing classroom rules and expectations or creating a class contract together.[28]

Do What You Are Doing

Many of us step out of bed in the morning directly onto a treadmill that does not stop until we crash into bed again at night. We tell ourselves that we have so much to do that we cannot afford to stop, even for a moment. Some have suggested that our chronic busyness is a symptom of our fallen condition. Octavio Paz, winner of the Nobel Prize for Literature, speaks of our "exile from the present moment."[29] Picking up on this image, Father Stinissen reflects, "It seems we have been banished from the paradise of the now. We are always somewhere other than where we ought to be."[30] We worry about things in the past that we cannot change and things in the future that we can do nothing about right now. Holding these many things in our heads contributes to our feelings of fragmentation, feeding our stress and anxiety.[31] The reality is that we can control only what we do in this present moment[32]—nothing more—and our efforts to do multiple things at once tend to be counterproductive.[33]

This is not the life God intended for us. Yet even now, we can return from our self-imposed exile and reenter the kingdom of God's

28. Being known by name is essential to students feeling that they belong in a class or other group. See Josh Packard et al., *Belonging: Reconnecting America's Loneliest Generation* (Bloomington, MN: Springtide Research Institute, 2020).

29. Quoted in Stinissen, *Eternity in the Midst of Time*, 146.

30. Stinissen, *Eternity in the Midst of Time*, 146.

31. Susan Nolen-Hoeksema, Blair E. Wisco, and Sonja Lyubomirsky, "Rethinking Rumination," *Association for Psychological Science* 3, no. 5 (2008): 400–424.

32. Of course, one thing we can do in the present moment is plan for the future, but planning is distinct from unproductive worrying.

33. Reynol Junco, "In-Class Multitasking and Academic Performance," *Computers in Human Behavior* 28, no. 6 (2012): 2236–43.

time. The entry point into that kingdom is the present moment. God in God's wisdom created us such that we can only live one moment at a time. Consequently, Stinissen notes, the present is the only place where we actually encounter God.[34] For this reason, every moment deserves our full attention. "We ought never to have the feeling that we have 'much' to do," writes Stinissen. "Right now, we have only *one single thing to do*."[35] If we are attentive to what God is asking us to do right now, we do not have to worry about what happens next.

We again see this wisdom instantiated in particular features of the monastic way of life. When a bell rings in a monastery, it calls the monks back from the dissolution of their mental wanderings to the present moment and the present task. As another aid to their re-collection, monastic communities have traditionally inscribed the phrase *Age quod agis* ("Do what you are doing") over their doorways. These are practices that translate easily enough into the school setting. While Latin inscriptions are less popular today, there are modern equivalents such as posters that remind us "Be. Here. Now." When our attention begins to float around the room, landing upon a poster such as this can help bring us back to the current task or material. Utilizing auditory reminders like bells and periodic "attention breaks" in the classroom can also help to keep us grounded in the present moment and focused on the task at hand.[36]

Many people today have discovered the mental health benefits of practicing present-moment awareness thanks in no small part to the popularity of mindfulness meditation.[37] Most of these people would be surprised to learn that Christian spiritual guides were offering similar advice centuries before it became trendy. According to Father Caussade, the spiritual life of our forebearers was simple: "All their attention was focused on the present, minute by minute. . . . Constantly prompted by

34. Stinissen, *Eternity in the Midst of Time*, 148.

35. Stinissen, *Eternity in the Midst of Time*, 160–61.

36. We will discuss attention breaks further in chapter 3.

37. See, e.g., James N. Donald et al., "Daily Stress and the Benefits of Mindfulness: Examining the Daily and Longitudinal Relations Between Present-Moment Awareness and Stress Responses," *Journal of Research in Personality* 65 (2016): 30–37.

divine impulsion, they found themselves imperceptibly turned towards the next task that God had ready for them at each hour of the day."[38] Caussade's spiritual classic *Self-Abandonment to Divine Providence* describes this "spirituality of all ages and all conditions" in simple, practical terms.[39] Stinissen offers similar advice to a contemporary audience: We find God in the present moment. When our minds stray from the present, we get wrapped up in ourselves, our disappointments, and our illusions.[40] Stinissen goes on to explain that we find peace in the present moment because we experience wholeness when all our attention is focused on one single task.[41] When we enter fully into the present moment, time opens up and we can even seem to touch eternity.

Transitioning and Letting Go

Many of us begin the day with a sprint out of the gate, and we find it very hard to break stride once we are off and running. However, always running from one thing to the next is a bad habit for several reasons. For one, it is stressful and negatively impacts our health.[42] For another, we tend not to do things as well when we rush. Even if we recognize these downsides, it can be very difficult to break this habit, rooted as it is in our desire for control. We always want to send one last email, polish off one more paragraph, grade one more paper.[43] It gives us a sense of satisfaction and control when we can tick

38. Caussade, *The Sacrament of the Present Moment,* 1.

39. Caussade, *The Sacrament of the Present Moment,* 4. This text is the same as *Self-Abandonment to Divine Providence* but with a different title.

40. Stinissen, *Eternity in the Midst of Time,* 151.

41. Mihaly Csikszentmihalyi lends research-based support to this observation in his book *Flow: The Psychology of Optimal Experience* (New York: Harper & Row, 1990).

42. We will examine relevant research when we explore practices of rest in chapter 6.

43. Somewhat counterintuitively, some writers and researchers recommend leaving a simple task unfinished as an effective strategy for increasing motivation and making it easier to resume work after a break. See Pink, *When,* 138.

these things off our to-do list. Of course, circumstances frequently prevent us from accomplishing everything on our list. Rather than accepting our limitations, we try to retain control mentally by ruminating on things even when there is nothing we can do about them. So it is that we are often still thinking about the last conversation or an incomplete task when we have physically moved on to another task or location. As a result, we are not really present to this task, this person, this moment. Recognizing these tendencies underscores why we need to be intentional about moments of transition.

Although schools are busy places, some features of the school environment are naturally conducive to a healthy daily rhythm. Take school bells, for example. Typically the sounding of the bell between classes functions like a starter's gun, prompting students and teachers to sprint off to their next destination. Although we have been conditioned to respond in this way, this is a bad habit that we need not indulge. Inspired by the monastic tradition, a school community might recondition itself to pause for a moment of silent reflection and thanksgiving before everyone begins to move. Punctuating the day with special moments of pause can help to reinforce this habit. Jesuit schools often pause in the middle (or end) of the school day to pray the examen. Other schools pray the Angelus at midday. Another possibility would be observing a "Great Silence" in the middle of the day—five minutes of stillness and quiet to remind us of the presence of the divine Mystery in the midst of all our activity. Dimming the lights at such times signals that we are all entering into a different kind of time for a different purpose.

Even within a single class period, there are many opportunities to pause and recenter. Every time the class transitions from direct instruction to individual work or from group work to a whole class discussion is an opportunity for the class community to pause, take a breath, be still for a moment, and perhaps say a brief prayer. These kinds of breaks add a negligible amount of time and yet can significantly reduce our feelings of hurry. What is more, taking breaks has been found to boost creativity and even test scores.[44]

44. Hans Henrik Sievertsen, Francesca Gino, and Marco Piovesan, "Cog-

Of course, no school day ever goes perfectly according to plan (much to the consternation of type A teachers everywhere). But there can be a grace in interruptions, too. The Rule of Benedict instructs monks to welcome unexpected visitors as they would Christ himself.[45] In the same spirit, we educators can bear in mind that the messenger at the door or the tardy student might be bringing an unanticipated gift from God. Like the tolling of the bell, unexpected interruptions can serve as opportunities to loosen our grip and open ourselves to God's will. Speaking from experience as one whose initial reaction to interruptions is seldom delight, I have often looked back at day's end and realized that the impromptu conversation I had with a stressed-out colleague in the hallway or with the student who missed my regular office hours was the most important thing I did that day.

When we create openings for God's light to shine upon the seeds that are the moments of the school day, it bears fruit in many ways. We experience time as *kairos* time, the eternal present, rather than the inexorable march of *chronos* time. We feel less rushed and less stressed. We avoid the interpersonal conflicts that arise due to our distractedness or to negative feelings lingering from an earlier incident. God offers us countless gifts every day, but we miss many of them because we plow through the day with our heads down, fixated on our own agendas. When we take advantage of the natural moments of transition in the day to pause, reflect, and pray, we open ourselves to the good things only God knows the day has in store for us.

Entering Time Anew

The passage of time is a reality of life, and schools are not exempt from this reality. Classes have to begin and end. We have assignments to complete and deadlines to meet. Given these realities of school life, we cannot expect to exist perpetually in a state of detached contem-

---

nitive Fatigue Influences Students' Performance on Standardized Tests," *Proceedings of the National Academy of Sciences* 113, no. 10 (2016): 2621–24.

45. Rule of Benedict 53.1.

plation, no matter how intentional or contemplative we are. But it is still possible to experience something of the eternal in the everyday, perhaps more possible than we imagine. Rowan Williams offers, "if the eye has been opened . . . to 'ever,' at least we may be delivered from the futile resentment of time lost, the futile anxiety about time to be filled. We have touched time as grace."[46] It is my hope that the reflections and meditations in this chapter might open our eyes to "ever" and dispose us to recognize it in the day-to-day.

God in God's great wisdom created us as beings who live within time. That fact should be enough to assure us that it is good that we live our lives according to hours and days and seasons. We do not need to fret or race against the clock. Our task is simply to discern how God intends us to make use of the hours and days God has given us. Living this way requires humility. That is to say, it requires accepting ourselves for what we are, namely, temporal beings who do not control time. Still, even if we are not masters of time, we are in league with the One who is. When we align ourselves with God's will, we find that somehow we always have enough time and no time is ever wasted.

Drawing upon the wisdom of the Christian tradition in this chapter, we have explored some concrete ways of entrusting our time in school to God. For ease of reference, I have summarized these and other practical suggestions below.

Contemplative Practices for Living and Learning on God's Time

For starters:[47] Enter with intentionality: Pause as you enter your office or classroom. Give thanks for this place, these tools, and the work

46. Rowan Williams, *A Century of Poetry: 100 Poems for Searching the Heart* (London: SPCK, 2022), 104.

47. These contemplative practices can seem so different from the ways we normally do things that it can be intimidating to even begin. Seasoned spiritual guides commonly give the advice to work on one new practice until it becomes habit and then gradually add others. Following this wisdom, I will in each chapter recommend one practice "for starters" among other practices that can be added when the time is right.

that happens there. Say a prayer for the people you will encounter there today.

Beginning: Consider some of these practices for beginning the day and each activity from an awareness of God's presence rather than from a sense of pressure to get things done.

- Wake up and get up: Get out of bed as soon as the alarm rings as if God were summoning you.[48]
- Pray through the commute: Use your commute as an opportunity to transition intentionally from home to work. Take in the scenery. Pray the Jesus Prayer, the Lord's Prayer, the rosary, or meditate on the daily readings or another Scripture passage.[49]
- Begin from prayer together: Begin the school day by coming together for worship or prayer at morning assembly. Alternatively, schools can begin with a reflection, prayer, or spiritual reading over the intercom.

Do what you are doing: Utilize some of these visual and temporal markers to bring your attention back to God throughout the day:

- Visual reminders: Put up posters of phrases that will remind everyone to be present to the divine Mystery, each other, and the task at hand (e.g., *Age quod agis* or "Be. Here. Now.").
- Heed the bell: Use a timer to keep time instead of watching the clock.[50] When the bell chimes, pause to breathe, stretch, pray, and be aware of God's presence.

48. Father Josemaría Escrivá calls this the "heroic minute." *The Way* (New York: Image Books, 2006), no. 191.

49. Phone apps such as Hallow (https://hallow.com/) make it easy to listen to the daily readings or pray a meditation while commuting.

50. Timers can be found on YouTube as well as on phone apps like the Mindfulness Bell (https://tinyurl.com/35njknej).

- Practice the presence of God:[51] During the moments of the day when no active thought is required (e.g., waiting for the computer to turn on or for copies to print), steal a little time with the Lord by repeating the Jesus Prayer or another simple prayer.

Transitions: We spend too much of our days running from one thing to the next. Take advantage of transition moments as opportunities to recenter on God.

- Pause in between: During minor transitions (e.g., between class activities or emails), take a deep breath, stretch, and say a brief prayer. During major transitions, stop in the chapel, sit in prayer for a few minutes, or take a walk. When moving from one place to another, walk in a prayerful, mindful manner.
- Plan to pause: Identify times in your day when you know you can take a break. Write them into your planner or set alarms on your phone. Consider praying the Liturgy of the Hours.[52]
- Pause together: Build opportunities to pause into the school schedule, for example, praying the Angelus at midday or the examen at the end of the day and pausing for a moment of recollection when a class period ends. Alternatively, plan to meet up with a colleague for a walk or to pray or meditate together.
- Let go: When it is time to move to the next class, meeting, or task, take a moment to let go mentally. Say a prayer of thanks for the work God has done in you, commend it into God's hands, and move on.

51. Brother Lawrence, *Practice of the Presence of God*, Christian Classics Ethereal Library, accessed October 30, 2024, https://tinyurl.com/2nrvbhbh.

52. Daily prayers for the Liturgy of the Hours can be found at https://tinyurl.com/muybhb4z.

3

Teaching and Learning

Sharing the Fruits of Contemplation

As we saw in chapter 1, Christian schools grew out of monasteries and materialized an education motivated by "the love of learning and the desire for God."[1] These monasteries and schools were (often if not always) places of wisdom, peace, order, and love. This is rarely our experience in modern schools, and it is hard not to feel that something has been lost. Certainly we have lost the sense of leisure and living on God's time that characterized medieval monastic study. Reflecting further upon our experiences in the classroom today might help us to identify what else has been lost and—we may hope—what we might yet recover.

Struggles in the Classroom

If you are a teacher like me, a typical class often looks something like this: I arrive on campus later than I wanted and have to quickly print out my notes and run to class. When I walk into the classroom, a few students are already there, sitting in the darkened room scrolling on their phones, not talking to each other. I flip on the lights, offer a perfunctory "Good morning," and hurriedly connect my laptop to the

1. Jean Leclercq, *The Love of Learning and the Desire for God: A Study of Monastic Culture*, trans. Catharine Misrahi (New York: Fordham University Press, 1961).

display and arrange my notes on the podium. More students trickle in. Most do not make eye contact or acknowledge the others in the room. They simply make their way to their usual seats and immediately take out their phones.

The clock strikes the top of the hour, I ask everyone to put away their phones, and I begin. A few more students trickle in late. I do not react visibly, but I feel my muscles tense. I am irritated at this distraction, especially since we are now well into the semester and they should know better. I make a note to talk to the tardy students after class while trying (unsuccessfully) not to break my stride.

I review key points from the previous lesson, introduce the day's topic, and pose a question with the intention of stimulating discussion. Twenty-two sets of eyes look down at the desks in front of them. I notice one set of eyes angled more sharply. This student has already taken out his phone again, five minutes into class. The muscles in my shoulders tighten further. I rephrase the question, and eventually a hand rises reluctantly. The student offers a comment, and I ask a follow-up question, inviting the student to connect her comment to the assigned reading. From her response, it is evident that she has not done the reading. As the class goes on, it becomes clear that neither have most of her classmates. I notice that several more students are now staring into their laps, their arms twitching rhythmically.

I give up on the Socratic approach and revert to lecture. Time is running out, and they need to know the material. Only a week and a half remains before all first-year core students will take the common midterm exam. With five minutes left in class, several students begin packing up their things. I point out that class has not yet ended and ask for their attention. My speaking accelerates as I attempt to get to the last of my talking points. Yet again we will not get to the comprehension-check questions I had planned. As the final minute slips away, students stand up, most reaching instinctively for their phones. I bark a few last-minute reminders as they walk out and begin packing up my own things. I notice my notes from earlier to talk to the tardy students, and, looking up, curse to myself when I see that they have already gone. "Just as well," I tell myself. I have to run to a department meeting.

What Happened to the Joy of Learning?

The scene I have just described will no doubt feel familiar to many teachers. The classroom can be a place of joy, connection, and insight, but for teachers and students alike the classroom is also frequently a place associated with tension, frustration, and hurry. In due course we will explore how joy and calm might be more frequent experiences in the classroom, but for the moment I want to examine these frustrations. Why is teaching and learning so often like this?

If you ask just about any veteran teacher, that educator will tell you that the current crop of students seems different from those in years past. Recent research offers evidence that these perceived changes are objective realities, not just the nostalgic projections of teachers yearning for an imagined golden age.[2] What teachers note most is the decrease in attention spans.[3] Students struggle to sustain attention on presentations and to complete even short reading assignments. Research points to students' use of smart phones and social media as the primary culprit. These technologies rewire users' neural circuitry in such a way that they are conditioned to shift attention rapidly from one thing to the next.[4] Psychologist Gloria Mark observes that this "kinetic" form of attention is the brain's way of adapting to the flood of information and distractions we now encounter on a daily basis, but there are significant downsides to kinetic attention.[5] For example, we easily succumb to "attention traps" that distract us from more important tasks.[6] Furthermore, being wired for

2. I will engage this research in the footnotes throughout the chapter.

3. By some measures, attention spans have shrunk by 70 percent in the last twenty years. See Kim Mills, "Episode 225: Why Our Attention Spans Are Shrinking, with Gloria Mark, PhD," *Speaking of Psychology Podcast*, accessed August, 17, 2024, https://tinyurl.com/ypf4behe.

4. See Gary Small and Gigi Vorgan, *iBrain: Surviving the Technological Alteration of the Modern Mind* (New York: Collins, 2008), 1.

5. Gloria Mark, *Attention Span: A Groundbreaking Way to Restore Balance, Happiness, and Productivity* (Toronto: Hanover Square Press, 2023), 46.

6. Mark, *Attention Span*, 55. Examples of these attention traps include mind

kinetic attention comes at the expense of more focused and sustained attention required for much academic and professional work (writing, researching, listening, etc.).[7] In the socio-emotional domain, if social media offers valuable opportunities for instantaneous connection with peers, it appears to come with the double edge of increased anxiety, depression, and loneliness.[8]

While it is easy for teachers to blame students for being rude and inattentive, the more difficult truth is that these "digital natives" have been conditioned for these behaviors all their lives. Like all of us, they seek meaning and personal connection, and the most readily available means of satisfying these needs are digital devices and social media.[9] Internet search engines and social media platforms that limit expression to short posts and video clips and reward rapid clicking

---

wandering and aimless clicking, addictive games and social media, and our own mistaken judgments about our ability to redirect and refocus our attention. Some of these traps are natural, but others are the result of tech developers' deliberate design of their products. These designs are so effective that many people now find it more difficult to refrain from using social media than from consuming tobacco, coffee, alcohol, and food. See Wilhelm Hofmann, Kathleen D. Vohs, and Roy F. Baumeister, "What People Desire, Feel Conflicted about, and Try to Resist in Everyday Life," *Psychological Sciences* 23, no. 6 (April 30, 2012).

7. Neuroscientist Andrew Huberman explains that acclimating to constant dopamine hits, which social media is engineered to deliver, makes normal activities feel less rewarding and therefore more difficult to do. Andrew Huberman, "Dr. Jonathan Haidt: How Smartphones & Social Media Impact Mental Health & the Realistic Solutions," *Huberman Lab Podcast*, June 10, 2024, https://tinyurl.com/bdeytmpj.

8. Jean Twenge, *iGen: Why Today's Super-Connected Kids Are Growing Up Less Rebellious, More Tolerant, Less Happy—and Completely Unprepared for Adulthood* (New York: Atria Books, 2017). While the effects of social media usage on mental health are still somewhat debated among researchers, there is ample evidence of its harm for at least some people (especially girls) in some circumstances.

9. For two helpful discussions of how the basic human need for connection motivates social media use, see Andrew Zirschy, *Beyond the Screen: Youth Ministry for the Connected but Alone Generation* (Nashville: Abingdon, 2015),

condition them to consume content rapidly and superficially. Cultural and parental pressure to succeed academically and professionally contributes to packed extracurricular schedules and little time for play and rest.

Our schools often reproduce this culture of busyness and distraction. Even when a school or teacher succeeds in compelling students to store away their phones, other technology is usually present. Smart boards, AV equipment, computers, and tablets have become fixtures in many classrooms. To be sure, educational technology has its benefits. However, more technology does not necessarily translate into better learning and can actually be detrimental.[10] The fact that the word "school" derives from the Greek for "leisure" (*scholē*) would strike most educators today as comical. In the era of teaching to the test, teachers fly through material chapter after chapter with no occasion to dwell upon the hidden stories of history, the marvels of the solar system, or the elegance of a geometric proof. Students return home each day with piles of homework that they hurry to complete (or not) in between after-school extracurriculars.

Teachers fare no better, shouldering the burden of an ever-growing list of curricular requirements, parental demands, and intensifying student needs. Although university professors spend fewer hours in the classroom than elementary or secondary teachers, they experience other burdens including committee work and research expectations.[11] In the "publish-or-perish" culture of academia, conscientious faculty devote extra time to lesson prep and student meetings at their professional peril. And they are the fortunate ones. Less fortunate are the ever-growing hordes of underpaid and uninsured

---

and James Lang, *Distracted: Why Students Can't Focus and What You Can Do About It* (New York: Basic Books, 2020), especially page 99.

10. Joe Clement and Matt Miles, *Screen Schooled: Two Veteran Teachers Expose How Technology Overuse Is Making Our Kids Dumber* (Chicago: Chicago Review Press, 2017).

11. See Maggie Berg and Barbara K. Seeber, *The Slow Professor: Challenging the Culture of Speed in the Academy* (Toronto: University of Toronto Press, 2016).

adjunct faculty, who are forced to teach multiple courses at multiple universities in order to make ends meet. As most universities have come under financial stress in recent decades, fewer full-time faculty lines have been replaced and the remaining faculty are forced to absorb the workload of their departed colleagues.

There is much about this state of affairs that just about everybody involved—educators, students, parents—finds frustrating, yet we have a hard time seeing our way out of it. We feel powerless to overcome the deeply entrenched culture of busyness and ubiquitous technology. Of course, there are pragmatic concerns to confront. Students and parents demand that their schools provide the skills (or at least the credentials) necessary for securing students' livelihoods. Schools need to meet those demands in order to stay open and support their employees. It is hard to fault anyone here, and yet we might question if we are seeing the whole picture. Might it be possible to see this reality differently and therefore to educate in a different way?

I contend that, despite all of these challenges, the classroom need not be a place of hurry and frustration. I know this to be a possibility because I and others have experienced it to be true and because current research confirms our experience. Radical change often begins with a simple action. For me, it has made all the difference when, rather than cramming in a few last-minute changes to the lesson plan, I stop in the chapel or pause for a moment of silent prayer before making my way to the classroom. There in the silence and stillness, I have encountered something that changes me and changes how things go in the classroom. I invite you to come and see for yourself. Join me in the chapel for a meditation that just might help us see the classroom and our students in a different light.

A Meditation on Growth

In this meditation, I will invite you into the chapel of my home institution to meditate on some images we find there. We will meditate on these images, which you see on page 67, according to the practice of *visio*

The Chapel of the Immaculate Conception at Seton Hall University

Detail of archway above the chapel sanctuary

divina (divine seeing). *Visio divina* is like *lectio divina* (mentioned in chapter 1) except that instead of praying with Scripture we pray with artwork, icons, and other images. It involves four steps—*visio* (seeing), *meditatio* (meditation), *oratio* (prayer), and *contemplatio* (contemplation).

The Chapel of the Immaculate Conception lies at the heart of Seton Hall University's campus, just off the campus green. Thanks to the hospitable spirit of the current director of campus ministry, the front doors of the chapel are always flung open in welcome. When we step through a second set of doors, the buzz of the campus outside subsides and we enter into a reverent stillness. Sitting down, we hear the pew creaking like a tree bending in the wind. The wooden floors, pews, and support beams give the space a sylvan feel. Decorative foliage bursts forth all throughout the chapel—lining the communion rail, tracing along the walls, up to the ceiling. Green painted vines climb the arch above the sanctuary. They grow outward from the sanctuary where God, the source of life, dwells and run down and outward along the walls of the chapel. Red berries hang upon them, a sign of their fecundity. Take a moment to gaze (*visio*) upon this image of the vine in the bottom photograph. What do you notice about it?

Next I invite you to meditate (*meditatio*) upon this image. What thoughts does it elicit? What meaning do you find in this symbolism? For me, the vine brings to mind Jesus's words in John 15:

> "I am the true vine, and my Father is the vine-grower. . . . Abide in me as I abide in you. Just as the branch cannot bear fruit by itself unless it abides in the vine, neither can you unless you abide in me. I am the vine, you are the branches. Those who abide in me and I in them bear much fruit, because apart from me you can do nothing." (John 15:1, 4–5)

This passage captures the reason we come to a place like the chapel—to be grafted onto Christ and abide in him. The images of growth that adorn this space make visible what happens invisibly within the people who come here. When we receive Christ in the Eucharist, a seed of new life is planted inside. When we abide with him during adoration or a quiet moment of prayer, this seed is nourished and begins to bear fruit.

Follow wherever your thoughts lead. However, if it serves your meditation, you might ponder these questions:

- Do you see any connections between these images or the text of John 15 and your experiences of teaching and learning?
- What happens in the classroom and to the people who gather there? What kind of growth occurs? How does it occur?
- Do these images suggest possibilities different from the experience of the classroom described earlier? What are those possibilities?
- Would it be possible to experience in the classroom something of the calm, peacefulness, and sacredness that we have experienced here in the chapel? How?

Take some time to meditate on these questions.

The final two steps of *visio divina* involve bringing these reflections to prayer. We are invited to go beyond our own thoughts and enter into conversation with God about what we are seeing and thinking. In this sense, *visio divina* is not a solitary exercise; it is an opportunity to grow in relationship. Speak with God (*oratio*) about what was emerging for you in your meditation. What seemed significant? What questions came up? What is in your heart at this moment?

Finally, take a moment simply to rest in God's loving presence (*contemplatio*). Let your mind settle. Cease any effort to make sense of the images. Say nothing more. Be still. Listen. Know that God is near.

When you have finished, you might offer God a word of thanks for this moment of prayer.

Seeing People as Growing Beings

Let's return to the classroom now that we have fortified our vision through this exercise of *visio divina*. How might we see and experience people, time, space, objects, and activities in the classroom differently?

We will begin with our students. Students come to school to learn and grow, but to learn what exactly? To grow in what way? Often our educational institutions and practices reflect muddled thinking about what is good for the human person and how education should contribute to that good. In the face of such confusion, education often gets reduced to the lowest common denominator, namely, career training or college prep in the case of certain high schools. This approach reflects an implicit (sometimes explicit) materialism, a misguided assumption that achievement and material acquisition will lead to happiness.[12] Even many Christian schools, which we would expect to pursue higher aims, get caught up in this trend.

We see how such materialistic thinking has affected our schools in the extent to which they often function like factories. The "factory owners" (accrediting agencies, school boards, administrators) determine the desired "product" or outcome and design the learning process accordingly. The student is regarded as passive material to be molded like metal on a conveyor belt or to be programmed like a robot. Teachers, for their part, play the role of technicians or programmers, shaping or programming students according to predetermined specifications. They control the knowledge, the timeline, and the process.[13]

How does our meditation invite us to look at the teacher-student dynamic differently? For one thing, the images of growth that we encountered in the chapel may suggest a more fitting understanding

12. See Iain McGilchrist, *The Master and His Emissary: The Divided Brain and the Making of the Western World* (New Haven: Yale University Press, 2019), 434–35, for a summary of research demonstrating that increase in material well-being contributes to happiness in only a limited way.

13. I am generalizing a bit here. Education today is far more learner-centered than it was in generations past. That being said, there remain in our educational system many practices that seem more the product of bureaucracy than of concern for learners' needs (e.g., standardized test-driven curricula and school schedules).

of the human being from which to develop our pedagogical practices. Consider how the methods of a gardener tending to living plants differ from those of a factory technician working with steel or stone. The former would seem a better analogy for education since people are living, growing beings, not inanimate objects to be bent and shaped according to someone else's designs.[14] The analogy is even more apt for Christian education, as it touches upon a fundamental component of Christian anthropology. As Christians, we believe that each and every human being possesses unique dignity, value, and freedom deriving from his or her creation in God's own image and likeness (Gen. 1:26–27). The most nonnegotiable of Christian moral teachings is that we love our neighbor as we love ourselves (Mark 12:31). To objectify another person in any way is a violation of the other's human dignity and of this most central tenet of Christian faith.

In order for gardeners to know how to help a plant grow to its full potential, they must know what kind of plant it is. They cannot produce a maple tree from a geranium seed or a rose bush from a pumpkin seed. The same is true for educators and students. As Christian educators, we recognize that human beings are created, not primarily for goods production or for profit but rather for divine communion. Accordingly, Christian schools should be places where, in addition to learning academic subjects and professional skills, students learn what it is to be persons-in-communion created in the image and likeness of the triune God.[15]

Given these convictions, Christian educators can affirm Alfred North Whitehead's identification of freedom and discipline as two

14. This view of the human person is fully consistent with contemporary neuroscience, which has helped us to understand how the human brain continues to change and grow throughout our lives. Neuroscientists even employ naturalistic language like "dendritic" (having a branching structure like that of a tree) and "pruning" to describe neural structures and growth.

15. See Lynn E. Swaner and Andy Wolfe, *Flourishing Together: A Christian Vision for Students, Educators, and Schools* (Grand Rapids: Eerdmans, 2021), chapter 5.

essential components of education.[16] On the one hand, we must support students in developing genuine freedom and personal agency, a basic requirement of becoming mature adults. From a Christian perspective, this respect for students' agency is essential because our human fulfillment hinges upon our free response to God's offer of loving communion and to the particular vocation to which God calls each of us. Unfortunately, too often our schools succeed only in producing people who, in the stinging words of Thomas Merton, are "literally unfit for anything except to take part in an elaborate and completely artificial charade which they and their contemporaries have conspired to call 'life.'"[17] Practically speaking, promoting students' agency might involve inviting them to set their own learning goals and giving them some choice over class activities, projects, groups, etc., whenever possible.[18] Research suggests this element of choice also has the benefit of increasing students' engagement and motivation to learn.[19]

On the other hand, we all require some support in this work of self-discovery, that is, some form of "discipline." Saint Augustine observed that we become like the things we desire.[20] We are like

16. Alfred North Whitehead, *The Aims of Education and Other Essays* (New York: Free Press, 1967), 30. For a Christian articulation of these same principles, see Luigi Giussani, *The Risk of Education: Discovering Our Ultimate Destiny* (New York: Crossroad, 1996).

17. Thomas Merton, "Learning to Live," in *Love and Living*, ed. Naomi Burton Stone and Brother Patrick Hart (San Diego: Harcourt, 1985), 11.

18. A radical example is "ungrading," in one version of which teachers establish a learning contract with students at the beginning of the course identifying the grade each student desires to earn and the work required to earn that grade. For more see Susan D. Bloom, ed., *Ungrading: Why Rating Students Undermines Learning (and What to Do Instead)* (Morgantown: West Virginia University Press, 2020).

19. See Mihaly Csikszentmihalyi, *Flow: The Psychology of Optimal Experience* (New York: Harper & Row, 1990).

20. James K. A. Smith has elaborated upon Augustine's insight at length, drawing out implications for Christian universities in his books *Desiring the Kingdom: Worship, Worldview, and Cultural Formation* (Grand Rapids: Baker

vines that wrap themselves around whatever support with which they come into contact. If we wrap ourselves around the idealized images and materialistic messages we see on social media, our self-image and lifestyle come to reflect those things. However, if we conform ourselves to Christ—to his teachings, his example, the church that is his body—we become like Christ. Self-awareness of this feature of our humanity is what led monastic founders such as Pachomius the Great and Saint Benedict to develop "rules" that served as a spiritual trellis for their communities and the individuals who constituted them.[21] There is wisdom here for school communities as well. Providing students with the right kind of structure is as important for helping them live into their vocation as respecting their freedom. Solid Christian teaching, a structured schedule, communal rituals, and clear expectations for conduct all serve to provide such support.

When schools strike this balance between freedom and structure, students glimpse a vision of life at its fullest and feel it is possible to achieve it.[22] More than a sequence of obligatory classes and assignments, school becomes a training ground and an adventure in realizing their full human potential.

Community as Soil for Our Souls

We have been exploring a crucial anthropological insight for Christian education, namely, that humans are growing beings. Like plants reaching up to the sun, we grow toward something in particular. That light toward which we grow (and also the soil in which we grow) is love. Current research confirms that relationship building creates the

---

Academic, 2009) and *You Are What You Love: The Spiritual Power of Habit* (Grand Rapids: Brazos, 2016).

21. In fact, the Greek word for "rule" is related to the word for trellis.

22. Harvard psychologist Robert Kegan similarly attests, "people grow best when they continuously experience an ingenious blend of support and challenge." *In Over Our Heads: The Mental Demands of Modern Life* (Cambridge, MA: Harvard University Press, 1996), 42.

foundation and the context within which the most meaningful learning happens.[23] Students are more likely to learn from teachers whom they admire and who they know care for them. Nurturing such caring relationships creates an ideal learning environment in which our students, like Jesus's and Anthony's disciples, can learn from our lived example and way of being in the world in addition to learning from our explicit instruction. On the flip side, if we teachers are frustrated with our students' lack of interest in the class, perhaps our first response should be to take more of an interest in them and see how they respond.

Although the gardener clearly plays an important role, many other things impact the health of the garden. Each plant is affected by every plant around it, not to mention the insects, animals, soil, and air. Similarly, teachers are not the only formators of the students. Students play a significant part in forming each other, just as do fellow monks in a monastery or siblings in a family. Recognizing this dynamic, teachers and administrators can endeavor to create structures and conditions wherein loving relationships and friendships form among students. As we will see in chapter 4, much of this work happens through schoolwide practices and rituals. However, a great deal of community building happens at the more local level of the classroom.

One powerful means of building community is storytelling. Stories—both personal and communal stories—are water for the soul and for our communities. In listening to another person's story, it becomes easier for me to see this other person as someone like myself and therefore to feel compassion for him or her. Stories are catalysts for creating a classroom culture where everyone enjoys a sense of security and belonging.[24] Some young people come to our schools with heart-wrenching stories, and, as educator Mary Rose O'Reilly

23. Josh Packard et al., *Belonging: Reconnecting America's Loneliest Generation* (Bloomington, MN: Springtide Research Institute, 2020); Swaner and Wolfe, *Flourishing Together*, 69–70.

24. The effect is particularly powerful for individuals who might otherwise feel like outsiders. See Gregory M. Walton and Geoffrey L. Cohen, "A Brief Social-Belonging Intervention Improves Academic and Health Outcomes of Minority Students," *Science* 331, no. 6023 (2011): 1447–51.

says, it is very hard for them to learn until the weight of their story is pulled off them (i.e., shared).[25] Storytelling can be incorporated in the classroom throughout the year and can be as simple as giving students a few minutes at the start of the week to talk with each other about their weekend. However, sharing stories is particularly valuable at the beginning of the year or semester when the classroom culture is just being established. Here teachers might invite students to share a biographical story that will give their classmates an insight into who they are or to relate their personal story to the "story" of the course.

Besides storytelling, there are many other ways of building community. Another tested and true method is working together on a shared task. This is the principle behind team-building exercises and retreats, but it is not always practical for a class to go to a retreat center or a high-ropes course. Simply working on a project together (ideally something fun, creative, and playful) can work very well. Group work tends to be most effective and meaningful when teachers provide clear goals and instructions regarding the process and expected product, ensure interaction among group members as well as group and individual accountability, and offer frequent feedback.[26] Exchanging physical signs of affirmation such as high fives not only promotes connection but also enhances individual and group performance.[27] Singing together (for example, chanted hymns, Taizé-style music,[28] or even students' favorite songs) also has a way of unifying a group.[29]

25. Mary Rose O'Reilly, *Radical Presence: Teaching as Contemplative Practice* (Portsmouth, NH: Boynton/Cook Publishers, 1998), 28.

26. "Guidelines for Using Groups Effectively," Center for Research on Learning and Teaching, University of Michigan, accessed October 30, 2024, https://tinyurl.com/mvzan8ze.

27. Michael W. Kraus, Cassy Huang, and Dacher Keltner, "Tactile Communication, Cooperation, and Performance: An Ethological Study of the NBA," *Emotion* 10, no. 5 (2010): 745–49.

28. You can experience the beautiful musical prayer of the Taizé community in France on their YouTube channel: https://tinyurl.com/36c4h3sz.

29. See Resmaa Menakem, *My Grandmother's Hands: Racialized Trauma and the Pathway to Mending Our Hearts and Bodies* (Las Vegas: Central Recovery Press, 2017), 184. Studies have shown that people's heart rates actually syn-

Several of my colleagues at the university begin every class with music and testify to how it transforms the dynamics of the class.

These practices are effective because they correspond to who we are most essentially—beings created for communion. As Jesus said, the branch that remains connected to the vine bears much fruit (John 15:5–6). A branch cut off from the vine withers.

The Classroom as a Place of Growth

Let's return to the chapel for a moment. As we leave behind the activity of the campus and pass through the wooden doors and into the stone confines of the chapel, we immediately recognize that this is a different kind of place with a different kind of purpose. The reverent silence, the flickering candles, the religious symbols, the orderliness and cleanliness of the space all point to the presence of something sacred and invite us to respond accordingly.

The classroom, too, is a place set apart. For Christian monastics, study was hallowed work that led to divine union, and the spaces they used for study were designed to suit that purpose. This sort of appreciation for the sacredness of space seems less common in our own day. Modern architecture is often more concerned with utility and efficiency than with raising hearts and minds to divine contemplation.[30] Such utilitarian designs reflect certain assumptions about the people

chronize when they sing together. See Björn Vickhoff et al., "Music Structure Determines Heart Rate Variability of Singers," *Frontiers in Psychology* 4 (2013): 334. The same thing can happen to people listening to a story together. See Pauline Pérez et al., "Conscious Processing of Narrative Stimuli Synchronizes Heart Rate Between Individuals," *Cell Reports* 36, no. 11 (2021), https://doi.org/10.1016/j.celrep.2021.109692.

30. John Skillen criticizes the "leveling of space" in modern design, enumerates the costs of this dissociation of space design from designated action, and offers guidance on how to design school spaces in ways that further the school's mission. *Making Schools Beautiful: Restoring the Harmony of Place* (Camp Hill, PA: Classical Academic Press, 2020), 1.

who occupy these spaces.[31] If we think of students as products to be assembled or programmed, a space designed for the efficient distribution of information will suffice. But students are not machines. They are growing beings, and growing things need a particular kind of environment in order to thrive.[32] How might our classrooms and schools be different if we took this aspect of our human nature more seriously?

To begin with the most obvious, we might reconsider the ways we decorate our classrooms (or don't) and the messages we send to our students thereby. Walk into any elementary- or middle-school classroom today, and you are likely to see posters reinforcing principles of socio-emotional learning ("Treat others the way you want to be treated") and a growth mind-set ("Mistakes are proof that you are trying"). While these messages are perfectly appropriate for Christian schools, we have a more profound message to share.[33] At the heart of

31. As Anne Taylor and George Vlastos say, the built environment constitutes a "silent curriculum." *School Zone: Learning Environments for Children*, 2nd ed. (Corrales, NM: School Zone, Inc., 1983).

32. On this topic, I recommend Matthew Crawford's book *The World Beyond Your Head: How to Flourish in an Age of Distraction* (New York: Penguin Books, 2015), wherein the author presents a number of examples of "well-ordered ecologies of attention and action . . . that can support some low-to-the-ground, perfectly attainable moments of human flourishing" (112). Crawford's reflections are highly instructive for educators considering how schools and classrooms might serve as such well-ordered ecologies. The Montessori method of education, pioneered by Catholic educator Maria Montessori and developed for religious instruction by Sofia Cavalletti, also gives great importance to the learning environment. See Maria Montessori, *The Montessori Method* (Mineola, NY: Dover Publications, 2002), and Sofia Cavalletti, *The Religious Potential of the Child: Experiencing Scripture and Liturgy with Young Children*, trans. Patricia M. Coulter and Julie M. Coulter, ed. Rebekah Rojcewicz, 3rd ed. (Chicago: Catechesis of the Good Shepherd Publications, 2020). Although Montessori and Cavalletti were primarily concerned with the education of children, Jared August has drawn out implications for adult education in his article "Montessori, 'Formation,' and the Adult Learner," *Religious Education* 119, no. 1 (2024): 3–16, https://doi.org/10.1080/00344087.2023.2283668.

33. For an explicitly Christian approach to social-emotional learning, see

the good news of Jesus Christ is the truth that each of us is a beloved child of God. All students should hear this message loud and clear in what they see and hear in their classroom.

Now, consider what messages your classroom sends. If college pennants or posters of potential careers predominate, what message does that send? Is there anything that signals to students that they are good and lovable regardless of what they achieve?

Even the arrangement of seats and other furnishings sends a message. Recall, if you can, what it felt like as a child to walk into your elementary classroom where desks were arranged in straight rows. What did your body anticipate as you sat down? How were you supposed to behave? The unspoken message would seem to be that the important person is at the front of the room and that is where students should focus their attention. Arranging chairs in a circle or around tables, by contrast, invites learners into conversation, exploration, and community. My point is not that rows are always bad and circles are always good. Derek Bruff, former director of the Vanderbilt Center for Teaching, argues that the most important technology in the college classroom is "chairs on wheels" because movable furnishings give teachers the ability to reconfigure the classroom to best suit the kind of learning that will happen.[34] Generally speaking, as Christian educators, we should ask ourselves, *What arrangement and features of the learning environment will dispose my students to engage the subject matter and one another deeply and to be aware of the presence of Mystery?*

More subtle features of the learning environment can also have significant effects on students. Research shows that creating a visually stimulating environment and changing the classroom appearance regularly correlate with attention and engagement.[35] Lighting qual-

---

the "Insight" professional development program produced by the Institute for the Transformation of Catholic Education (https://tinyurl.com/4n58er7j).

34. Derek Bruff, *Intentional Tech: Principles to Guide the Use of Educational Technology in College Teaching* (Morgantown: West Virginia University Press, 2019), 1.

35. Glenn Whitman and Ian Kelleher, *Neuroteach: Brain Science and the Future of Education* (Lanham, MD: Rowman & Littlefield, 2016), 90.

ity can affect students' psychological state, behavior, and academic achievement.[36] Natural sunlight and full-spectrum fluorescent lamps are best for student focus and health.[37] The presence of plants has similarly been shown to improve mood and well-being.[38] Other studies draw attention to the ways noisy classrooms can negatively impact students' and teachers' cognitive processing, academic performance, and behavior.[39] This research suggests that quiet is a key ingredient not only for spiritual growth but also for psychological health and learning and therefore something teachers should strive to preserve in their classrooms. Playing music from time to time can also enhance cognitive performance, behavior, and motivation.[40]

Christian educators should be similarly discerning when it comes to the place of technology in the classroom.[41] Although technology can certainly be helpful in certain subjects at certain times, it does not always promote learning and it should not be our default pedagogical

36. Mark Winterbottom and Arnold Wilkins, "Lighting and Discomfort in the Classroom," *Journal of Environmental Psychology* 29, no. 1 (2009): 63–75.

37. W. E. Hathaway, "Non-visual Effects of Classroom Lighting on Children," *Educational Facility Planner* 32, no. 3 (1994): 12–16; Lisa Heschong and Carey Knecht, "Daylighting Makes a Difference," *Educational Facility Planner* 37, no. 2 (2002): 5–14.

38. See Charlotte Gunn, Maria Vahdati, and Mehdi Shahrestani, "Green Walls in Schools: The Potential Well-Being Benefits," *Building and Environment* 224 (2022): 109560, https://doi.org/10.1016/j.buildenv.2022.109560.

39. Julie E. Dockrell and Bridget M. Shield, "Acoustical Barriers in Classrooms: The Impact of Noise on Performance in the Classroom," *British Educational Research Journal* 32, no. 3 (2006): 509–25.

40. Larry Scripp, "An Overview of Research on Music and Learning," in *Critical Links: Learning in the Arts and Student Academic and Social Development*, ed. Richard Deasy (Washington, DC: Arts Education Partnership, 2002), 132–36.

41. Space limitations do not allow me to discuss online learning in any depth here. However, I refer readers to discussions of this topic in Daniel P. Barbezat and Mirabai Bush, *Contemplative Practices in Higher Education: Powerful Methods to Transform Teaching and Learning* (San Francisco: Jossey-Bass, 2014), 121–22, and Agnieszka Palalas et al., "Mindfulness Practices in Online Learning: Supporting Learner Self-Regulation," *Journal of Contemplative Inquiry* 7, no. 1 (2020): 247–78.

approach.[42] As we have already discussed, young people's constant interfacing with their personal devices is rewiring their brains for a kinetic form of attention that impedes their ability to engage one another, God, and the created world attentively, thoughtfully, and lovingly. Schools (especially Christian schools) should be places that remediate this attenuating of attention rather than contributing to it. Many schools have already established tech-free zones and times. Evidence for the benefits of removing phones from the school entirely is mounting as concerns about students' mental health intensify and increasing numbers of schools take this drastic measure.[43] It is important to discuss these practices and their rationale with students so they do not perceive them as punitive. Better yet, we can engage students in exercises and conversations that raise their awareness of the pros and cons of technology.[44]

While even one class can make a difference, students grow best when fully immersed in a beautiful, well-ordered environment. In this regard, the culture of the whole school takes on great importance. When we spend time in a place where the architecture of the buildings and the interior spaces are thoughtfully designed and crafted, where the rooms are bathed in natural light, and where artwork and other beautiful things adorn the walls, we feel inspired, smarter, and more whole. These are not just feelings. As the above-cited research shows, these elements of design have significant psychological effects on the people who occupy such spaces and therefore merit serious attention from educators. Possibilities exist whatever a school's budget. A school may not be able to afford museum-quality prints, but teachers can surely display their students' artwork in classrooms and

42. See Whitman and Kelleher, *Neuroteach*, 134.

43. Jonathan Haidt and Z. Rausch, "The Effects of Phone-Free Schools: A Collaborative Review," unpublished manuscript, New York University (ongoing), https://tinyurl.com/mj6sph2v.

44. Felicia Wu Song describes several such exercises in her book *Restless Devices*, for example, asking students to keep a record of their technology habits for a day or a week and then reflect on these habits.

hallways. If a school does not have the budget or the space for a community garden, it is probably nevertheless possible to liven up the grounds with some well-placed potted plants.

Learning as the Fruit of Contemplation

We now come to the heart of the matter of teaching and learning. Here it is crucial to return to that central question: What are we educating for? When we talk about promoting our students' growth, what is it we believe they are growing toward? Often our educational institutions and practices reflect muddled thinking about what is good for the human person and how education should contribute to that good. For us as Christian educators, how we answer these questions—whether explicitly or implicitly in the way we teach—should flow from what God has revealed to us about ourselves.

The core truth of our humanity is that we are created for loving communion with God and one another. The ultimate goal of our Christian schools, therefore, is to facilitate our students' entering into this loving communion. This goal suggests a different way of thinking about our teaching. Jesus invites us to abide in him so that we can bear much fruit (John 15:5). The Dominicans offer a model of education that begins from this assumption, approaching teaching as a means of sharing the fruits of contemplation. Following their lead, we will now explore numerous contemplative practices through which we can invite our students to abide in the divine Mystery and consider the fruit they might bear as a result.

Meaning and Staying Connected to the Vine of Life

We Christian educators generally expect our students to master the same academic subjects studied by their peers in secular schools, but our hopes for them extend much further. Christian schools have historically been committed to the education of the whole person (body, spirit, mind, heart), and we aspire to nothing short of students living into the fullness of life.[45] This commitment is more important now than ever in light of the ever-narrowing and often incoherent education offered in public schools. It is no wonder that so many young people currently suffer from "dysthymia" (a low-grade feeling that life is unfulfilling),[46] depression, and a sense of meaninglessness in life.[47] Some, like Iain McGilchrist, argue that the narrow, analytical thinking emphasized in modern education has contributed directly to the host of mental health disorders we see today.[48] In the face of such troubling trends, I do not think Thomas Merton is being dramatic when he writes that the very function of the university (or any Christian school) is to help men and women save their souls from the "hell of meaninglessness."[49]

These problematic trends in modern education reflect a superficial understanding of the human person and our deepest needs that coheres

45. For example, Jesuit schools emphasize this priority in the language of *cura personalis*, or care for the whole person. "Characteristics of Jesuit Education," Jesuit Resource, accessed October 30, 2024, https://tinyurl.com/4xc28xxu, 9. Benedictines found their schools with the aim that they should be places rooted in love that nurture all persons "to cultivate habits of mind and behavior that are life-giving and contribute to the good of all." "Education within the Benedictine Wisdom Tradition," Association of Benedictine Colleges and Universities, accessed October 30, 2024, https://tinyurl.com/ahf2vv7e.

46. Lisa Miller, *The Awakened Brain: The New Science of Spirituality and Our Quest for an Inspired Life* (New York: Random House, 2021), 25.

47. Josh Packard et al., *Meaning-Making: 8 Values That Drive America's Newest Generations* (Bloomington, MN: Springtide Research Institute, 2020), 125. Aaron Antonovsky and others have shown that, when people lack a "sense of coherence" in life, mental health declines. See Aaron Antonovsky, *Unraveling the Mystery of Health: How People Manage Stress and Stay Well* (San Francisco: Jossey-Bass, 2010).

48. McGilchrist, *The Master and His Emissary*, 403–7.

49. Merton, "Learning to Live," 4. Merton's choice of wording is apt. A community of educators working together rather than individual teachers working in isolation has the best chance of offering students the support they need. Especially when it comes to issues of mental health, teachers must know the limits of their competency, coordinate with school counselors and other professionals, and refer out when necessary.

no more with psychological research than it does with Christian teaching. The work of Abraham Maslow, for example, explains that once we satisfy our basic physiological and safety needs, we seek to meet higher-order needs such as self-actualization and self-transcendence.[50] Viktor Frankl likewise affirms that self-actualization is possible only as a side effect of self-transcendence.[51] In Christian terms, we would say that we humans desire the infinite, the fullness of reality that is found only in God. Nothing finite or partial will ever satisfy us.

An authentically Christian education not only provides skills for making a living but also proposes to students what might be worth living for. It was with this aim in mind that Christian education since the time of the monastery schools has included studies in philosophy and theology in which students could think deeply about the meaning of life and integrate their learning into a coherent vision of the whole.[52] That many Christian universities have in recent decades reduced or eliminated requirements in these subjects reflects a significant mission drift and departure from traditional wisdom. The monastic tradition also recognized literature as an important source of humanization.[53] Not only theology and philosophy but also great works of fiction and poetry open up new intellectual vistas and serve as conversation partners as we reflect on life's big questions: What is the meaning of life? What does it mean to be human? Why do we suffer? Is there a greater power at work in the universe, and what is our relationship to it?[54] Of course, much depends on the person teaching

50. Abraham H. Maslow, "A Theory of Human Motivation," *Psychological Review* 50, no. 4 (1943): 370–96, https://doi:10.1037/h0054346.

51. Viktor Frankl, *Man's Search for Meaning* (Boston: Beacon, 2006), 133.

52. For two classic articulations of this vision for education, see Josef Pieper, *Leisure: The Basis of Culture*, trans. Gerald Malsbary (South Bend, IN: St. Augustine's Press, 1998), and John Henry Newman, *The Idea of a University* (Notre Dame: University of Notre Dame Press, 1982).

53. See Leclerq, *The Love of Learning and the Desire for God.*

54. The classical Christian education movement offers a witness to the distinctive value of Christian education today. Classical Academic Press offers

the texts. Most of us have been assigned a "classic" by a teacher who does not really appreciate it and know that there is nothing life-giving about such an experience. For this reason, schools serve their students best by providing ongoing faculty development in the Christian tradition, which has the added benefit of nurturing the hearts, minds, and souls of the faculty members.[55]

Capacity for Loving Relationships

Perhaps the single most important element in a life worth living is our relationships. I think Thomas Merton again hits the mark when he writes that the purpose of education is to help us define ourselves "authentically and spontaneously" in relation to our world, that is, to understand ourselves in relation to the people and things of this world and the Mystery at the source of it all.[56]

Our exploration of the world starts from our own body and soul. We can begin no other way. Learning who we are therefore constitutes the foundational task of education. This kind of self-exploration is work most young people are eager to do. Unfortunately, the resources most readily available to them—social media, the disjointed messages of pop culture, the opinions of equally naive peers—tend to be more confusing than helpful. As Christian educators we have more genuine wisdom to share. For example, we can share the writings of great Christian authors, including theologians, popes, and models of inner exploration such as Saint Augustine, Dorothy Day, and Merton himself.[57] An appropriate level of personal sharing and witness by the teacher may hit home with students even more. Teach-

---

curriculum recommendations for schools and teachers interested in this approach: https://tinyurl.com/t2s5e24v.

55. The Scala Foundation (https://tinyurl.com/3cxuzhx4) and the Portsmouth Institute (https://tinyurl.com/8aeydkuc) are two institutions that provide such enrichment for teachers.

56. Merton, "Learning to Live," 3.

57. See Augustine's *Confessions*; Day's *The Long Loneliness* (San Francisco:

ers can help students to apply these reflections from class to their own lives by providing time for writing, drawing, and other forms of creative expression. Current research demonstrates the many benefits of journaling, including improved content comprehension, metacognition, self-efficacy, and, in some cases, improved mental health.[58] Every subject provides opportunities for students to grow in self-knowledge—in discerning wherein lie their gifts, passions, and weaknesses, if nothing else. Indeed, Merton suggests that the purpose of all learning, in whatever discipline, is to ignite "the inner 'spark' of the fully conscious and free human being."[59]

In these words Merton echoes an important truth about our human nature that is emphasized throughout the Christian tradition. Centuries earlier John of the Cross put it simply: "The soul's center is God."[60] When someone comes into contact with this divine spark within him, says Merton, he has discovered "the ground of his own personality as it opened out into the center of all created being, found in himself the light and wisdom of his creator, a light and wisdom in which everything comprehensible could be comprehended."[61] To know ourselves truly is to recognize the Mystery present within us

---

HarperCollins, 1997); and Merton's *The Seven Storey Mountain*, fiftieth anniversary ed. (San Diego: Harcourt Brace & Co., 1998), respectively.

58. Krista K. Fritson, Krista D. Forrest, and Mackenzie L. Bohl, "Using Reflective Journaling in the College Course," in *Promoting Student Engagement*, ed. Richard Miller et al. (n.p.: Society for the Teaching of Psychology, 2011), 1:157–61; Philip M. Ullrich and Susan K. Lutgendorf, "Journaling about Stressful Events: Effects of Cognitive Processing and Emotional Expression," *Annals of Behavioral Medicine* 24, no. 3 (2002): 244–50. Student journals also provide an opportunity for teachers to check on their students individually since it is often not feasible to have one-on-one conversations with every student on a regular basis.

59. Merton, "Learning to Live," 10.

60. John of the Cross, *The Living Flame of Love*, in *The Collected Works of St. John of the Cross*, trans. K. Kavanaugh and O. Rodriguez (Washington, DC: Institute of Carmelite Studies Publications, 1979), 583.

61. Merton, "Learning to Live," 9.

and all around us. Such an encounter with the divine Mystery is the highest aim of our life and learning, and yet coming to know this Mystery is unlike how we know anything else. This knowledge beyond all ideas and images—*theōria* or "contemplation," ancient Christians called it—is the fruit of *contemplatio* in the sense of prayerful communion with the Beloved. It is the only way we can know God truly. "Of God Himself no man can think," says the author of *The Cloud of Unknowing*, but God "may well be loved" and in this way known.[62] This notion of *contemplatio* is essential to understanding Christian contemplative education and what distinguishes it from secular notions of contemplative pedagogy.

We do not obtain such knowledge from books. Neither can teachers engineer students' discovery of the divine within themselves. At best we can direct students' attention, like a guide pointing out a rare bird before it flies away. We can point out how God was at work in the lives of the saints and authors we read and is at work in students' own lives. We can point out how the structure of a cell or the laws of the universe reflect God's creative work. We can engage students with art, music, and poetry, which are more adequate to capturing something of the ineffable than propositional statements. Above all, we can invite students into silence where they might encounter the divine Mystery, not as an idea to be recorded in their notes, but as Someone with whom they come face-to-face and heart-to-heart. This fertile silence need not always take the form of extended periods of prayer. Sometimes it suffices to let words cease for a moment so the class can sit in awe after reading a beautiful poem or completing an elegant mathematical proof. In this way, we may come to know the meaning of stillness to be worth more than a library full of books, as suggests the Egyptian monk John Climacus (ca. 579–ca. 649).[63]

62. *The Cloud of Unknowing*, Christian Classics Ethereal Library, accessed October 30, 2024, https://tinyurl.com/2p82xvff.

63. Paraphrase of John Climacus in Martin Laird, *A Sunlit Absence: Silence, Awareness, and Contemplation* (Oxford: Oxford University Press, 2011), 102.

To know this Mystery is to know all things in relation to it, including other people. Like the spokes of a wheel drawing closer together as they approach the center, so too do we draw closer to one another as we approach our common center.[64] Entering more deeply into ourselves and discovering the Mystery in our inner depths, we recognize that this Mystery is no less present in other people. The illusion of separation falls away. We see that we are all one. Such awareness of our connectedness flowers in proportion to the time we spend united with the Ground of our being and deepens as we enter into relationship with one another.[65] This is another reason (besides the benefits for learning)[66] to give students time to engage in the kinds of community-building activities described earlier in the chapter. Especially in an age when our relationships are so often mediated (and fractured) by digital media, it is vital that we have time to be physically and emotionally present to one another, to attend deeply to the same things, to speak one heart to another, to share in life together.

It is important to add a caution here: Silence is fertile, but it can also be frightening. Because their lives are filled with constant noise, students (and many adults) often find it awkward and discomforting when they are initially invited into silence. It helps for the teacher to explain the purpose and benefits of silence (as I do in this chapter), to acknowledge the awkwardness, and thereby to demystify and normalize the experience. When the silence is part of a prayer or meditation, inviting rather than commanding students into silence

64. I borrow this image from Martin Laird, *Into the Silent Land: A Guide to the Christian Practice of Contemplation* (Oxford: Oxford University Press, 2006), 12.

65. Besides ample testimony of this phenomenon in contemplative literature, the connection between contemplative practice, compassion, and sense of connectedness is well documented in contemporary research. See Daniel Goleman and Richard Davidson, *Altered Traits: Science Reveals How Meditation Changes Your Mind, Brain, and Body* (New York: Avery Books, 2018), 109.

66. Marjan Laal and Seyed Mohammad Ghodsi, "Benefits of Collaborative Learning," *Procedia-social and Behavioral Sciences* 31 (2012): 486–90.

assures them that their grade will not be affected and that we are not attempting to control their interior life. They should be free to enter into the silence however they wish as long as it does not distract others. Trauma-informed practice also recommends providing students with guidance for what they should do if the silence triggers a troubling reaction, for example, regrounding themselves through their feet or quietly stepping out of the room.[67] While we must take due precautions, in my experience such instances are rare and most students are grateful for the opportunity to be still once they get over the initial awkwardness.

Cultivating Attention

Becoming aware of God's presence within us and being present to others both require attention.[68] In fact, our capacity to attend is the foundation for virtually all our thinking and acting. How we attend to the people and things around us changes our experiences of them and even changes the things themselves.[69] How and what we attend to also changes us. It is not exaggeration when researcher Chris Bailey says, "The state of our attention determines the state of our lives."[70]

Given the importance of attention, the distractedness of today's culture is a crisis of the highest order. Our attention is a finite re-

67. See David Treleaven, *Trauma-Sensitive Mindfulness: Practices for Safe and Transformative Healing* (New York: Norton, 2018). In cases where a traumatized student is triggered, it is usually best for the teacher to refer the student to a mental health professional rather than trying to address the issue in the classroom.

68. Regarding how cultivating attention in school enhances our capacity for prayer and for relationship with others, see Simone Weil's classic "Reflections on the Right Use of School Studies with a View to the Love of God," in *Waiting on God* (New York: Fontana Books, 1959), 66–76.

69. McGilchrist, *The Master and His Emissary*, 28.

70. Chris Bailey, "How to Get Your Brain to Focus," TEDxManchester, accessed October 30, 2024, https://tinyurl.com/ymjh5mms.

source. We can only attend to so much at a time. When our attention is overloaded, we become frustrated and overwhelmed. Such attention overload has become a routine experience in our day not only due to the increasingly complex demands of living in the modern world[71] but, more insidiously, due to highly sophisticated technologies and advertising techniques designed to capture and sell our attention.[72] In the face of these challenges to cognitive coherence, it has become a matter of self-preservation that we learn to strengthen and intentionally direct our attention lest our attention become captive to those forces that would direct it for their own gain. Well before the emergence of social media and digital marketing, William James wrote, "An education which should improve this faculty [of attention] would be *the* education *par excellence*."[73] In James's time, it was a matter of strengthening a capacity that most people exercised routinely. The same cannot be said today. Personal devices have so thoroughly rewired our young people's neural circuitry that many struggle to sustain attention in class for the briefest of periods. Recognizing this new reality, a host of educators and researchers (myself included) are now insisting that the rehabilitation of attention has become the most pressing task for education today.[74]

In theory there is no better place for this training, for an "ascetics of attention," than a school.[75] Unfortunately, we have in many ways set up our schools to diminish attention rather than strengthen it. As

71. Robert Kegan describes these demands and the effects of cognitive overload in his book *In Over Our Heads*.

72. See Tim Wu, *The Attention Merchants: The Epic Scramble to Get Inside Our Heads* (New York: Knopf, 2016).

73. William James, *The Principles of Psychology*, vol. 1 (New York: Holt, 1890), 424.

74. See, for example, Mark, *Attention Span*; Lang, *Distracted*; and D. Graham Burnett, Alyssa Loh, and Peter Schmidt, "Powerful Forces Are Fracking Our Attention. We Can Fight Back," *New York Times*, November 24, 2023, https://tinyurl.com/4vz8afas.

75. Crawford, *The World Beyond Your Head*, 15.

far back as 1929, Alfred North Whitehead criticized the modern education system for fragmenting knowledge into distinct subjects resulting in an "unrhythmic collection of distracting scraps."[76] Looking at typical high school schedules today, we might legitimately ask how a student is supposed to enter deep into thought when attending eight fifty-minute classes in a single school day. Further complicating the matter, tech developers have now produced devices that monitor and refocus attention by transmitting noises to distracted students' brains or generating a strong vibration. Presented as a solution to students' attention-deficit issues, such technologies further diminish students' agency rather than actually strengthening their attention.[77]

The Christian contemplative tradition and current research suggest numerous possibilities for making schools fertile grounds for cultivating attention.[78] One of the most basic ways teachers can nurture students' attention is by inspiring love and awe for the subject matter. What we love determines what we pay attention to.[79] When something attracts us, we desire to know more about it. In this way, an encounter with beauty can lead us to know the world more truly. Knowing can become loving, as physicist Arthur Zajonc says, but loving also leads to knowing. It is in this sense that Walter Burghardt describes contemplation as "a long loving look at the real."[80] Even the greatest of scientific

76. Whitehead, *The Aims of Education*, 21.

77. Jac Mullen, "The Use of 'Attention Capture' Technologies in Our Classrooms Has Created a Crisis," *Nation*, April 22, 2024, https://tinyurl.com/yzm7nxsb.

78. I highlight here guidance from the contemplative tradition. However, we also find valuable guidance in the writings of contemporary educators and researchers like James Lang (*Distracted*), Gloria Mark (*Attention Span*), and Oren Ergas ("Attention Please: Positioning Attention at the Center of Curriculum and Pedagogy," *Journal of Curriculum Theorizing* 31, no. 2 [2016]: 66–81).

79. Again, I recommend to readers the writings of James K. A. Smith on this crucially important insight into our human nature.

80. Walter Burghardt, "Contemplation: A Long Loving Look at the Real," in *An Ignatian Spirituality Reader*, ed. G. W. Traub (Chicago: Loyola Press, 2008), 187–202.

minds—people like Marie Curie and Albert Einstein, whom we associate with disciplined, scientific reasoning and method—were motivated by a sense of beauty and awe of the natural world. Our students, too, are more likely to attend to their learning deeply when they see their teachers seized by something beautiful and are themselves given freedom to pursue their passions in their studies. Besides motivating learning, this *via pulchritudinis*, or way of beauty, may be the path most likely to lead modern people to God, at least as far as Pope Benedict XVI was concerned.[81] Benedict's successor, Pope Francis, has expressed similar sentiments: "Rather than being too concerned with communicating a great deal of doctrine, let us first try to awaken and consolidate the great experiences that sustain the Christian life . . . 'when we experience a great love . . . everything else becomes part of it.'"[82]

Educators can employ many other means to help their students build their capacity for attention. Beginning class with contemplative prayer (for example, a few moments of silence) is good preparation for this work because it requires students to repeatedly refocus their attention on God when their mind starts to wander. Research suggests that people who engage in similar practices spend more time on task than those without such training.[83] Christian practices like *lectio divina* and *visio divina* offer inspiration for various forms of deep reading, viewing (artwork and film), and listening (to music, nature, or one another).[84] For example, some teachers have students study

81. Benedict XVI, "General Audience," Castel Gandolfo, August 31, 2011, https://tinyurl.com/ffrcdw4m.

82. Francis, *Christus Vivit*, Vatican, 2019, https://tinyurl.com/3vpetjcp, #212.

83. David M. Levy et al., "The Effects of Mindfulness Meditation Training on Multitasking in a High-Stress Information Environment," *Proceedings of Graphics Interface 2012*, Toronto, 45–52. Teachers might also consider utilizing exercises specifically designed to strengthen attention, for example, Jon Kabat-Zinn's famous raisin meditation or Arthur Zajonc's paperclip meditation on pages 70–71 of *Meditation as Contemplative Inquiry: When Knowing Becomes Love* (Great Barrington, MA: Lindisfarne Books, 2009).

84. See chapter 5 for more detailed guidance for practices of slow reading.

the same piece of art for fifteen, thirty, or sixty minutes or multiple times throughout the semester.[85] Long-form art projects, science projects, math problems, and writing assignments can likewise provide challenging but valuable opportunities to stretch the attention of students who are accustomed to multitasking and swiping for new content every few seconds. There are limits, however, to how far we can stretch students' attention. Attentiveness generally declines the longer a class goes on. Therefore, these kinds of attention-building exercises are most effective when balanced with attention-renewing activities like posing a question or a problem for students to solve, physical movement, or a nature break.[86]

We have everything to gain by rehabilitating attention in our schools. We modern people know that we are distracted and fragmented, and we desire to be whole. Christian schools have the potential to facilitate the healing that so many seek today. Andrew Sullivan recognizes as much: "If the churches came to understand that the greatest threat to faith today is not hedonism but distraction, perhaps they might begin to appeal anew to a frazzled digital generation."[87] I believe Sullivan is right. By focusing resources on this pressing need, Christian schools could become places of refuge where weary, distracted people reclaim a sense of wholeness.

Bearing Fruit in Our Living

As Christians we believe "the word of God is living and active" (Heb. 4:12). The letter of James enjoins all disciples of Christ to be

85. One example is the practice of "picture study" in the Charlotte Mason philosophy of education. See Charlotte Mason, *A Philosophy of Education: Charlotte Mason's Original Home Schooling Series*, vol. 6 (Lawrenceville, GA: Simply Charlotte Mason, 2017).

86. See Lang, *Distracted*, 145–73, for more examples of learning strategies that sustain and renew attention.

87. Andrew Sullivan, "I Used to Be a Human Being," *New York*, September 19, 2016, https://tinyurl.com/4yp237c2.

"doers of the word, and not merely hearers" (James 1:22), making it clear that we are deceiving ourselves if we acquire knowledge but do not put it into action. More than academic centers, Christian schools in their origins were schools for conversion of life (*conversatio morum*) and "for the Lord's service."[88] By this standard, a Christian school has surely fallen short of its calling if its students graduate with their heads filled with knowledge but their lives unchanged.

One crucial component in such a conversion of life concerns how Christians evaluate the situations they find themselves in and make decisions. Drawing upon the traditional language of moral theology, we could say that one of the aims of a Christian school is that its students become prudent persons. A person of prudence not only knows the truth in an abstract way but also knows how to act on that truth in the right way at the right time. It would thus seem essential that Christian education involve training in the art of discernment, the exercise of prudence in the midst of daily life.[89] The essence of Christian discernment can be encapsulated in one simple question: What is God asking of me here and now?[90] It is the mark of a Christian realist to understand and accept God's will, as Jesus did (see Luke 22:42), rather than trying to force reality to conform to our ideas or desires.[91] When we earnestly ask what God wants of us, more often than not we will know the right course of action in a given situation. However, educators can find more detailed guidance for discerning decisions in Ignatius's *Spiritual Exercises* and derivative materials developed by the Jesuits.[92]

Discerning God's will is an important step, but knowing is not the same as doing. Many things can intervene between thought and action,

88. Rule of Benedict, Prologue, 45.

89. See Francis, *Christus Vivit*, chapter 9.

90. Caussade, *The Sacrament of the Present Moment*, 43.

91. Iris Murdoch, Matthew Crawford, and others have observed that being drawn out of ourselves in this way is key to psychological health. See Crawford, *The World Beyond Your Head*, 173–75.

92. The website Ignatian Spirituality is a good place to begin: https://tinyurl.com/3czxf7d3.

and, for a Christian, mere knowing is not enough.[93] The Epistle of James warns, "If a brother or sister is naked and lacks daily food, and one of you says to them, 'Go in peace; keep warm and eat your fill,' and yet you do not supply their bodily needs, what is the good of that?" (James 2:15–16). This is why the desert monastics endeavored not only to study Scripture but also to purify the distorted desires and habits that prevented them from living in accord with what they read. Thomas Aquinas understood the matter similarly. Building on the thought of Aristotle, Aquinas taught that we do not become virtuous (just, temperate, etc.) merely by studying the virtues.[94] We become virtuous by doing virtuous things, by developing virtuous habits.[95] Cultivating a life of prayer, living in accord with Christ's teachings, and participating in the sacraments are all part of the work of becoming people who know and live in the truth.

The pedagogical implication of the above is that students require both explicit instruction in Christian moral teaching (for example, in a morality course) and opportunities to apply their learning.[96] The Cardijnian model of "See–Judge–Act" is one tried and true method of engaging people in such thinking grounded in Catholic social teaching and social ministry.[97] Following this process, a group

93. Contemporary research confirms this ancient wisdom. For example, one study found that divinity students who were assigned to read and preach on the parable of the good Samaritan were no more likely to stop to help a man who was bent over moaning in pain than students in a control group. See Goleman and Davidson, *Altered Traits*, 102.

94. Thomas Aquinas, *Summa Theologica* II-I, q. 52, a. 3., trans. Fathers of the English Dominican Province, New Advent, 2017, https://tinyurl.com/y8jjwaef.

95. Even some modern scientific researchers acknowledge that understanding the world rightly depends upon the moral foundation of the knower. See Zajonc, *Meditation as Contemplative Inquiry*.

96. Recent research on character formation confirms this insight. See Larry Nucci and Elliot Turiel, "Capturing the Complexity of Moral Development and Education," *Mind, Brain, and Education* 3, no. 3 (2009): 151–59, https://doi.org/10.1111/j.1751-228X.2009.01065.x

97. See Erin Brigham, *See, Judge, Act: Catholic Social Teaching and Service Learning* (Winona, MN: Anselm Academic, 2013).

or individual discerns an action in three steps: (1) See—reflecting on what we know about a situation (what is happening, who is involved, what is the context), (2) Judge—analyzing the causes of the situation in conversation with Scripture and Christian teaching, and (3) Act—formulating and enacting a plan to respond to the situation. Regardless of whether educators use this model or another process, it is crucial that students have opportunities to develop the skill of discernment by thinking through Christian moral teaching with respect to the situations they encounter in their own lives and in the world around them. A regular meditative practice may also help to translate school learning into compassionate action. Research on the compassion meditation, for example, indicates that repeating positive wishes for another person in a mantra-like fashion is an exceptionally effective means of translating empathic thoughts into concrete actions that serve others.[98]

Time to Grow

Besides sunlight, water, soil, and nutrients, another ingredient—often unnamed but no less essential—is required for the health of a garden, namely, time. Living things need time to grow. This is no less true of human beings than it is of plants, and even more so. Recognizing this truth about ourselves, we see how unfortunate it is that our schools and classrooms are so often places of hurry—hurry to get all the lecture points in before the bell rings, hurry to move from one class to the next, hurry to cover all the material before the testing date. This culture of hurry runs counter to what we know to be best for our students from educational research. That research shows

98. Goleman and Davidson, *Altered Traits*, 121. By "compassion meditation," Goleman and Davidson mean specifically the "loving-kindness" meditation (also known as "metta"). Although the most common form of this meditation is Buddhist in origin, it is fully consistent with the Christian value of *agapē*. We will experience a Christian version of this meditation at the beginning of the next chapter.

that scores improve dramatically when students take a twenty-minute break before a test[99] and that taking periodic breaks from focused work boosts idea production.[100] If our educational practices fail to align with what the research tells us, perhaps that is because we remain beholden to inaccurate images of the human person (the human mind as a computer, etc.). We persist in feeding students data and demanding output on a predetermined timeline when we should be providing a trellis and the time they need to grow.

The monasteries that gave birth to Christian schools honored time in this way. As noted in chapter 2, the monastic ideal is for the monks to give themselves fully to the present task, whatever that may be, and to practice detachment by stopping an activity immediately when the bell summons them to the next one. One activity does not run into the next. This is an aspect of our spiritual and educational heritage that we would do well to recover. For starters, we might apply this practice in our classrooms by honoring our need for periodic pauses and resisting the ever-present temptation to push through.[101] Pausing to wonder at something beautiful or awe-inspiring—a poem, a story, a piece of art, the clouds passing overhead—has a way of slowing down our experience of time.[102] It also encourages a kind of learning that touches the person more deeply and makes a more lasting impact. As Jesuit educators have noted, what is most important for Christian education "is not the quantity of course material covered

99. Pink, *When*, 57.

100. Sophie Ellwood et al., "The Incubation Effect: Hatching a Solution?," *Creativity Research Journal* 21, no. 1 (2009): 6–14.

101. I would again refer the reader to James Lang's helpful recommendations for attention-renewing activities such as reflecting on a question, moving around, or taking in natural beauty. See *Distracted*, chapter 6.

102. Melanie Rudd, Kathleen D. Vohs, and Jennifer Aaker, "Awe Expands People's Perception of Time, Alters Decision Making, and Enhances Well-Being," *Psychological Science* 23, no. 10 (2012): 1130–36.

. . . but rather a solid, profound, and basic formation. ('Non multa, sed multum.')"[103]

That formation is all the more profound when the entire school community inhabits God's time in this way. In this sense, the school schedule is potentially one of the most formative aspects of Christian education. Inspired by Christian wisdom and current research, a growing number of schools are implementing block schedules, which at least in some cases have contributed to reduced failure rates and improved grades, student satisfaction, and retention rates, with historically disadvantaged learners especially benefiting.[104] While block scheduling may not be ideal for every age group and setting, the general principle of devoting more class time to fewer subjects at a time helps students to go deeper.[105] Slowing things down in our schools is not just academically beneficial; more importantly, it responds to a profound need rooted in our human nature. We are beings with finite limits to our energy, attention, and capacity to make sense of all the information entering our consciousness. Making time and mental space to process and think deeply helps us to integrate our learning and experience a sense of wholeness.

103. "Characteristics of Jesuit Education," #163.

104. See "What the VU Block Model Means for the Future of Education," Victoria University, accessed October 30, 2024, https://tinyurl.com/5b4w7bkc, and Sarah Silverman et al., "Time for Change: Findings from a Survey of Time Use in Schools," *Unlocking Time*, 2020, https://tinyurl.com/6s7s7726. There are potential downsides of the block schedule, however. For example, some express concerns that moving university courses to block scheduling is prohibitive of long-term assignments, experiments, and projects.

105. Research from the Education Endowment Fund suggests that "how teachers use the time they are allocated is more important than the length of lesson or the schedule of lessons." Andrew Watson, "The Best Length of Time for a Class," Learning & the Brain, October 7, 2018, https://tinyurl.com/3atwntnf.

Bringing Class (and the Chapter) to a Close

Human beings are living, growing beings, not machines. Our Creator has created us to be grafted onto the Son, who is the vine, to draw our life from him, and to bear fruit by abiding in him (John 15:1–4). Jesus modeled for us the way of life that facilitates such growth, and those who follow him have practiced and developed this way of life for two thousand years. This tradition is an invaluable source of guidance for educating our students in ways that will help them to grow into vibrant, Christlike people. What is more, current research shows that when we heed this wisdom, our students are healthier, learn better, and develop better relationships with God and one another. Modern education has largely abandoned this wisdom in its pursuit of more utilitarian ends, and our students have suffered as a result. It is incumbent upon us as Christian educators to recover what has been lost and to give our students the good things they need to grow and flourish.

One particular piece of Christian wisdom is relevant here at the end of this chapter. Just as beginning well is important, so too is ending well. The final moments of a class are particularly precious, but too often we squander this precious time when we try to cram in a bit more information and our students start pulling out their phones. We are much better served by taking a moment to be still. That stillness might take the form of a moment of prayer or a simple act of giving thanks for the learning that has occurred.[106] Whatever it looks like, taking a moment to pause helps us to bring our racing minds back to God. Having sown the seeds of growth during class, we trust that God will make them grow even if we know not how (Mark 4:27). In so doing, we prepare ourselves to move on to the next class, activity, or meeting with intentionality and grace.

106. Cultivating gratitude has been found to make students more alert, focused, creative in problem solving, and appreciative of learning. See Jane Taylor Wilson, "Brightening the Mind: The Impact of Practicing Gratitude on Focus and Resilience in Learning," *Journal of the Scholarship of Teaching and Learning* 16, no. 4: 1–13, https://doi.org/10.14434/josotl.v16i4.19998.

Contemplative Practices for Teaching and Learning

For starters: Introduce periodic silent pauses for prayer or for reflecting on students' contributions or something that the class has just heard, read, or viewed.

Nurturing students' humanity: Affirm students in their God-given goodness and nurture the divine life within them by:

- Above all, conveying care and concern for students. Their worth does not depend on their academic achievement or even their behavior.
- Empowering students' sense of agency by giving them choices about assignments, activities, partners, etc., whenever possible.
- Providing the structure and support students need in the form of clear expectations, modeling, and solid Christian teaching.
- Fostering community and caring relationships in the classroom by using each person's name, sharing stories, working on common tasks, singing together, and exchanging physical signs of affirmation (e.g., high fives).
- Giving students access to sources of meaning and wisdom (e.g., classic texts, Christian exemplars, Christian teaching) and providing opportunities to explore them in a personal way (e.g., writing, discussion, creative projects).

Environment: Create a learning environment in the classroom and the school that encourages calm, deep thinking, and awareness of God's presence.

- Adorn the classroom and the school with signs, decorations, posters, etc., that convey Christian messages about God, community, and the human person.
- Arrange seating with a mind to pedagogical aims and promoting community.
- Adjust the lighting to suit the activity. In general, natural sunlight and full-spectrum fluorescent lamps are best for focus and health.

- Be mindful of the noise level in the classroom. Regularly carve out periods of quiet for prayer, reflection, and deep thinking.
- Consider whether technology-free zones or times, or even banning phones completely, might be necessary for creating an undistracted environment for learning, prayer, and personal connection.
- Beautify the classroom and the school by means of greenery, artwork, and keeping spaces clean and orderly.

Contemplative learning: In Christian schools, we hope that students will be transformed in the fullness of their being—heart, mind, body, and soul. Some practices that facilitate such holistic transformation include:

- Contemplative reading, for example, following the steps of *lectio divina*.
- Deep listening to texts, music, and other people.
- *Visio divina* with religious artwork and icons and patient beholding of artwork and nature.
- Contemplative writing and drawing as a means of reflecting more deeply upon class material.
- Bodily movement such as walking around the room to read excerpts or look at images rather than taking notes while seated.
- Memorizing, reciting, and performing texts.[107]
- Breaks for physical movement and play, especially before tests.
- Learning and practicing the art of discernment, for example, using the Ignatian process for decision making.
- Reflecting on learning and experiences using a process like the See–Judge–Act model.
- Practicing compassion meditation in order to prime students for assisting people in need.

107. For examples, see Mary Keator, *Lectio Divina as Contemplative Pedagogy: Re-appropriating Monastic Practice for the Humanities* (New York: Routledge, 2018), 103–4.

Many of the above practices strengthen essential powers of attention. Others include:

- Contemplative prayer.
- Long-form art projects, science projects, math problems, and writing assignments.
- Attention-renewing activities such as posing a question or a problem for students to solve, physical movement, or a nature break.

4

Committees and Community

Our Common Labor of Love

As I leave class and make my way to the faculty meeting, my head is not in the best space.[1] *Let's get this over with,* I think, *so I can get back to my work.* I enter the conference room. Most of those already inside are locked on to their computer screens, catching up on emails and other tasks. More people trickle in, and then it is time to get started. The department chair calls us to order and invites a faculty member to offer a prayer. The prayer is perfunctory. When everyone gives their "Amen," I wonder to myself if I have actually just prayed.

We begin with the first item on the meeting agenda. The chair makes a brief presentation and opens the floor for discussion. Then it begins. Someone starts talking, and after a few minutes it becomes clear that the person did not read the materials that were circulated before the meeting. Before calling on the next person, the chair reminds no one in particular to read the emails he sends before meetings, assiduously avoiding eye contact with the person who has just been speaking. Another faculty member begins speaking and continues for the next ten minutes, straying considerably from the topic. By now every-

1. The following is a partially fictionalized amalgam of experiences with different groups over the years. I am blessed to work with wonderful colleagues in my current position.

one is looking down at the agenda, knowing that, once again, time will run out before we address all the items listed. Another faculty member jumps into the conversation (or rather the series of monologues) and criticizes what the preceding speaker just said, again without directly addressing him or making eye contact. The rest of us shift uncomfortably in our seats. A few people who had been tapping away at their computers look up for the first time since the meeting began.

The chair intervenes, attempting to defuse the tension in the room. With the first agenda item still unresolved, he says we must move on to the next in the interest of time. He invites another faculty member to speak on the proposal being brought forward. After she finishes, a heated exchange ensues with multiple faculty members volleying rebuttals, amendments, and counterproposals. I look up at the clock to see how much longer I must sit through this. I have little patience for the current conversation, knowing that this new policy proposal is all about one individual feeling slighted by something that happened the previous semester. Rather than going to speak to the offending party directly, that individual drafted a ten-page memo and is now consuming valuable meeting time.

After twenty minutes of debate, nothing has been resolved. The chair proposes that an ad hoc committee be formed to pursue the matter. He calls for volunteers. Only the individual who proposed the new policy volunteers. After an interminable minute of awkward silence, two more hands go up, and the committee is formed. We will hear a report from this committee at the next faculty meeting in addition to addressing the agenda items we did not get to today. Everyone stands up to leave. Most bolt out of the room back to their offices or classrooms. A few linger in the conference room, clumping together in opposite corners to spout opinions about what has just transpired.

Why Can't We All Just Get Along?

Whether you are an elementary teacher, a college professor, or an administrator, meetings are a fact of life like taxes and rush hour traffic.

Why are they often so difficult? Certainly some meetings are just not run well, and there are techniques and procedures that can help with that. But something much bigger is at issue here. These meetings are a microcosm of our society. We all yearn for connection, and coming together with others can be a source of joy and rejuvenation. However, we also frequently experience our personal and work relationships as a source of frustration. Our Christian tradition tells us that this brokenness is rooted in humanity's first sin. From the beginning, human beings have found relationships hard. The third chapter of Genesis depicts the first humans struggling with their dependence on an Other and then breaking relationship in an attempt to seize life on their own terms. When confronted about their sin, they blame each other rather than repenting and reconciling. Since that time, we human beings have lived our relationships in a tension between our desire for communion and our desire for control. We draw close and then push each other away.

Saint Augustine described sin as the condition of being curved in on oneself. Although this has always been a human tendency, changing social conditions and developing technology have given us modern persons enhanced abilities to protect and isolate ourselves.[2] With the proliferation of personalized electronic entertainment in our homes, civic involvement and in-person interactions have steadily declined for decades.[3] When we cannot avoid being around others (for example, when at work or school), we form camps and social circles often defined against other groups. Social media platforms

2. danah boyd has offered an explanation of how changing social realities (e.g., suburban sprawl) have created new barriers to children and young people gathering in person. See danah boyd, *It's Complicated: The Social Lives of Networked Teens* (New Haven: Yale University Press, 2014).

3. See Robert D. Putnam, *Bowling Alone: The Collapse and Revival of American Community* (New York: Simon & Schuster, 2000), and Jean M. Twenge, Brian H. Spitzberg, and W. Keith Campbell, "Less In-Person Social Interaction with Peers among US Adolescents in the 21st Century and Links to Loneliness," *Journal of Social and Personal Relationships* 36, no. 6 (2019): 1892–1913.

like Facebook and TikTok not only make it possible but actively engineer our enclosing ourselves within virtual tribes of the like-minded.[4] The forced isolation, social distancing, masking, and pivot to virtual work and school that defined life during the COVID-19 pandemic have had a particularly dramatic effect on how young people relate to others. Early studies on the pandemic's impact on children are detecting significant developmental delays, and most teachers will tell you anecdotally that their students seem to have a harder time connecting with each other postpandemic.[5]

Technology presents new problems and imperfect solutions. On the positive side, modern technology offers us possibilities for social connection and access to information that would have been unfathomable to previous generations. Connecting with friends and family over social media, Zoom, and FaceTime was literally a lifesaver during the days of COVID. However, the power technology affords us does not always work to the good of our relationships and communities. As Felicia Wu Song points out, social media posts and text messages offer us the gratification of instant connection while also giving us ability to "dial down" people's access to us.[6] We get to choose how and when we interact with people through these media rather than having to interact spontaneously and face-to-face, which involves more emotional energy and possibly anxiety.[7] As notes Song, it is far easier to open up

4. Eli Pariser, *The Filter Bubble: How the New Personalized Web Is Changing What We Read and How We Think* (New York: Penguin Books, 2011).

5. Sarah B. Mulkey, Cynthia F. Bearer, and Eleanor J. Molloy, "Indirect Effects of the COVID-19 Pandemic on Children Relate to the Child's Age and Experience," *Pediatric Research* 94, no. 5 (2023): 1586–87, https://doi:10.1038/s41390-023-02681-4.

6. Felicia Wu Song, *Restless Devices: Recovering Personhood, Presence, and Place in the Digital Age* (Downers Grove, IL: IVP Academic, 2021), 178–79, summarizing Sherry Turkle's research.

7. Today many young people experience even unexpected phone calls as anxiety-inducing events. See Aphrodite Papadatou, "Phone Fear Affects over Half of UK Office Workers," *HR Review*, May 17, 2019, https://tinyurl.com/4cd4wd9t.

The sanctuary of the Chapel of the Immaculate Conception

an app than strike up a conversation with the person next to us, even if it is less fulfilling.[8] We yearn for communion, but we are settling for connection.[9] Engaging less and less in embodied interactions, we are losing our facility with this most basic of human activities.

Genuine communion is hard to find and hard to maintain, so we settle for cheap alternatives that are more within our control—"views" instead of a human gaze, "likes" instead of love, and "followers" instead of true friends. The inconvenient truth is that we cannot have both total control and authentic communion, which is possible only through personal encounter and vulnerability.[10] We must be willing

8. Song, *Restless Devices*, 81.

9. Song, *Restless Devices*, 5. For two helpful discussions of how the basic human need for connection motivates social media use, see James Lang, *Distracted: Why Students Can't Focus and What You Can Do About It* (New York: Basic Books, 2020), especially p. 99, and Andrew Zirschy, *Beyond the Screen: Youth Ministry for the Connected but Alone Generation* (Nashville: Abingdon, 2015).

10. See Brené Brown's in-depth exploration of the importance of vulnerability in *Daring Greatly: How the Courage to Be Vulnerable Transforms the Way We Live, Love, Parent, and Lead* (New York: Avery Books, 2015).

Stained glass windows with Saint Jerome and Saint Augustine

to see and hear the person on the other side of the phone, desk, or conference table in all of that person's complexity, beauty, and brokenness. It is "this encounter," says Pope Francis, "that returns to each person their dignity as children of God, the dignity of living."[11]

Is it possible to see each other like this in today's world? It is possible, and it is what God calls us to. But for us to realize this possibility, we must lay down our masks and shields—our phones, titles, protocols—and let ourselves be seen for who we are. If nowhere else, this should be possible in the church community Christ founded. Let us enter the chapel once more and see if we might catch a glimpse of this reality.

A Meditation on Communion

When we enter a church, we are never alone, even if there is no one else seated in the pews. In many churches a red candle burns perpetually in the stillness of the sanctuary, calling our attention to the presence of an Other. There are signs of other presences as well. Take a look. As we approach the sanctuary of our campus chapel, several faces slowly come into view (see the photographs on pages 106 and 107). On either side of the altar we are greeted by some of our ancestors in faith. Many of Seton Hall's first students were seminarians, and the saints who reside in these stained glass windows are companions of special significance for priests and those preparing for the priesthood. To one side is Saint Thomas Aquinas, his eyes nearly closed in contemplation. He holds a book in one hand, symbolizing the voluminous theological works he wrote, the fruits of his contemplation. Nearby Saint Jerome is focused intently on a book of his own, quill in hand as he translates the Bible. Next to him is Saint Augustine, who holds not only a book but also a burning heart, a visual reminder that our hearts

11. Francis, "Morning Meditation in the Chapel of Domus Sanctae Marthae: For a Culture of Encounter," *L'Osservatore Romano*, September 23, 2016, https://tinyurl.com/55ny9mrh.

are restless until they rest in God.[12] Across the way stand the four evangelists, Matthew, Mark, Luke, and John, bearing the Gospels that they wrote and that preachers proclaim every week from the pulpit.

The sanctuary of this chapel is unusually long because, in its early years, this is where the soon-to-be-priests would lie prostrate during their ordination. In that moment, they were surrounded not only by living members of their community but also by those memorialized in the stained glass windows who had gone on to eternity. The communion of saints was also made present in the singing of the litany of the saints during the ordination ceremony.

This moment in the life of a priest is like a little glimpse of heaven. The veil between this life and the next is lifted. Eternity breaks into our time. The people of God, living and dead, are united to do what we were all created to do, namely, to worship our Creator. Although most of us will never be ordained, we all experience something like this every time we gather for worship. There we, too, gather in the company of the saints. The eucharistic prayer of the Catholic liturgy reminds the congregation explicitly that their praise is joined to that of a larger community: "And so, with the angels and all the saints we declare your glory, as with one voice we acclaim: Holy, holy, holy, Lord God of hosts. Heaven and earth are full of thy glory, Hosanna in the highest. . . ."

I invite you now to enter into the embrace of the communion of saints and to feel them supporting you. If you have any icons or pictures of saints, set them up where you can see them. If you do not have any such images, pull one up on your phone, computer, or tablet. Lie or sit down. Listen to (and maybe sing along with) this recording of the litany of the saints: https://youtu.be/kIdoNBvNiCk?si=EbKAho_cqrAmyxDg.

As you sing the name of each saint, imagine the saint there with you, praying for you, looking at you with love, maybe even wrapping you up in a hug. Know that the saints see you through God's eyes,

12. See Augustine, *Confessions* 1.1.

that they see straight through to your heart. They know everything about you and love you with all of your faults and imperfections.

Now take a few minutes to absorb their love. Quietly speak each one of the following phrases (or a variation that feels right to you) with every breath you take: "I am loved." "I am whole." "I am at peace." Repeat these phrases for several minutes. Now bring to mind someone you know who might be in need of prayer and direct these same words to that person: "May you be loved." "May you be whole." "May you be at peace." Repeat these prayers for several minutes.[13]

When you are ready, open your eyes and conclude with a prayer of gratitude for the gift of being part of the communion of saints. Remember this experience the next time you gather with your brothers and sisters in Christ for worship.

After completing this exercise, reflect on the following:

- How does it feel knowing that you are part of a community of holy men and women who love you and pray for you?
- How well does your school community embody this sense of communion?
- Who are the people in your school community who might be most in need of your prayer, love, and support? Who are the people who are hardest for you to love?

Made for Communion

Christianity offers us a different way of understanding ourselves and our relationships than what mainstream culture typically presents to us. To repeat Felicia Wu Song's apt phrase, we are created for communion but

13. This is a modified version of the "loving-kindness" or *metta* meditation mentioned in chapter 3. This form of meditation has been studied extensively and found to yield benefits for anxiety, depression, PTSD, feelings toward others, cell health, and much more. See Daniel Goleman and Richard Davidson, *Altered Traits: Science Reveals How Meditation Changes Your Mind, Brain, and Body* (New York: Avery Books, 2018), 87, 104, 177–79, 236–38, 250–52.

settling for connection. We all know this about ourselves on some level. At least we are aware of our desire for love, attention, and belonging. Although many of our contemporaries pay little heed to Christian teachings, virtually no one would dispute the words of Genesis 2:18, "It is not good that the [hu]man should be alone." We all feel this to be true of ourselves. When we arrive in a new community and encounter welcome and love, it draws us in. We want to be a part of it.

Where opinions diverge is in the ways we make sense of these desires and the ways we attempt to satisfy them. Technology developers have exploited our desire for connection, designing their products to deliver quick gratification in the form of likes, shares, and instant messaging. Because they are so instantly gratifying, smart phones and social media have become for many people their primary conduit for social interaction. But no one is really satisfied by this form of connection. It is fleeting, superficial, and frequently exhausting.[14] Despite their dissatisfaction, many young people do not see any alternative. They fear that changing their technology habits would cause them to incur unbearable social costs.

Our Christian faith tells us that we are created for something much deeper. We understand that our desire for connection derives from our being created in the image of the Trinitarian community of love. Our fulfillment depends upon imitating and entering into the exchange of self-giving love that occurs among the Father, Son, and Holy Spirit. Dorothy Day put it this way: "We have all known the long loneliness and we have learned that the only solution is love and that love comes with community."[15] Our whole being is oriented to this end, and, as current research shows, our flourishing in virtually every

14. Social media contributes to stress among those who feel obligated to keep up on the latest. See Julie H. Aranda and Safia Baig, "Toward 'JOMO': The Joy of Missing Out and the Freedom of Disconnecting," *MobileHCI '18: Proceedings of the 20th International Conference on Human Computer Interaction with Mobile Devices and Services*, September 2018, https://doi:10.1145/3229434.

15. Dorothy Day, *The Long Loneliness* (San Francisco: HarperCollins, 1997), 286.

domain of life depends not on the number of people following us on social media but on forming intimate, loving relationships.[16] That includes flourishing academically and in our school communities.[17]

This chapter is the most important in the book. I hope at this point you can appreciate why. We cannot achieve the fullness of life God wants for us apart from loving communion. By extension, our schools can only fulfill their *raison d'être* if they nurture such loving community, no matter how many awards they win or how many students they send on to Ivy League universities and prestigious careers. Forming people with the capacity for healthy relationships is a dire need in today's world. Mainstream American culture constantly reinforces a distorted image of the human person as a separate self, feeding an epidemic of loneliness.[18] Our Christian schools should be places where students hear a different message and are formed in a more fulfilling self-image. As communities built upon the model of the divine community of love, Christian schools are ideally equipped to help students (and employees) experience authentic loving communion and understand themselves in this light. This goal ought to remain in constant focus in our schools. Everything else depends on it.

Fortunately, we have models in our tradition for building "the beloved community."[19] Indeed, Christians have been engaged in this

16. Robert Waldinger and Marc Schulz, *The Good Life: Lessons from the World's Longest Scientific Study of Happiness* (New York: Simon & Schuster, 2023). Feelings of belonging even boost job satisfaction and performance. See Daniel H. Pink, *When: The Scientific Secrets of Perfect Timing* (New York: Riverhead Books, 2018), 191.

17. When schools prioritize supportive relationships, students experience gains in academic outcomes, reduced bullying, and improved physical health, all of which benefit students from disadvantaged backgrounds. See Lynn E. Swaner and Andy Wolfe, *Flourishing Together: A Christian Vision for Students, Educators, and Schools* (Grand Rapids: Eerdmans, 2021), 70.

18. "Our Epidemic of Loneliness and Isolation: U.S. Surgeon General's Advisory on the Healing Effects of Social Connection and Community," Office of the U.S. Surgeon General, 2023, https://tinyurl.com/46j626r3.

19. Martin Luther King Jr., "'The Birth of a New Age,' Address Delivered

labor of love for two thousand years. As people were first hearing the good news of Jesus Christ from Paul and the other apostles, a new kind of community was taking shape. The Acts of the Apostles reports:

> All who believed were together and had all things in common; they would sell their possessions and goods and distribute the proceeds to all, as any had need. Day by day, as they spent much time together in the temple, they broke bread at home and ate their food with glad and generous hearts, praising God and having the goodwill of all the people. (Acts 2:44–47)

Acts and Paul's epistles also make it clear that there were plenty of challenges to sustaining this kind of community, but the Way of Jesus Christ appealed to people's desire for deeper communion and Christians have worked out ways of nurturing community through the centuries. We see this effort reflected in the rules that guided the common life of the early desert and monastic communities and in the founding documents of the various religious orders. More recently, we see it reflected in the organization and life of new lay ecclesial movements and associations and in new monastic communities such as the Rutba House and the Catholic Worker.[20] In the following sections, we will draw wisdom and inspiration from this tradition as we endeavor to envision a more loving community in our Christian schools.

Forming a Community of Attention

How does a school forge a community of love in the midst of a climate of hyper-individuality and ephemeral interactions? What can

on 11 August 1956 at the Fiftieth Anniversary of Alpha Phi Alpha in Buffalo," Stanford University, accessed October 30, 2024, https://tinyurl.com/2s3rkc7a; see also 1 John 4.

20. Readers can learn more about the story of Rutba House in Jonathan Wilson-Hartgrove, "Costly Hospitality: Learning Trust at Rutba House," *Christian Century*, October 30, 2013, https://tinyurl.com/mrxesbvv.

we learn from the efforts of Christians in ages past to build the beloved community? Genuine community—as distinct from a collection of individuals who happen to occupy the same space or engage in related activities—is the product of shared attention and shared love. We all have some experience of this. Think of the bonding that happens when a group of people are caught up together in the drama of a sporting event. People who entered the stadium as perfect strangers leave arm in arm chanting songs together. That such experiences have become less common in our day has not a little to do with the divisions we see in our society. With our attention divided among different screens, social media bubbles, and news networks, we live in different realities with shockingly divergent views on what is true and what values matter. We struggle to understand or empathize with the perspectives of others, much less enter into communion with them. Given the current trajectory of society and technological development, it is hard to imagine a future in which an entire country or even an entire city reclaims the kind of shared attention we once enjoyed.[21] Shared attention does remain a real possibility within individual school communities, however.

In a Christian school the collective attention of the community should focus primarily on the divine Mystery at the heart of the community's life, even more so than on academic achievement or financial stability. How does a Christian school focus its attention this way? The most important way is by bringing together the community for prayer and worship. Especially when the presider and liturgical ministers celebrate the liturgy in a reverent manner, when the preaching touches our hearts, when the music stirs our souls, and when pregnant silence raises our awareness of the presence of Mystery, liturgy can arrest our attention. Under such conditions, Rowan Williams suggests, we get

21. For a poignant reflection on how shared attention used to form communities and what has been lost in modern society, see Joshua Whitfield, "The Spiritual Place and Moment of Listening," *Church Life Journal*, June 27, 2023, https://tinyurl.com/3ajerav9.

the feeling that "*this is it*—this is the moment when people see one another and the world properly: when they are filled with the Holy Spirit and when they are equipped to go and do God's work."[22]

Since most schools do not gather for worship every day, other forms of communal prayer are necessary to maintain the community's collective focus on God. Many schools recite certain traditional prayers on a daily basis such as the Angelus or prayers particular to their founding charism such as Saint Ignatius's "Prayer for Generosity" or Saint Francis's "Prayer for Peace." Researchers have found that praying and singing together (for example, during worship or in Taizé-style services) are two particularly powerful ways of harmonizing groups, not only in terms of feelings of connectedness but even on the level of their heart rates and brain waves.[23] The potential impact of these moments of prayer and worship cannot be overestimated. Young people who have experienced a sacred moment in their lives report higher rates of belonging, flourishing, and life satisfaction.[24]

Clearly praying together is essential to a school community maintaining its collective focus on the divine Mystery. However, because most of the school day is spent doing things other than prayer, schools also need to be attentive to what their members see and hear as they move through the day. School mottos and mission statements are in-

22. Rowan Williams, *Being Christian: Baptism, Bible, Eucharist, Prayer* (Grand Rapids: Eerdmans, 2014), 58.

23. See Lisa Miller, *The Awakened Brain: The New Science of Spirituality and Our Quest for an Inspired Life* (New York: Random House, 2021), 198–200, and Pink, *When*, 195. Pink adds that singing in groups has been found to calm heart rates, boost endorphin levels, improve lung function, increase pain thresholds, increase immune function, improve mood and self-esteem, reduce stress and depression, enhance sense of meaning and purpose, and increase sensitivity toward others.

24. *The State of Religion and Young People 2023: Exploring the Sacred*, Springtide Research Institute (Winona, MN: Springtide Research Institute, 2023), 31. This profound sense of connection to one another and to our common Source is not a benefit typically attributed to mindfulness meditation, whatever its other benefits.

tended to form the community around a shared sense of identity and purpose. Are they displayed strategically throughout the school so that students, teachers, and staff see them every day? Do administrators, teachers, and staff refer to them in a meaningful way at meetings and school events? Pictures of school members engaged in activities that contribute to that mission (teaching, studying, serving) can help reinforce this message. Religious artwork, statues, crosses, and other sacramentals serve as visual reminders that we are ever in the presence of divine Mystery.

We also need to be intentional about the stories that are told within our school walls. If school leaders do not embrace their role as storytellers, unwelcome stories will inevitably fill the vacuum—gossip about teachers and students, tales about what happened over the weekend, fantasies about the life of luxury and success that awaits students upon graduation. A Christian school has a far more salutary story to tell about humanity's creation, fall, and redemption and God's unsurpassable love for us. This larger Christian story becomes more personal and compelling when told in the local dialect, that is to say, when it is refracted through the lens of the school's particular history and charism. Hearing from colleagues and peers whose personal stories reflect something of this larger story (for example, during prayer services, retreats, and special lectures) helps others to see themselves as protagonists in that story. School orientations are opportune moments for telling these stories, but orientation should not be the last time a community member hears them. Anniversaries, reunions, and other celebrations offer opportunities for everyone to hear these stories again and to reflect on them in new ways.

Finally, a school community forges shared attention through the things community members do together.[25] A school's story becomes written on people's hearts through school rituals and practices, just as God prescribed certain rituals and observances to concretize Israel's

25. On the importance of spiritual practices for forming Christian identity and faith, see Dorothy Bass and Miroslav Volf, eds., *Practicing Theology: Beliefs and Practices in Christian Life* (Grand Rapids: Eerdmans, 2001).

relationship with their Lord. Beginnings and endings are particularly important. For example, students at Saint Ignatius High School in Cleveland, Ohio, mark the beginning of each new academic year by walking from the school to the cathedral downtown for the Mass of the Holy Spirit. When students from an affiliated middle school, the Welsh Academy, transition into the high school, the Saint Ignatius community welcomes them with the symbolic presentation of the blue blazers that Ignatius students wear for special occasions. Similarly, first-year students at Saint Benedict's Preparatory School in Newark, New Jersey, exchange their school-issued grey hoodies for black ones when they have earned recognition as full members of the school community.[26] Graduations and year-end liturgies present additional opportunities to remind the whole school community what they are about.

As important as are beginnings and endings, much formation happens in between. The school's "ways of proceeding" (to borrow a Jesuit phrase) imprint the school's mission on everyday tasks such as beginning classes and meetings, addressing interpersonal conflict, and completing work. For example, students in some schools write "JMJ" (for Jesus, Mary, and Joseph) or "AMDG" (*ad majorem Dei gloriam*—to the greater glory of God) on all their assignments.[27] Engaging in these actions together, hearing these stories, and seeing these visual reminders week after week form members of the school in a shared vision and sense of abiding together in the presence of our loving God.

The School as a Community of Communities[28]

We have been discussing some ways that entire school communities can be collectively focused (and refocused) on the divine Mystery

26. This school tradition imitates how novice Benedictines change habits upon making their final vows.

27. For more practical strategies for forming a community of attention in the classroom, see chapter 4 of James Lang's book *Distracted*.

28. I borrow this phrase from Pope Francis, who envisions the parish as a community of smaller communities. *Evangelii Gaudium*, Vatican, 2013, https://tinyurl.com/bdd6926h, #28.

by what members see, hear, and do together. These things are important because they unite us in the common Ground of our being. However, we need something more for us to feel like we truly belong to a community, namely, intimate one-to-one relationships and small communities. It is no coincidence that such small communities—monasteries, ecclesial associations, *comunidades de base*, faith-sharing groups—have so often been sources of renewal throughout the history of the church. Christian schools, too, can and have served as such communities. However, this does not happen by accident. Community members experience belonging when school leaders nurture the proper conditions and community members buy in.[29]

Community is the number-one priority for the Benedictines of Saint Benedict's Prep in Newark, and it shows in the organization of the school. Every student belongs to a "group" of about twenty students. Groups sit together at morning convocation and reassemble during group time at the end of the school day. At morning convocation, each group leader (an older student) takes attendance. If someone is absent, the group leader calls the missing student or a parent to find out where the student is. Group leaders later announce to the entire school body assembled in the gym who is missing and why.[30] This practice ensures that no one goes unnoticed at Saint Benedict's. Every single student is noticed and named, and the collective community acknowledges that it is incomplete when someone is missing.[31]

29. More specifically, Swaner and Wolfe offer that school communities flourish when leaders "share good news regularly, make routine deposits in their colleagues' emotional bank accounts, clear blockages in relationships, and make their teams' jobs easier." *Flourishing Together*, 97.

30. More information about groups, convocation, and other aspects of school life can be found in *Creating a Successful Urban School Culture: A Summary of the Principles, Programs, and Practices of Saint Benedict's Preparatory School* (Newark, NJ: Benedictine Abbey of Newark, 2014).

31. This practice aligns with recent research by the Springtide Institute that found that three elements were essential for nurturing a sense of belonging in

Think for a moment about the impact these practices have on the students over time. Before coming to Saint Benedict's, many students had drifted through schools where no one paid them much attention. Imagine their surprise the first time they are sick or decide to play hooky and they get a text from their group leader: "Hey, everything all right? Why aren't you here?" Someone actually noticed. Imagine their reaction when an older student slides over during group time and asks, "How's it going in algebra? I remember that was a tough class." "Yeah, it's pretty rough." "Want some help with the homework?" Initially the student might wonder, *Why does he care?* However, as things like this happen again and again, he comes to accept that this is the way it is here. We are a family; we take care of one another. Other high schools employ similar means of forming small communities, for example, homeroom, the *tutorías* of el Colegio San Benito in Chile,[32] and the "houses" at schools like Holy Spirit Prep School in Atlanta, Georgia,[33] and Saint James Academy in Lenexa, Kansas.[34]

Colleges, universities, and boarding schools have the added advantage of the residential life system. The dorm truly becomes a home for some college students, and their fellow residents, an extended family. This is more likely to happen when community is intentionally cultivated through dorm rituals and events, training of hall staff, and initiation of new members.[35] The dorm can also provide a natural set-

---

a community, namely, being noticed, named, and known. Josh Packard et al., *Meaning-Making: 8 Values That Drive America's Newest Generations* (Bloomington, MN: Springtide Research Institute, 2020).

32. To learn more about the *tutorías* at el Colegio San Benito sponsored by the Manquehue Community in Chile, see "Hora de Tutoría," Colegio San Benito, accessed November 9, 2024, https://tinyurl.com/mvwb3vbm.

33. "The House System," Holy Spirit Preparatory School, accessed November 9, 2024, https://tinyurl.com/2peu74jt.

34. "Community System," St. James Academy, accessed November 9, 2024, https://tinyurl.com/ytmcravy.

35. The University of Notre Dame does this exceptionally well: "Residence Halls," University of Notre Dame, accessed November 9, 2024, https://tinyurl.com/mr282w52.

ting for Bible studies, faith-sharing groups, and other kinds of small groups. Living learning communities (LLCs), wherein students integrate their academic studies with social and extracurricular lives, can provide particularly transformative experiences.[36] Campus Ministry and other student life organizations also frequently support intimate student communities.

This last example points to the valuable role adults can play in nurturing student communities. An abundance of research describes how much young people benefit from the mentorship of adults, perhaps even more so than from peer relationships. The presence of trusted adults in a young person's life correlates with decreased levels of loneliness, isolation, and stress.[37] The more trusted adults young people have in their lives, the better they do. School sports and clubs provide common opportunities for mentoring relationships to develop both among young people and with adults. The "affinity courses" offered at Welsh Academy in Cleveland present another highly promising model.[38] These short-term after-school courses provide a hands-on introduction to new activities (e.g., martial arts, shop, cooking, film, creative writing) that help students discover their talents and passions by learning from local experts. They are highly formative experiences in which students learn to work together, solve problems, and develop relationships with caring adults.

Of course, students are not the only ones who need community. Adults benefit as well, especially when we nurture peer relationships with others at a similar stage in life and with whom we can share things that would be inappropriate to divulge to students. Faculty

36. For numerous examples of LLCs, see Ashley Mowreader, "Residential Spaces Combine Living and Learning in New Ways," *Inside Higher Ed*, February 19, 2023, https://tinyurl.com/yzyt44c7.

37. Josh Packard et al., *Belonging: Reconnecting America's Loneliest Generation* (Bloomington, MN: Springtide Research Institute, 2020), 45, 48. See also Swaner and Wolfe, *Flourishing Together*, 70.

38. See "Affinity Courses," Saint Ignatius, accessed November 9, 2024, https://tinyurl.com/8p6h495j.

and staff retreats are one tried and true means of building community among colleagues (real retreats, not daylong meetings labeled as retreats). In universities where the faculty is large and individuals can feel like cogs in a big machine, creating opportunities for small communities becomes even more important. Some universities offer "affinity groups" or "learning communities" that bring together faculty and staff around a common interest in a particular author, issue, or practice. In a Christian university, such groups can include opportunities to learn about the school's mission and heritage, to grow in faith, and to form Christian community (for example, mission seminars, reading groups, and prayer groups).

Being Christian means being friends to one another as Jesus is a friend to us (John 15:12, 14, 17). Applied to the life of a Christian school, this means all those within should feel that they are not merely members of an institution or a particular team or club but also part of a community of friends who care about one another.

Hospitality

As Christians, we can hardly talk about nurturing community without mentioning hospitality. Hospitality is arguably the most important value in the Old Testament and remains of vital importance in the New Testament and in the subsequent life of the church. Jesus conveys the importance of hospitality in his instructions to welcome the outcast and the marginalized and manifests it in his own practice of table fellowship. The Rule of Benedict commands, "All guests who present themselves are to be welcomed as Christ, for he himself will say: I was a stranger and you welcomed me (Matt. 25:35)."[39]

Christian schools can practice hospitality on multiple fronts. On a basic level, a school's admissions policies and practices can be an expression of hospitality.[40] Each school needs to discern thoughtfully

39. Rule of Benedict 53.1 (hereafter cited as RB).

40. For more on this point, see Swaner and Wolfe, *Flourishing Together*, 65.

how diverse a population of students it can welcome given the realities of the school's resources and context. If certain people are being excluded, a Christian school ought to ask itself why and whether something needs to change. Visits from outsiders (people from the surrounding community, athletic teams from other schools, etc.) should be recognized as special opportunities to practice hospitality by, for instance, assigning a student guide to show visitors around and answer questions. Such occasions are also opportunities for students to cultivate the virtue of hospitality.

However, hospitality is not only for visitors. As Christians we also strive to be hospitable to members of our own community. When new students and employees arrive at the school, the school community should make every effort to help them feel welcome, known, cared for, and to help them learn the ropes. Crafting and implementing rules, policies, and practices that create a safe, welcoming environment is another way of practicing hospitality.[41] The roll call system at Saint Benedict's Prep (described above) is one good example. Others include educating about bullying and various stereotypes and being deliberate about including members with disabilities in school decision making, initiatives, and events.[42]

Embracing the virtue of hospitality can also serve as an authentically Christian way of approaching issues of diversity, equity, and inclusion (DEI). DEI issues are fraught for many Christian institutions. On the one hand, Christian hospitality has traditionally included a particular concern for people who exist on the margins of society.[43] On the other hand, Christians often feel varying levels of discomfort with certain

41. Unsurprisingly, Swaner and Wolfe have found in their research that inclusive, welcoming practices correlate highly with students' flourishing in school. See *Flourishing Together*, 70.

42. For more examples, see Swaner and Wolfe, *Flourishing Together*, 69–74.

43. To say that Christianity has traditionally invoked a special concern for the marginalized is not to say that Christians and Christian institutions have always lived up to this value. On this point see Willie James Jennings's books *The Christian Imagination: Theology and the Origins of Race* (New Haven: Yale

aspects of the mainstream DEI movement that they view as inconsistent with their Christian values (e.g., affirming same-sex marriage and preferred pronouns). Christian schools today are thus faced with the challenge of thoughtfully discerning what inclusion and hospitality look like within their particular context and ecclesial commitments.

If we are faithful to our Christian identity, we are uniquely well equipped to ensure that every person in our schools feels welcome, valued, supported, and loved. The reason is that our primary motivation to create an inclusive community does not come from political pressure or the mandates of accrediting agencies. It comes from our Christian conviction that each and every human person possesses inalienable dignity and worth rooted in being created in God's own image. Bearing this fundamental truth in mind, we are able to approach diversity, to quote Stephen Murphy-Shigematzu, not "as a problem to be fixed" but rather "as a mystery to be appreciated."[44] This recognition of the infinite worth and potential of every person is the starting point for everything that goes on in our schools, including initiatives explicitly aimed at inclusion. Every member of the community is to be honored as a little Christ, to be treated with love, respect, and compassion. Full stop.

What practical resources does the Christian tradition offer school communities for promoting hospitality and inclusion? To begin by building on earlier reflections, the practice of attentive listening is a simple but powerful way of creating a hospitable, inclusive environment.[45] When a school like Saint Vincent's College in Latrobe,

---

University Press, 2010) and *After Whiteness: An Education in Belonging* (Grand Rapids: Eerdmans, 2020).

44. Stephen Murphy-Shigematzu, *From Mindfulness to Heartfulness: Transforming Self and Society with Compassion* (Oakland: Berret-Koehler, 2018), 179. Murphy-Shigematzu's sentiments are consistent with Scripture. First Corinthians 12, for example, speaks of diversity as a gift God has given us for the health of our communities.

45. On the effectiveness of sharing and listening to personal stories for promoting a sense of security and belonging, see Gregory M. Walton and Geof-

Pennsylvania, makes a point of teaching their students and professors to listen well to one another, it creates a space where everyone's voice can be heard and appreciated, including those voices that are most easily silenced.[46] Following the wisdom of Saint Benedict, it is important for school leaders to listen to members of the community before making major decisions or changes to school policies and to communicate to the community what they have heard and why a particular decision was made.[47]

Although we as Christians should strive to be loving and hospitable at all times, experience has proven that it is beneficial to establish special times and spaces where we practice hospitality in a more intentional way. Research shows that historically marginalized persons (for example, first-generation college students, racial minority groups, and LGBTQ students) benefit from coming together for mutual support in learning communities and other small groups.[48] Important as these supports are, we as Christians can never be content

---

frey L. Cohen, "A Brief Social-Belonging Intervention Improves Academic and Health Outcomes of Minority Students," *Science* 331, no. 6023 (2011): 1447–51.

46. For other examples of how teachers at Christian schools have encouraged their students to be more inclusive, see Jonathan Nash, "Practicing Benedictine Values to Create an Inclusive Learning Environment," *Headwaters* 30 (2017): 223–41, https://tinyurl.com/yn438anw, and J. D. Whitt, "Teaching Attentiveness in the Classroom and Learning to Attend to Persons with Disabilities," *International Journal of Christianity and Education* 19, no. 3 (2015): 215–28, https://doi.org/10.1177/2056997115588869. For a more general treatment of research-based inclusive education strategies, see David Mitchell and Dean Sutherland, *What Really Works in Special and Inclusive Education: Using Evidence-Based Teaching Strategies* (New York: Routledge, 2020).

47. See RB, chapter 3. Father Timothy Radcliffe describes how similar practices guide governance in the Dominican Order in *Listening Together: Meditations on Synodality* (Collegeville, MN: Liturgical Press, 2024), 154, 165.

48. Paul B. Thayer, "Retention of Students from First Generation and Low Income Backgrounds," *Opportunity Outlook*, May 2000, 2–8; Giselle Bonet and Barbara R. Walters, "High Impact Practices: Student Engagement and Retention," *College Student Journal* 50, no. 2 (2016): 224–35.

with "accommodating" the "special needs" of certain members of the community. We are all less whenever a member of the community is deprived or suffering. Because our goal is the full communion of everyone involved, we also need designated times and spaces where the entire community is constituted and reconstituted together. The Eucharist plays a central role in this formation of community while school assemblies and other gatherings provide supplementary means of addressing the business of the community.[49]

Because sin is inevitable, Christian schools need means of repairing the community when trust is broken—when valuables go missing from students' lockers, when comments in a faculty meeting get personal, or when parents are upset by an administrative decision. The first and most important point, agreed upon by ancient desert monastics, psychologists, and neuroscientists, is not to attempt to address conflict when angry. Besides this cardinal rule, neuroscientists Andrew Newberg and Mark Robert Waldman recommend a number of strategies for restoring peace based on hundreds of studies in psychology, conflict mediation, and peacemaking.[50] Some of the most important include choosing a time and place where all parties are comfortable, not blaming or insulting, being specific about issues and proposed solutions, and allowing all parties to take a time-out when they need to.

In cases where an issue has affected much or all of the school community, a communal healing service might be in order. As theologian Father Brian Massingale highlights, four elements are essential in this kind of communal healing: recognizing the humanity of the other and the roots of the conflict, taking responsibility for the harm done, healing psychological wounds, and repairing material dam-

49. See Brian Massingale, *Racial Justice and the Catholic Church* (Maryknoll, NY: Orbis, 2010), 124–25, regarding the role of the Eucharist in forming people for compassion and solidarity.

50. For the full list of strategies, see Andrew Newberg and Mark Robert Waldman, *How God Changes Your Brain: Breakthrough Findings from a Leading Neuroscientist* (New York: Ballantine Books, 2009), 231–39.

age or losses.[51] Such healing services are most effective when they can draw on relational capital accumulated over months and years of shared meals and activities, praying together, and learning about one another. If a community has done this prior work of relationship building, its members will be able to be vulnerable with each other, challenge one another, and lovingly call each other out on mistakes without the conversation devolving into an unproductive cycle of blame and retaliation.

Learning to Do Community

Real community does not just happen. It requires the commitment and active participation of everyone involved. It is easy to take community for granted, which is why Saint Benedict mandated that anyone seeking admission to the monastic community should first have the rule read to him "so that he may know what he is entering."[52] The entering monk heard the rule read again after six months, and then again four months after that. Likewise, when a school is hiring new employees, it is common (and prudent) practice to explain the mission of the school and ask potential hires how they think they can contribute. Some schools require prospective students to visit before being admitted so they know exactly what they are committing to. Schools often require students and employees to provide a signature indicating that they have read the appropriate guides and handbooks.[53] Schools treat these practices as formalities at their own

51. Massingale, *Racial Justice*, 97–98.

52. RB 58.9–16.

53. At their best, such documents are not merely legalistic compendia of rules and policies but living documents that paint a picture of the kind of community the school aspires to be. It is instructive to look at the commitment cards Dr. Martin Luther King Jr. distributed to volunteers in the civil rights movement: "MLK Commitment Card," Love Out Loud, accessed November 8, 2024, https://tinyurl.com/32mueetn. Felicia Wu Song suggests doing something similar in schools. See *Restless Devices*, 202, 205.

risk. Regardless of how well crafted the school's policies, they are not worth the paper they are written on if community members do not understand them or feel no sense of commitment to them.

Following initiation into the school community comes the hard work of building, maintaining, and repairing community day in and day out. While structures and resources can support community, much depends on the individual members' capacity for relationship, and that capacity is something most of us need to develop.[54] Jesus offers us a model for the required inner work. Jesus's public teaching and healings were always preceded by a time of turning inward to abide with his heavenly Father, and he told his disciples to do likewise. On the one hand, he instructed them to go to their inner room to pray (Matt. 6:6). On the other, he commanded them to go out to make disciples of all the nations (Matt. 28:19). By turning inward, they were prepared to go out to others. In the following two sections, we will explore this double movement as it relates to our living and work in our schools.

Turning Inward

Why did Jesus so frequently retreat from the crowds to deserted, lonely places? Why did the desert fathers and monastics do likewise throughout the centuries? Thomas Merton offers that we do not go into the "desert" to escape from people but rather to learn how to do them the most good.[55] We might ask why this is the case. How do we learn to do others more good by withdrawing from them?

To begin with, the better we understand ourselves, the better we are able to enter into relationship with others. As often as not, our difficulties with another person stem more from some wound within

54. Fortunately our brains seem to be disposed/wired for relationship. As Goleman and Davidson say, "Just as with speaking, the brain seems primed to learn to love." *Altered Traits*, 111.

55. Thomas Merton, *New Seeds of Contemplation* (New York: New Directions, 1961), 80.

ourselves than from any fault in the other person. We expect the new administrator to run roughshod over the faculty because that is what previous administrators did. A colleague offers a compliment, and we assume that person has some secret agenda because our parents never offered us any affirmation. So long as we operate out of these wounds and expectations, we will always struggle to form healthy, trusting relationships and to work well with others. As Richard Rohr has put it, "If we do not transform our pain, we will always transmit it."[56] The only way to fully transform our pain is by encountering God's unconditional love for us and thereby knowing ourselves as lovable. God has already taken the first step in our healing process: "In this is love, not that we loved God but that he loved us and sent his Son to be the atoning sacrifice for our sins" (1 John 4:10). The Father has made his love known to us by giving us his Son. We accept that love by spending time with him in prayer. When we thus receive God's perfect love, we find the courage to love others, even those who do not love us in return (1 John 4:11).

Awareness of our inner workings also helps us to interact with others in healthier ways. There is now greater recognition of the value of such inner work since social-emotional learning (SEL) has found a place in many school curricula.[57] SEL involves the development of skills and attitudes for managing emotions and achieving personal and collective goals, showing empathy for others, and establishing and maintaining supportive relationships. While novel in this particular form, this new educational movement reflects ancient Christian wisdom about the human person as found, for example, in the desert fathers' teachings on *apatheia*.[58] Not to be confused with our modern

56. Richard Rohr, *Dancing Standing Still: Healing the World from a Place of Prayer* (Mahwah, NJ: Paulist, 2014), 80.

57. Tim Walker, "The Truth about SEL? It Works," *NEA Today*, January 19, 2023, https://tinyurl.com/4da2z92r.

58. Another example is Saint Ignatius's guidance on the "discernment of spirits," which includes detailed instructions for cultivating awareness of one's feelings and discerning their types and causes. See *The Spiritual Exercises of St.*

concept of apathy, *apatheia* was understood by the ancients as "that state in which you are aware of your reflexes and responses in such a way that you can think through them, sense your way towards a goal that is not purely self-protective or acquisitive."[59] When possessed of *apatheia*, we are able to recognize clearly what is happening within ourselves and respond to internal and external events deliberately rather than reacting impulsively. We are able to interact with others out of concern for their good rather than projecting onto them our own pain. This is what Evagrius means when we writes that love is the offspring of *apatheia*.[60]

The first step toward achieving *apatheia* is cultivating a habit of inner watchfulness (*nēpsis*, as the ancients called it) over our inner thoughts and feelings. A hundred times a day some provocation kicks up a cloud of afflictive thoughts (*logismoi* in Greek) that start swirling in our minds: "No one recognizes all the work I do." "Everyone else on faculty is a better teacher than I am." "That's just like him to do something like that." Indulging such thoughts compounds our suffering.[61] This is why Evagrius counsels, "Be the door-keeper of your heart and do not let any thought come in without questioning it."[62] How do we prevent meddlesome thoughts from entering our hearts? After noticing that we are having these thoughts, we meet them with the Jesus Prayer or some word from Scripture, as Jesus did when

---

Ignatius, ed. Louis J. Puhl (Chicago: Loyola Press, 1951), #313–36. One of the founders of SEL, Daniel Goleman, has himself been profoundly influenced by religious contemplative traditions.

59. Williams, *Being Human*, 75–76.

60. Evagrius Ponticus, *Praktikos and Chapters on Prayer*, trans. John Eudes Bamberger (Kalamazoo, MI: Cistercian Publications, 1981), chapter 81.

61. Fixating on negative thoughts activates the sympathetic nervous response, causing stress. For a research-based discussion of these thought patterns and prayerful ways of dealing with them, see chapter 1 of Gregory Bottaro, *The Mindful Catholic: Finding God One Moment at a Time* (North Palm Beach, FL: Beacon Publishing, 2018).

62. Cited in Anthony M. Coniaris, *Philokalia: The Bible of Orthodox Spirituality* (Minneapolis: Light and Life Publishing, 1998), 104.

Satan tempted him in the desert. In this way, says Martin Laird, we move from being victims to being witnesses of our reactions.[63] This spiritual practice enables us to cope better not only with negative thoughts in our heads but also with the frustrating words and behaviors of other people. If we have learned to meet our inner chatter with prayerful stillness, we will be able to do the same with the tension we experience when we find ourselves in a frustrating meeting or uncomfortable encounter.[64]

Going Out

We have now seen how turning to our "inner room" helps us to grow in self-awareness and capacity for healthy relationships. Still, self-awareness is not an end in itself. Jesus also commands us to "go out" (Matt. 28:19). Fulfilling this command means emptying ourselves for others as Jesus has done for us. Perhaps no passage captures this dynamic better than the *kenōsis* hymn in Paul's letter to the Philippians:

> Let each of you look not to your own interests, but to
> the interests of others.
> Let the same mind be in you that was in Christ Jesus,
> who, though he was in the form of God,
> did not regard equality with God
> as something to be exploited,
> but emptied himself,

63. Martin Laird, *Into the Silent Land: A Guide to the Christian Practice of Contemplation* (Oxford: Oxford University Press, 2006), 95.

64. According to one study, participants experienced decreased reactivity in the amygdala after just thirty hours of meditative practice. See Goleman and Davidson, *Altered Traits*, 250. Other embodied practices such as chanting and deep breathing help to relax the vagus nerve that relays fight-or-flight messages and also relaxation signals throughout the body. See Resmaa Menakem, *My Grandmother's Hands: Racialized Trauma and the Pathway to Mending Our Hearts and Bodies* (Las Vegas: Central Recovery Press, 2017), chapter 10.

> taking the form of a slave,
> being born in human likeness.
> And being found in human form, he humbled himself
> and became obedient to the point of death—even
> death on a cross. (Phil. 2:4–8, layout altered)

What does this *kenōsis*, or self-emptying, look like concretely? One of the simplest and most concrete ways of giving ourselves to another is by listening to one another.[65] Good listening requires giving another person our undivided attention, being patient, and listening without judgment or an agenda.[66] When someone listens to us lovingly and attentively, we feel seen and valued. It can be a source of profound healing. Unfortunately, we rarely listen to one another this way today. Our students are often so busy consuming each other's content on social media that they are oblivious to the living person sitting right next to them in class. We teachers can be just as guilty, fixating so much on our learning objectives and curricula that we allow no room for our students' questions, concerns, and goals to surface. Recognizing the importance of listening and inspired by the opening line of the Rule of Benedict,[67] some Benedictine schools have identified listening as a core competency to be developed in their curriculum.[68] Their teachers strive to model good listening for

65. For a beautiful and honest reflection on the importance of deep listening and its relevance for teaching, see Mary Rose O'Reilly's slim book *Radical Presence: Teaching as Contemplative Practice* (Portsmouth, NH: Boynton/Cook Publishers, 1998).

66. Howard Thurman, mentor to Martin Luther King Jr., writes, "there must be a sense of leisure out of which we relate to others. . . . We cannot be in a hurry in matters of the heart. The human spirit has to be explored gently and with unhurried tenderness." *Disciplines of the Spirit* (San Francisco: Harper & Row, 1963), 126–27. See also Francis, *Christus Vivit*, Vatican, 2019, https://tinyurl.com/3vpetjcp, #292.

67. "Listen carefully, my son, to the master's instructions, and attend to them with the ear of your heart" (RB, Prologue 1).

68. Take, for example, the "Listening Seminar," the first of three core

their students, and the students intentionally practice this skill in their classes. Activities outside the classroom provide other opportunities for practicing listening. Cultivating this ability is an explicit aim of the *lectio divina* groups at Benedictine schools such as Portsmouth Abbey School in Rhode Island and San Benito in Chile.[69]

To love one another as Christ loves us means not only listening to one another but also acting to alleviate each other's needs and suffering. Numerous times in the Gospels we read that, just before performing a miracle, Jesus was "moved with compassion" for someone.[70] Jesus makes it clear that he expects his followers to extend the same kind of compassion to others (Matt. 9:13). In this vein, Saint Paul writes to the community in Corinth, "If one member suffers, all suffer together with it; if one member is honored, all rejoice together with it" (1 Cor. 12:26).[71] Most of us require some training to develop the capacity to feel what another person feels and to respond with compassion. The more time we spend listening to others, the more attuned we become to their perspectives and feelings. We can also develop empathy by means of Ignatian reading of Scripture in which we imagine ourselves as the people in the stories of the Bible, attempting to see, hear, and feel as they do.[72] Regular practice of the compassion meditation, like the one at the beginning of this chapter, is a highly effective means of promoting not only feelings of empathy but also compassionate action.[73] These classroom practices can form us in a

---

courses taken by all students at Saint Vincent College in Latrobe, PA: "Explore the SVC Core," Saint Vincent College, accessed November 8, 2024, https://tinyurl.com/2ur4ekwh.

69. For more on the Manquehue method of *lectio divina*, see The Weave of Manquehue Prayer, *Pathways to Lectio Divina: Methods from the Weave of Manquehue Prayer* (Weave of Manquehue Prayer, 2021).

70. For example, Mark 1:41; 8:2; Matt. 9:36; 20:34; Luke 7:13.

71. Saint Benedict's Prep in New Jersey has fully embraced this mentality, adopting as their school motto Whatever Hurts My Brother or Sister Hurts Me.

72. Thank you to Erin Conway at Welsh Academy for this suggestion.

73. Goleman and Davidson, *Altered Traits*, 121.

habit of going out of ourselves to respond to each other in our need. When members of a community nurture these capacities, everyone is more likely to flourish and many conflicts are avoided or at least resolved in a healthier manner.

The Committee as Community

At the beginning of the chapter I described the familiar scene of a faculty meeting where people were not at their best and where sense of community was lacking. Let's return to that space and imagine how things could be different if those present utilized the kinds of contemplative practices we have been exploring.[74]

As we saw in chapter 3, how an event begins often has a significant effect on its outcomes, so taking a few minutes to get the meeting off on the right foot is well worth a bit of extra thought and time.[75] A simple, thoughtful gesture can make all the difference. For example, it is a custom in some Benedictine schools to begin meetings by bowing to each other in an acknowledgment of the divine present in every person.[76] This embodied gesture serves as a concrete reminder that we enter the meeting not as adversaries but rather as fellow members of

74. Although I do not have the space to discuss it here, it is worth considering how the physical (or virtual) environment influences our mental states and behaviors during meetings. Parker Palmer offers some suggestive examples in his chapter "Transformative Conversations on Campus," in *The Heart of Higher Education: Transforming the Academy Through Collegial Conversations*, ed. Parker Palmer and Arthur Zajonc (San Francisco: Jossey-Bass, 2010).

75. For example, Daniel Pink cites research on the high-impact practice of "pre-incision timeouts" during which surgical teams review instructions and regain their collective focus (*When*, 52). If this simple practice can dramatically reduce errors in surgery, as it has, similar rituals such as those I describe here can surely help faculty members to avoid impulsive decisions or saying something they later regret.

76. Stephen Adobato, "Ascetics in the City," *American Benedictine Review* 69, no. 4 (2018): 366–74. Adobato reports that this ritual typically happens at the end of meetings and classes, but it can work just as well at the beginning.

the communion of saints. The ritual bow might be followed by a moment of silence during which we pray for one another, perhaps in the style of the compassion meditation. This is just one example of how a meaningful moment of prayer and reflection (not just a rushed, perfunctory prayer) can help us enter into a better mental space before beginning a meeting. Other possibilities include inviting people to set their intention for the meeting; reflecting on a passage of Scripture, a mission statement, or some other seminal text; envisioning how the meeting might go well; or simply observing a few minutes of silence. Beginning with intentionality rather than rushing in gives us the opportunity to reconnect with the divine in us and others, recenter ourselves, and become aware of any emotions, tensions, or other unwanted "guests" that we may be bringing with us into the meeting.

Becoming aware of ourselves and others is a good beginning, but it is only a beginning. Ideally we strive to give our full attention to one another for the entirety of our time together, whether we are meeting in-person or virtually.[77] On this point, Saint Ignatius advises, "Be slow to speak, and only after having first listened quietly, so that you may understand the meaning, leanings, and wishes of those who do speak. Thus you will better know when to speak and when to be silent."[78] More generally, good listening involves making eye contact, not multitasking or thinking about what we want to say next, summarizing for ourselves what the speaker is saying, and trying to understand the speaker's intention. When we establish and maintain this kind of human connection, we are better able to understand and

77. Many of the subtleties of personal interaction are lost when communicating via screens. If you must meet virtually, establish practices and commitments to help everyone engage each other thoughtfully and attentively, for example, by keeping cameras turned on and committing to not multitasking during the meeting.

78. This advice comes from a letter Ignatius wrote to some fellow Jesuits who were to attend the Council of Trent, "On Dealing with Others," Woodstock Theological Library at Georgetown University, 1546, https://tinyurl.com/5xe5p92f.

speak directly to one another rather than talking past one another or around the real issue.[79]

Even when everyone comes to the meeting with the best of intentions, tensions will sometimes arise. My experience is that, more often than not, people do not address the mounting tension but instead simply push through the agenda driven by a sense of hurry. Ironically, we more often than not lose ground by running ahead. Here Evagrius's teaching on watchfulness proves highly useful. He and other desert fathers learned that, by training ourselves to be constantly vigilant over our interior workings, we can more quickly notice the body tensing and the negative thoughts spinning in our heads (perhaps in response to a colleague's unhelpful comment or long-winded monologue).[80] Left unchecked, these negative thoughts can lead us into a downward spiral terminating in an emotional response or at the very least distract us from the real business of the meeting. We can prevent this outcome by meeting negative thoughts and feelings with silence—that is to say, with a simple prayer word such as the Jesus Prayer—when we notice them. Alternatively, we can reground ourselves in our bodies by focusing on our breathing or the sensation of our feet on the floor. After a minute or two, our minds and bodies will usually settle down and we are able to make a deliberate decision about how best to respond. In extreme cases when we are not able to reclaim our equilibrium, it is best to excuse ourselves and step out of the room for a minute until we are able to be present again.[81]

79. That such deliberate practices improve communication has been confirmed in the research of Andrew Newberg and Mark Robert Waldman. For a detailed guide to their "compassionate communication" exercise and its benefits, see *How God Changes Your Brain*, 214–26.

80. Those who invest time in prayer outside of work hours will find that they are better able to maintain their composure and recover more quickly. See Margaret E. Kennedy et al., "Contemplative/Emotion Training Reduces Negative Emotional Behavior and Promotes Pro-social Responses," *Emotion* 1, no. 2 (2012): 338.

81. By the same token, it can help to take an upset student for a walk before trying to talk through the issue.

Because we are naturally attuned to other people's bodily and emotional cues, practicing this kind of self-regulation benefits not only us but also those around us. A settled body settles other bodies, and, conversely, an agitated body agitates other bodies.[82] A prime example of this phenomenon is yawning. Yawning is famously contagious (you might even yawn simply because you read this) and, it turns out, has manifold benefits, including enhancing alertness and concentration, lowering stress, relaxing every part of the body, and increasing empathy and social awareness.[83] So the next time you are in a meeting and tensions are running high, just pause and have good yawn.

While one person yawning (or breathing deeply or silently meditating) may seem odd or rude, it is a different matter if everyone does it together. In this regard, meeting facilitators can play an important role in shaping group dynamics. When facilitators notice things getting tense and exchanges becoming less productive, they should recognize that people may be running up against the limits of their attention.[84] It may be time to take a break to stretch the legs, breathe some fresh air, and grab a snack.[85] Better yet, facilitators can head off tensions by taking a break anytime a meeting runs over an hour. Sometimes there may be more behind the tension than dropping blood sugar levels. Legitimate differences of opinion and personal wounds also come into play. Facilitators must hold these tense moments carefully when they arise. They and everyone involved should be prepared to slow down and even fall into silence. As the Quakers know well, silence often

82. Menakem, *My Grandmother's Hands*, 182.

83. Newberg and Waldman, *How God Changes Your Brain*, 155–59.

84. Studies show that overworked workers have enlarged amygdala and weak connections between areas in the prefrontal cortex that regulate the amygdala, which results in reduced ability to regulate their emotional reactions. Goleman and Davidson, *Altered Traits*, 92.

85. Hunger-related moods happen to the best of us. One study found that judges consistently issued more severe rulings as lunchtime approached and were significantly more lenient following a break. See Pink, *When*, 58–60. This is a good reason to offer food at meetings, besides being a gesture of hospitality.

gives birth to wisdom that is stifled by too much talking.[86] "The way opens in silence," they say.[87] In the silence we permit God to reenter the room and our ideas to mature.[88] Allowing for periods of silence not only yields wiser decisions; it also preserves our relationships by preventing harmful words spoken in haste.[89]

As with their beginnings, our meetings are more fruitful when we end with intentionality. So many end in a flurry of activity and a profusion of words with everyone trying to speak their piece before time runs out, but ending in this way can taint the experience as a whole. It is better to take a moment at the end of our meetings to sincerely thank our colleagues for their gifts and contributions, to offer a prayer, or perhaps to observe a moment of silence during which we mentally review what we have accomplished and how we have conducted ourselves. When we end in this way, we are likely to feel more positively about the meeting and be better prepared to move with grace to the next meeting or task.[90]

Conflict, Correction, and Reconciliation

When we come to our meetings and classes grounded in an awareness of God's loving presence within us and those around us, conflicts are

86. For more on Quaker meetings, see Elizabeth Molina-Markham, "Finding the 'Sense of the Meeting': Decision Making Through Silence Among Quakers," *Western Journal of Communication* 78, no. 2 (2014): 155–74, https://doi.org/10.1080/10570314.2013.809474.

87. O'Reilly, *Radical Presence*, 4.

88. Here the same principle applies as when teachers insert "wait time" after asking a question in order to allow all students to consider the question thoughtfully. See Mary Budd Rowe, "Wait Time: Slowing Down May Be a Way of Speeding Up!," *Journal of Teacher Education* 37, no. 1 (1986): 43–50.

89. For guidance from the Quaker and Ignatian traditions on group decision making, see "Decision-Making," Quaker.org, accessed November 8, 2024, https://tinyurl.com/3d472w64, and William J. Byron, SJ, "A Method of Group Decision-Making," Ignatian Spirituality, accessed November 8, 2024, https://tinyurl.com/mrxnkpuy.

90. For more on the benefits of such ending rituals, see Pink, *When*, 172.

less likely to arise. Even still, the brokenness of our human nature makes conflict somewhat inevitable. Friends will gossip, students will cheat on assignments, colleagues' comments will get personal when arguing over school policies. Knowing that such breakdowns in our relationships will occur, we need to be prepared to address failures, forgive one another, and repair bonds that have been broken.

Every school has its mechanisms for dealing with infractions of rules and conflicts between members. As with curricula and pedagogy, how these policies are crafted and enforced conveys often tacit messages about the school's values and its understanding of the human person. We Christians understand that human beings are created for communion, and that communion is the primary goal of the school. A Christian school operates in a manner consistent with this overall goal when its disciplinary and grievance policies aim to restore communion. Our model in this regard is God's own mission of reconciliation. When human beings broke relationship with God, God did not count our trespasses against us but rather "reconciled us to himself through Christ" and now regards us as a "new creation" in Christ (2 Cor. 5:17–18).

What does it look like to participate in this mission of reconciliation as we address conflict in our Christian schools? The first important principle is that any instance of discipline or mediation in the school begins from a presumption of communion. When a student talks out or one colleague offends another, we should resist labeling the person as a problem or falling into an us-versus-them mentality. Rather, our presumption remains that this person is a beloved child of God and part of the community, even if the person has put himself or herself at odds for the moment. Practically speaking, the best way to maintain this mind-set is to reground ourselves in Christ with a moment of prayer before responding to an incident. In the words of Martin Laird, when we can enter a grounding awareness through contemplation, we are "free and gracious enough to welcome and respond to the present moment however it happens to be."[91] Beginning

91. Laird, *Sunlit Absence*, 82. These are more than pious sentiments. Studies

from a mind-set of communion rather than adversity, we are able to respond to the situation with the good of the other person in mind.

We see this common concern for the good of the human person reflected in the ways different founding orders approach student formation and community life. At Jesuit schools, student discipline is understood as part of a comprehensive framework of *cura personalis*, or care for the whole person. In practice, *cura personalis* can involve facilitating students' growth and healing in the community by working with counselors, spiritual conversations and prayer, restorative mediation sessions between individual students or with whole classes, and providing other resources. Similar methods can be appropriate for dealing with conflicts among adults. By creating opportunities for direct dialogue between disputing parties and learning more about individuals' needs and struggles, restorative practices for disciplinary issues and interpersonal conflict go beyond punishment or legalistic adjudication of grievances to create opportunities for forgiveness, reconciliation, and growth.[92]

Community life in Benedictine schools is guided by (or at least inspired by) the Holy Rule, which Benedict describes as "advice from a father who loves you."[93] He assures members of the Benedictine community, "In drawing up its regulations [for a school for the Lord's service], we hope to set down nothing harsh, nothing burdensome. The good of all concerned, however, may prompt us to a little strictness in order to amend faults and to safeguard love."[94] This concern

have found that intensive prayer strengthens neural functioning in the parts of the brain related to social awareness and empathy. See Newberg and Waldman, *How God Changes Your Brain*, 149.

92. For an overview of common restorative justice practices, see Jeanne Croteau, "What Is Restorative Justice in Schools? Everything Educators Need to Know," We Are Teachers, July 29, 2024, https://tinyurl.com/52p23hny. For a more in-depth treatment see Lorraine Stutzman Amstutz and Judy H. Mullet, *The Little Book of Restorative Discipline for Schools: Teaching Responsibility; Creating Caring Climates* (New York: Good Books, 2005).

93. RB, Prologue 1.

94. RB, Prologue 46–47.

for the good of both the individual and the community is evident in the approach of Saint Benedict's Prep to student discipline, which involves individualized responses to infractions and coordination among school administration, teachers, counselors, student leaders, and parents.[95] At Saint Benedict's students understand that they are bound together in a very real way. If one student misbehaves during convocation or steals from another student, the entire student body may have to stay after school until the issue is resolved and the community is again made whole.

Such practices embody wisdom revealed to us in the paschal mystery: preserving and healing communion in a broken world sometimes necessitates suffering on account of one another. To quote Saint Paul's words again, "If one member suffers, all suffer together with it" (1 Cor. 12:26). When he writes these words, Paul is emphasizing our oneness in Christ. By contrast, when we react to the harm another person has done to us, we are usually focusing on our separateness, on the harm *the other* has done to *me*. However, when we realize our essential oneness, we are able to look past *my* suffering to feel *our* suffering. If students or colleagues break relationship with the community, it is because they are suffering in some way. They feel afraid or excluded or inadequate. Maybe they have carried challenges at home with them into the school. Maybe they feel their voice is not heard among their colleagues. If we can enter into their suffering and feel it as our suffering, we are much more likely to respond in a way that will transform their pain rather than transmit it. This is what Jesus did. Even at the height of his suffering, he was able to go out of himself and feel compassion for those who were crucifying him: "Father, forgive them; for they do not know what they are doing" (Luke 23:34).

To be sure, this way is harder in the moment. When we have been hurt, our instinct is to react, perhaps to retaliate. However, retaliation only perpetuates the cycle of suffering. In contrast, Jesus offers us a model of abiding in the pain so as to transform it. He bore the weight of our sins so that we might be reconciled to God (2 Cor. 5:21). Civil

95. See *Creating a Successful Urban School Culture*, 15–16.

rights leaders such as Martin Luther King Jr. and John Lewis offer a model of how we can imitate Jesus in our own time. They were able to overcome the instinct to retaliate when they were being sprayed with fire hoses, beaten with clubs, and bitten by dogs because they had previously undertaken intensive mental and spiritual training to prepare for that moment.[96] They had learned how to abide in the pain, and their personal transformation catalyzed the transformation of the society of their time. Training students in similar practices (e.g., focused breathing and mantra-like repetition of a sound) has been found to reduce absenteeism, school rule infractions, and suspension days.[97] This is our model for dealing with conflict in Christian schools—prayer, compassion, forgiveness, and patience.

Responding to the World's Greatest Need

We are created for loving communion. This is our deepest identity and our greatest longing. Unfortunately, many elements of modern society—personal technologies, political polarization, decreased civic involvement—seem to be conspiring to isolate us from one another. The world desperately needs to find ways of repairing our fractured communities. What work could be more important for our Christian schools today than this? Fortunately, we have inherited a tradition that offers us the resources we need to carry out this work. School assemblies, student clubs, dorm-based activities, faculty meetings, and even disciplinary practices can all serve as opportunities to build and repair community and to grow in likeness of the Trinitarian community of love. The key to this communal and personal transformation is taking the time to abide in God's love. What seems to the world like inactivity, like wasted time, is in fact the one

96. These notes from a 1963 nonviolent training session provide some insight into the methods used to achieve this personal transformation: Bruce Hartford, "Notes from a Nonviolent Training Session (1963)," accessed November 8, 2024, https://tinyurl.com/4htk5k6w.

97. Newberg and Waldman, *How God Changes Your Brain*, 31.

thing necessary to loving one another, working well together, and reconciling when needed. All of a Christian school's activities flow from this reservoir of God's love. Below I summarize some of the contemplative practices highlighted in this chapter that assist us in this vital work of nurturing community.

Contemplative Practices for Community Building

For starters: Practice the compassion meditation described at the beginning of this chapter to increase your capacity to understand others' perspectives, feel their suffering, and respond to them with love rather than animosity or judgment.

Shared attention: Knowing that our hearts and minds are formed by the things we give our attention to, we can form the school community in a shared vision and love by:

- Spending time together in the presence of the divine Mystery (e.g., in the Eucharist, chapel services, eucharistic adoration).
- Engaging in communal rituals such as the Mass of the Holy Spirit at the beginning of the school year and bestowal of symbolic items (e.g., a blue blazer or black hoodie).
- Sharing stories about salvation history, the school's founding order, and members of the school community.
- Creating a school environment (posters, plaques, statues, photos, artwork) that constantly reminds members of the community that they are in the presence of Mystery.

Small communities: Nurture a sense of belonging by creating small communities within the larger school community where every person is noticed, named, and known. For example:

- teams, clubs, and affinity courses
- homeroom, groups, and *tutorías*

- residence halls, houses, and living learning communities
- affinity groups and learning communities for adults

Hospitality: Create a welcoming space for visitors and members alike by:

- Extending special hospitality to visitors by creating inviting reception areas and assigning student guides.
- Implementing school policies and practices that are inclusive of diverse groups to the extent possible given the school's resources and context.
- Training students, faculty, and staff in the art of attentive listening.
- Creating special times and spaces where everyone's voice can be heard and appreciated, including those voices that are most easily silenced.
- Creating support groups for historically marginalized persons such as first-generation college students, racial minority groups, and LGBTQ students.

Capacitation for community: Undertake the inner work needed to be capable of healthy relationships and communal life, including:

- Turning inward to receive God's unconditional love, understanding our personal histories and wounds, practicing watchfulness over our inner thoughts and feelings, and cultivating inner stillness by means of the Jesus Prayer or another prayer word.
- Going out to others by means of attentive listening and compassionate responding.

Contemplative meetings: Avoid frustration and strengthen community during meetings by utilizing the following practices:

- Beginning meetings with intentionality, for example, with a ritual bow or a meaningful moment of prayer.

- Listening to one another attentively and refraining from distractions such as checking emails during the meeting.
- Practicing watchfulness over thoughts and feelings and meeting negative thoughts and reactions with prayerful silence when they arise.
- Incorporating breaks in longer meetings (planned or as needed) during which time attendees can go for a walk, pray, or otherwise recenter.
- Falling into silence when tensions arise or when arriving at an impasse in the conversation.
- Ending with a moment of reflection or thanksgiving, a bow, prayer, or silence.

Resolving conflict: Conflict is inevitable in a broken world. The following practices can help us to heal the suffering in our school communities rather than perpetuating it:

- Creating special times and spaces where community members (especially the most vulnerable) can speak hard truths with the aim of restoring communion and without fear of reprisal.
- Responding to conflict and violations of school rules as a community rather than isolating the offending individuals. This may involve coordination among administrators, teachers, counselors, student leaders, and parents.
- Approaching student discipline and conflict mediation as holistic human formation rather than mere punishment. Specific interventions may include counseling sessions, spiritual conversations and prayer, restorative mediation sessions, and provision of resources.

5

Research and Study

Contemplating the Goodness of God's Creation

In the previous chapter, we explored how reappropriating the Christian contemplative tradition might help us to approach meetings and other communal work as a common labor of love rather than a chore. When we enter these moments together as departments, committees, or clubs with an awareness of God's abiding presence, they have the potential to knit us more tightly into a community that bears the likeness of the triune community of love. That is the hope. However, the truth is that many college professors perceive committee work (and even teaching) as distractions from their "real" work of research. I occasionally recognize this kind of thinking in myself even though I consider myself first and foremost a teacher. Follow me through a typical Friday morning, and you will see what I mean.

So Much for the Life of the Mind

The week has been a blur, but now it is Friday and I finally have time to get some writing done. I sit down at my desk and fire up the computer. When it turns on, I see a notification that I have new emails waiting to be read, and I make the mistake of checking what they are. Twenty minutes later I am cursing myself for getting sidetracked before I have even begun. I close out my email and open up the article I am working on. I scroll down to where I last left off but quickly realize that I will have to backtrack. I got dragged into meetings last Friday when I should have been writing, and now I have lost the thread of my argument. I take some time to reread the previous section and then resume writing. Eventually I get into a groove.

When I next look up, two hours have gone by. The thoughts start swirling: *Where is the time going?! I am not making enough progress! This article has to get done before the end of the semester if I am going to get it published this year. I have mid-tenure review coming up, and my department chair has already hinted that I need more publications.* I cast around my work space, looking for some source of consolation. My eyes land on the stack of books I had hoped to read as part of my research for this project. Instead of consolation, the sight of the books provokes a twinge of sadness and kicks up another dust storm of afflictive thoughts: *I'm never going to get to actually read these books. I don't have time. I will just have to pull out a few quotes so I can fill out the bibliography. I just have to get this thing done.*

Sadness gives way to shame. I never wanted to be this kind of academic, cherry-picking quotes and statistics to serve my purposes. What happened? When I was in grad school, I thought I would be living the dream once I secured a full-time position at a university. I thought that once I was done with coursework, comprehensive exams, and writing for a dissertation committee, I would be free to pursue my intellectual passions, but now I am just writing to get the next publication, the next promotion, the next raise. I have no time to learn anything new. I look at the clock again. I can't be indulging these kinds of thoughts right now. I need to get this section written because on Monday it's back to teaching and committee meetings.

The Tree of Knowledge and Its Bitter Fruit

My reading and conversations with colleagues assure me that this experience is all too common. There is widespread discontent regarding our experiences of research and study in the modern educational system. Many of us believe education is supposed to be about deepening and extending our knowledge, yet those golden learning moments seem rarer than we expect them to be. They have been crowded out by all the stuff we are required to do—tests, homework, publications, reports—by some impersonal authority. Other experiences contribute to our sense that something is amiss, including rampant cheating and plagiarism among students and a shocking number of professional researchers falsifying research data and study results.[1]

We teachers complain about our students taking shortcuts and grubbing for grades, but the truth is that our motivations for research and publishing can be equally utilitarian. We set out on our chosen research agenda out of a sense of fascination with a particular issue, topic, or need. We wanted to address social injustices, cure cancer, or lift up the insights of a thinker who inspired us. But as time has gone on, the cutting edges of our inquiry-driven thinking have been dulled by the practicalities of academic life. We compromise on which topics we write on, how we do our research, and where we publish in order to appease our committee members, stay in the good graces of senior colleagues, or earn a promotion. Little by little our passion cools, and research and writing feel more like work than a vocation.

Like our young people who feel ensnared in a technological web they are powerless to escape, we academics find ourselves trapped in an "iron cage" of technocracy, production, and efficiency.[2] Decision making in our corporatized universities is driven primarily by what can be readily quantified and assessed.[3] Research is valued according

1. Daniele Fanelli, "How Many Scientists Fabricate and Falsify Research? A Systematic Review and Meta-analysis of Survey Data," *PloS One* 4, no. 5 (2009): e5738.

2. Max Weber, *The Protestant Ethic and the "Spirit" of Capitalism and Other Writings* (New York: Penguin Books, 2002), 13.

3. See Stefan Collini, *What Are Universities For?* (New York: Penguin Books, 2012), and Maggie Berg and Barbara K. Seeber, *The Slow Professor: Challenging the Culture of Speed in the Academy* (Toronto: University of Toronto Press, 2016).

to the grant money it brings to the university.[4] Tenure and promotion are determined primarily by number of publications and the impact factors of the journals in which those publications appear. Colleges are judged according to their *U.S. News & World Report* rankings. This institutionalization of the utilitarian paradigm imposes intense pressure on researchers to adapt their research agendas to meet these narrow criteria and expectations. We feel that our careers depend on it.

In short, contemporary higher education has become obsessed with production and quantification—producing more knowledge, more publications, more grants—and this mentality has trickled down to the secondary and elementary levels as well. However, in the apt words of Stefan Collini, "Not everything that counts can be counted."[5] Collini's critique cuts to the heart of this contemporary educational crisis and draws attention to a detrimental shift from a focus on the development of the human person to production of things external to us.[6] This shift is the result of misguided assumptions about what contributes to the good of the human person. It is essentially the same error Adam and Eve succumbed to when they reached out to take the fruit from the tree of knowledge of good and evil. They believed that this act would give them knowledge and power and that this would make them happy. Unfortunately, they were only half right—they gained knowledge but were alienated from themselves, each other, their Creator, and their work.

4. Pushing back against this paradigm, Ernest Boyer has made a compelling case for why rewarding only a certain type of research is limiting and how other forms of scholarship make valuable contributions to the academy. See *Scholarship Reconsidered: Priorities of the Professoriate* (San Francisco: Jossey-Bass, 1997).

5. Collini, *What Are Universities For?*, 120.

6. In *Exiles from Eden*, Mark Schwehn points to Max Weber as the primary culprit in focusing the academy on instrumental motives (e.g., mastery, manipulation, control) and virtues (e.g., clarity, diligence, rigorous disciplinary procedures). *Exiles from Eden: Religion and the Academic Vocation in America* (New York: Oxford University Press, 1993).

Something similar has occurred in contemporary education. The fruit we grasped for has turned bitter in our mouths. Our knowledge has made us wealthier and more powerful but also more alienated. Corporatization and bureaucratization have made many universities wealthier and more efficient but at the cost of diminishing the humanity of the people who work in these institutions. Human acts of creativity, prudential judgment, and collaboration are increasingly replaced by standardized forms and procedures. Quantifiable production is increased while interior growth is neglected, even stifled.

Reflecting on the story of the tower of Babel sheds further light on our current predicament. According to Genesis 11, human beings got it into their heads to make a name for themselves by building a great city and tower that would reach into the heavens. The tragic result of their misguided efforts was that their language was confused and, no longer able to understand one another, they were scattered across the earth. There could be no more apt metaphor for what has happened in modern higher education. Ever more refined methods of inquiry have greatly advanced human knowledge but also fragmented universities into places where scholars from different disciplines no longer understand one another. Investment in technological development has yielded achievements that would seem godlike to our ancestors, but it has not been accompanied by corresponding development of the interior life needed to ensure that new discoveries be used for the authentic good of individuals and society.[7] We now live in fear of our creations (nuclear weapons, artificial intelligence, etc.) and how our enemies might use them against us. We can lament with T. S. Eliot, "Where is the wisdom we have lost in knowledge? / Where is the knowledge we have lost in information?"[8]

7. See John Paul II, *Ex Corde Ecclesiae*, Vatican, 1990, https://tinyurl.com/258cvtt6, #7.

8. T. S. Eliot, "Choruses from 'The Rock,'" in *The Complete Poems and Plays of T. S. Eliot* (London: Faber & Faber, 1969), 147. Expressing similar sentiments, Alfred North Whitehead writes, "The drop from the divine wisdom, which was the goal of the ancients, to text-book knowledge of subjects, which

Painting of the heavenly Father and stars above the sanctuary of the Chapel of the Immaculate Conception

Painting of the Holy Spirit and stars underneath the canopy above the altar

While these stories of humankind's beginnings may give us cause to despair that we will ever learn from our errors, they also offer us hope. God did not cast humans out of paradise and disrupt their tower building in order to block human development but rather to lift our sights to something even higher. It is the Tempter who seeks to obstruct our growth, and he is savvy. What he offers is "pleasing to the eyes" (Gen. 3:6 NABRE), though it leads to death. Every generation succumbs to the temptation to taste the fruit gained by our own effort. We not only want good things; we want to feel powerful. The trick in this temptation is that, when we fixate on what we can achieve by our own power, we limit ourselves to lower things. We confine ourselves to the earth, for indeed that is all we are on our own.[9]

God wants to raise us to higher things. Scripture makes that much clear. The question is: Are we willing to lift our eyes up from the things of this earth to something more ennobling, more wonderful, more mysterious? I invite you into the chapel once more to contemplate this possibility.

A Meditation on the Stars

God is always inviting us to raise our sights to higher things. Seton Hall's chapel is designed to do the same, as you can see in the photographs provided. As our gaze travels upward, the chapel's shining gold embellishments and polished woodwork give way to a dark blue reminiscent of the evening sky. Stars dot the ceiling, and we get the impression that we have arrived just in time to see them come out. The effect is to open up the confined space of the chapel onto something beyond. The stars are more numerous and more densely packed together toward the front of the chapel above the sanctuary where the

---

is achieved by the moderns, marks an educational failure, sustained through the ages." *The Aims of Education and Other Essays* (New York: Free Press, 1967), 29.

9. The Hebrew word for mankind in the Bible (*'adam*) literally means "earthling" or one created from the earth (*'adamah*) (Gen. 1:26).

heavenly Father is depicted surrounded by angels. Below the Father, on the underside of the canopy overhanging the altar, the Holy Spirit, in the form of a dove, descends out of a ring of fire with stars bursting forth all around. Here we encounter the origin of the stars flung across the sky. (Notably, we can only see this detail as we approach the sanctuary to receive the Lord in communion.)

These details from the chapel are an homage to our fascination with the heavens, a fascination that only deepens as time goes on. In 2022 NASA released new images from the James Webb Telescope, which allowed us to peer farther into space than ever before. What we see in these images is truly awe-inspiring. Some capture a span of space millions of light-years across. It is astounding to think that even this massive expanse represents only a small portion of the known universe, which astronomers estimate to be ninety-three billion light-years in diameter and growing larger every minute. When we look at these images of distant stars and galaxies, we are looking into the distant past, seeing light that took billions of years to reach us. Astronomers' best estimate is that the universe is 13.7 billion years old. We and the planet we live on are late-comers on the scene, the Earth only being formed about 4.5 billion years ago out of the dust of exploded stars. In that regard, to say that we humans are made of dust is only to tell part of the story. That dust is stardust. We are the products of a process of creation that has been under way for billions of years and of the creative force behind it all, "the Love that moves the sun and the other stars."[10]

I invite you to look at some of these images for yourself at https://webbtelescope.org. Take your time and notice as much detail as you can in each image. As you watch the video or behold different images, ponder the following:

- What thoughts and feelings do these images evoke in you?
- How does it feel knowing that everything on our planet and all that happens here is only a microscopic piece of this vast universe?

10. Dante Alighieri, *Paradiso*, 33.145, in *The Divine Comedy*, Digital Dante Edition, Columbia University, 2020, https://tinyurl.com/mpdnn2jm.

- Do you feel any differently about your concerns and to-do list for the day, having viewed these images?
- Do you think or feel any differently about God, knowing the vastness of God's creation? Ponder for a moment the workings of this divine mind (*Logos*) that works on a scale of billions of light-years and a timeline of billions of years.

When you have finished viewing the images, sit quietly for a few minutes. Know that you are in the presence of the Mystery behind all that you have just seen and that this Mystery is beholding you right now, loving you.

The Higher Calling of Christian Education

Our Christian faith assures us that we are not just creatures of the earth, that we are created for more than satisfying bodily desires and acquiring material goods. Our Creator beckons us to set our sights on the heavens. What does this calling mean for our work in Christian schools?

For one thing, this calling should shape the goals we set in our schools. Although there has been widespread agreement regarding the value of education for much of human history, why education is valuable and what purposes it serves are the subject of perennial debate.[11] In our own day, the aims of education are most often focused on the utilitarian—producing technology, acquiring skills, securing employment. However, I believe that any Christian educator who looks at his or her students with love, as Jesus once looked at a rich young man (Mark 10:21), will want much more for them. For all his wealth, the rich young man lacked something essential. Sadly, many of today's young people are lacking in the same way on account of the materialistic culture in which they live and the incomplete education they receive.

This state of affairs represents a narrowing of educational aims relative to the way education was conceived for much of history, in-

11. See Collini, *What Are Universities For?*

cluding in ancient Greece and medieval Europe. Aristotle, for example, recognized the value not only of *technē* or technical know-how (which modern education privileges) but also of other forms of knowledge including *epistēmē* (theoretical or scientific knowledge), *phronēsis* (practical prudence), and *sophia* (wisdom).[12] The eleventh-century Cistercian Saint Bernard of Clairvaux adverted to the many possible motivations for learning and made clear which he regarded as unworthy of a Christian:

> For there are some who desire to know only for the sake of knowing; and this is disgraceful curiosity. And then there are some who desire to know, that they may become known themselves; and this is disgraceful vanity. . . . And there are also some who desire to know in order to sell their knowledge, as for money, or for degrees; and this is disgraceful commercialism. But there are some who seek knowledge in order to edify others; and this is love.[13]

The words of Aristotle and Bernard are representative of a tradition of education that took as its goal the full flourishing of the human person (*eudaimonia*, in Aristotle's language). Such flourishing involves not only the satisfaction of biological needs and acquiring the means of making a living; it also includes a sense of meaning and purpose, personal integration, and (for Christians) loving relationships with God and other people. The knowledge that promotes this fuller kind of human flourishing is what Christians, following the ancient Greeks, have traditionally termed "wisdom" (*sophia*).

When we examine the scriptural understanding of wisdom, its absence in modern education becomes conspicuous. According to

12. See book 6 of Aristotle's *Nicomachean Ethics*, trans. D. P. Chase, Project Gutenberg, 2021, https://tinyurl.com/mv9av9vb.

13. From Bernard, Abbot of Clairvaux, "Sermon on the Song of Songs," in *The Steps to Humility*, trans. George Bosworth Birch (Notre Dame: University of Notre Dame Press, 1963), 37.

the book of Proverbs, wisdom entails insight, righteousness, justice, knowledge, prudence, and skill (1:2–6). It pertains not only to practical matters but also to eternal truths. The different forms of knowledge encapsulated in this concept of wisdom are essential to a fully human life and yet are rarely taught in contemporary schools. Focusing on information and technical skills, we neglect the wisdom our students need to know the meaning of the good life and the prudence they need to realize the good life in the midst of daily decisions. We do not teach them how to find meaning in life, nurture healthy relationships, or deal with suffering. We are so fixated on making them good students, doctors, and managers that we neglect the more fundamental task of helping them understand what it means to be a human being. This dehumanizing education is partly to blame for the widespread sense of meaninglessness and mental health problems we are currently experiencing.[14] In this respect, Pope Francis is right to say, "Today, above all, the right to a good education means protecting wisdom, that is, knowledge that is human and humanizing."[15]

An education that humanizes in the ways described above is fuller, more valuable, and ultimately more rewarding than mere career training. "Happy are those who find wisdom," reads Scripture, "for her income is better than silver, / and her revenue better than gold" (Prov. 3:13–14). And yet we need not imagine that these two modes of education are mutually exclusive. Students in Christian schools should strive to acquire the knowledge and skills required for the practicalities of life and work.[16] Christian scholars may pursue re-

14. According to a national survey conducted by the Springtide Research Institute, 25 percent of young people report that life rarely or never has meaning for them. Josh Packard et al., *Meaning-Making: 8 Values That Drive America's Newest Generations* (Bloomington, MN: Springtide Research Institute, 2020), 125.

15. Francis, *Christus Vivit*, Vatican, 2019, https://tinyurl.com/3vpetjcp, #223.

16. Franciscan University's College of St. Joseph the Worker, which forms students in the Catholic intellectual tradition while training them in a particular trade, is a shining exemplar of this synthesis. See https://tinyurl.com/yc6enc2j.

search in every field confident in the unity of all knowledge.[17] Still, as Thomas Merton and Simone Weil remind us, the crucial thing for a Christian education is that study of these various subjects contributes to the students' growth in holiness and relationship with God.[18] As we saw in chapter 1, Christians' desire to know and love God was the driving force behind the desert schools, monastery schools, and schools founded later by apostolic orders like the Jesuits and Dominicans. Students in Christian schools study the same natural phenomena with the same intellectual rigor as students in secular schools, but they study with an understanding that the things we can see and measure point beyond themselves to something more, to Someone.[19]

This reference to something beyond is the key to an authentically Christian education because, among other reasons, wisdom is not attainable by human efforts alone. True wisdom comes as a gift from God (Prov. 2:6). We receive the gift of God's wisdom in a particular way through the teaching and example of Jesus Christ, the incarnate Word, the divine *Logos*. Jesus, rather than a successful careerist, is our model of human fulfillment.[20] In the person of Jesus, we see most clearly that God's wisdom is self-giving love (*agapē*).[21] To be Christian

17. See John Henry Newman, *The Idea of a University* (Notre Dame: University of Notre Dame Press, 1982), 103, and John Paul II, *Fides et Ratio*, Vatican, 1998, https://tinyurl.com/d876ybdk, #34.

18. See Weil, "Reflections on the Right Use of School Studies," and Thomas Merton, "The Need for a New Education," in *Contemplation in a World of Action* (Garden City, NY: Doubleday, 1971).

19. Physicist Arthur Zajonc argues that this kind of contemplative approach (although not necessarily Christian for him) promotes better science and learning: "We require new and more embracing methods of inquiry that can accommodate the great advances of science but not be limited by the dogmatic perspective of materialism and its associated economics." *Meditation as Contemplative Inquiry: When Knowing Becomes Love* (Great Barrington, MA: Lindisfarne Books, 2009), 15.

20. See Paul VI, *Gaudium et Spes*, Vatican, 1965, https://tinyurl.com/yeyvvycn, #22, and *Ignatian Pedagogy: A Practical Approach*, Society of Jesus, accessed October 30, 2024, https://tinyurl.com/47avdk2p, #15.

21. See Benedict XVI, *Deus Caritas Est*, Vatican, 2005, https://tinyurl.

is to be conformed to the mind of Christ (Phil. 2:5), to be a person who "does the truth in love."[22] Indeed, God's wisdom cannot be acquired from books and lectures (although these might help) but only from living in conformity with the Truth and in relationship with Mystery. In the remainder of this chapter, we will unpack these seminal insights and explore what it looks like to seek wisdom through our research and study in Christian educational institutions.

Research as Seeking the Truth in Love

Imagine yourself sitting down at your desk or walking into your lab to pick up your work where you last left off. What thoughts and feelings arise as you enter this space—joy, anxiety, boredom? Do your thoughts gravitate toward thorny questions and exciting ideas or toward deadlines, funding, and evaluations? When you examine these thoughts and feelings, what do they reveal about your priorities and motivations for your research? Looking within, do you feel your heart is in the right place?

If our research has turned into toil and our institutions have become like corporations, that is perhaps because we have lost sight of our guiding star. Perhaps we have given over our hearts and minds to goals and concerns that are less than worthy. A scholar of the Jewish law once asked Jesus which was the greatest of the commandments (Matt. 22:36). I would suggest that Jesus's answer to that scholar offers important wisdom for scholars today. What is most important in our lives and our work? Loving God and loving our neighbor. As

---

com/2xbdw9j3, #13. Commenting on Benedictine education, Abbot Thomas Frerking, OSB, writes, "For the Christian, any knowledge, and any increase in knowledge, must always be such as to be accompanied by charity and to promote growth in charity. . . . Therefore, the love of Charity is the motive force of this ascent of the mind and heart to God." "Saint John Henry Newman on Benedictine Life and on Benedictine Schools," in *A Benedictine Education*, ed. Christopher Fisher (Providence: Cluny Media, 2020), 200.

22. Michael Himes, *Doing the Truth in Love: Conversations about God, Relationships, and Service* (Mahwah, NJ: Paulist, 2014).

Saint Bernard suggests, love is the proper motivation for our study. This was the guiding light the early Benedictines pursued in their learning. They studied Scripture and the church fathers but also the classical texts of antiquity because they wanted to know more deeply the One whom they loved, the One pointed to in these texts more or less directly. Likewise, it was love of neighbor that motivated the Dominicans' tireless pursuit of truth. They undertook study not merely for the sake of being learned but also so they could teach God's truth more clearly and thereby save souls.

What does it look like for us today to pursue learning in love as did the early Benedictines and Dominicans (and Jesuits)? It looks like legal scholars using their gifts to envision and implement processes of restorative justice. It looks like architects creating spaces that encourage people to linger together or to enter into reverent worship. It looks like scholars in diverse disciplines and institutions working together and applying their learning in ways that help others to become wiser and lead fuller lives.[23]

Doing research out of love for God and neighbor has real implications for the priorities we pursue and the methods we employ as researchers. While the modern academy typically assigns higher value to research and scholarship that generates new knowledge and innovation, for Christians the extent to which learning contributes to the love of God and the good of human persons is more important than how novel that learning is. By this I do not mean to suggest that Christians should not engage in innovative research. Christians have frequently been responsible for breakthrough discoveries that have benefited humanity.[24] My point is that the contemporary acad-

23. Doing something good for others also comes with the reward of making us feel better. Daniel Goleman and Richard Davidson, *Altered Traits: Science Reveals How Meditation Changes Your Mind, Brain, and Body* (New York: Avery Books, 2018), 108.

24. For example, Isaac Newton, the father of modern physics; Rev. Georges Lemaître, the father of the big bang theory; and Francis Collins, the former director of the National Human Genome Research Institute.

emy, in its fixation on novelty and innovation, tends to overlook the vital importance of the human subject. Albert Einstein, by contrast, clearly recognized the insufficiency of this approach to learning. Einstein writes:

> But let us not forget that knowledge and skills alone cannot lead humanity to a happy and dignified life. Humanity has every reason to place the proclaimers of high moral standards and values above the discoverers of objective truth. What humanity owes to personalities like Buddha, Moses, and Jesus ranks for me higher than all the achievements of the inquiring and constructive mind.[25]

Since so many of our peers are fixated on new knowledge, skills, and technologies, Christian institutions of learning have all the more responsibility to hand down the wisdom of the ages that stands to make us better people. They have a crucial role to play in today's world, supporting people's moral development and interior growth so that they can make good use of the new knowledge and technologies we are producing at an accelerating rate.[26]

Our fundamental human nature has not changed in the past several thousand years. For that reason, the wisdom of the ancient Greek philosophers, the desert fathers and mothers, and Christian

25. Quoted in Andrew Newberg and Mark Robert Waldman, *How God Changes Your Brain: Breakthrough Findings from a Leading Neuroscientist* (New York: Ballantine Books, 2009), 2.

26. In other terms, this educational approach involves valuing and nurturing what environmental scientist David Orr calls "slow knowledge" in contrast with the kind of "fast knowledge" that often typifies contemporary education, technology, and commerce. David Orr, "Slow Knowledge," in *Hope Is an Imperative: The Essential David Orr* (Washington, DC: Island, 2010), 13–20. Orr observes that our shortsighted focus on knowledge that produces novel technologies and immediate benefits has led to some of the most dogged problems of our day, including global warming, nuclear proliferation, and shortsighted economic policies.

monastics is just as relevant today as it was in their time. More than including pious language on a school brochure or website, being rooted in this tradition is what makes a school authentically Christian. Such rootedness is a gift that Christian schools have to offer a world that is forgetful of the wisdom of the past, wisdom that we urgently need to navigate the challenges of the present. Although tenure guidelines and college rankings seldom reflect it, this is one of the great gifts that Christian scholars and institutions have to offer the world—drawing forth from the Christian tradition things new and old (Matt. 13:52) in response to the pressing issues, questions, and challenges of our day.

Incarnating Wisdom

"Students today are only interested in getting jobs and making money." Such is the lament of many teachers with whom I work and correspond. "They have no interest in the life of the mind," they say. Yet my own experience and recent survey data paint a more nuanced picture.[27] It is clearly the case that current students are very concerned about getting jobs after graduation, but they also crave deeper conversations than they typically experience and are desperately hungry for meaning in their lives. If our students do not seem hungry for the Christian teaching we offer, we need to ask ourselves how effectively we are connecting that teaching to our students' experiences and concerns.

To do so in no way constitutes a watering down of Christian teaching. Wisdom as understood in the Christian tradition involves more than wise sayings preserved in books and committed to memory by readers. As Christians we believe that God has communicated God's wisdom to us most fully in the person of God's Son, the incarnate *Lo-*

27. See Packard, *Meaning-Making*, and *The State of Religion and Young People 2023: Exploring the Sacred*, Springtide Research Institute (Winona, MN: Springtide Research Institute, 2023).

gos (John 1:14). Given that God's wisdom has been revealed to us in words and deeds, flesh and blood, the kind of wisdom at the core of the Christian life is, as Dorothy Bass and company explain, closer to "embodied, situated knowing-in-action than to disembodied, theoretical knowledge."[28] Christian wisdom is wisdom for living. It is precisely the kind of wisdom today's young people seek, and, when they experience this living wisdom (emphasis on experience), it transforms them.[29]

God's wisdom is an incarnate wisdom. We recognize this wisdom most clearly and most fully when we encounter it in enfleshed form, that is to say, in other people. As Pope Paul VI once said, "Modern man listens more willingly to witnesses than to teachers, and if he does listen to teachers, it is because they are witnesses."[30] This is manifestly true of today's young people, who gravitate toward authenticity and shun traditional authorities. It is not enough for Christian educators to be knowledgeable about the content of the Christian faith. In order to communicate the wisdom of the Christian tradition to contemporary audiences, teachers must embody the values they teach and represent. Students must be able to look at their teachers and say, "I want to be like them." Every teacher has the potential to so inspire their students, whether they teach theology or math or physical education.

In this regard, a Christian scholar's human and spiritual formation is just as important as his or her academic training. As theologian Kathleen Cahalan notes, practical wisdom arises from how we pray and

28. Dorothy Bass et al., *Christian Practical Wisdom: What It Is, Why It Matters* (Grand Rapids: Eerdmans, 2016), 2.

29. Newberg and Waldman conducted one interesting study that exemplifies such transformation. This study found that the goals people identified for themselves became less materialistic and more intrinsic and spiritual after participating in an exercise where they imagined an intimate, compassionate conversation with another person. Newberg and Waldman, *How God Changes Your Brain*, 221–26.

30. Paul VI, *Evangelii Nuntiandi*, Vatican, 1975, https://tinyurl.com/4bn6tnyz, #41.

live.[31] It cannot be attained but through spiritual practice.[32] Sadly, this human and spiritual formation is not merely neglected in the typical academic preparation; academics are routinely formed in habits contrary to Christian values—habits of competitiveness, individualism, and self-aggrandizement. To be formed as a Christian, by contrast, is to be conformed to the mind of Christ, who did not grasp at glory but rather emptied himself to the point of death (Phil. 2:5–8).

The beginning of growth in Christian wisdom, therefore, is humility, the "mother" and "teacher of all the virtues."[33] The desert fathers recognized that a disciple would only derive spiritual benefit from his learning if he approached his studies with an awareness of the poverty of his knowing.[34] Seeking to instill humility in his monks, Saint Benedict devised a ladder of humility in twelve steps that include keeping the fear of God always before our eyes, seeking God's will rather than our own, and submitting to our superiors.[35] Each step presents a concrete way of opening our minds and hearts so that they may be filled, not with our ideas and desires, but with God's own wisdom. While it is good to work toward humility by such means, there is no better teacher than life itself. The fifth-century monastic John Cassian points out that humility comes through suffering, through encountering challenges and failing, and thereby confronting our limits.

The Christian tradition offers students and scholars other spiritual practices for growing in wisdom once we have cultivated a basic de-

31. Kathleen Cahalan, "Unknowing: Spiritual Practices and the Search for a Wisdom Epistemology," in Bass, *Christian Practical Wisdom*, 277. Arthur Zajonc makes similar assertions regarding the necessity of a solid moral foundation for conducting quality research. See Zajonc, *Meditation as Contemplative Inquiry*, chapter 2.

32. Dorothy Bass and her collaborators have explored the importance of spiritual practices in great depth in books like *Practicing Our Faith: A Way of Life for a Searching People* (Minneapolis: Fortress, 2019).

33. John Cassian, *The Conferences*, trans. Boniface Ramsey, OP (Mahwah, NJ: Paulist, 1997), 542, 670.

34. The Buddhist tradition similarly advises practitioners to adopt a "beginner's mind."

35. Rule of Benedict, chapter 7.

gree of humility and docility to God's work on us. The practice with perhaps the deepest roots, going back to the early desert monastics, is memorizing and reciting Scripture verses. Saint Pachomius enjoined his monks, "recite in your hearts the words of Scripture ceaselessly, resolving within yourselves to walk in them."[36] Repeating the words of Scripture not only in our hearts but also with our voices impresses the Scriptures upon us in a way that tends not to happen when reading silently.[37] Full integration requires enacting in our lives the words we read and recite, as Pachomius suggests.

Saint Dominic modeled another beneficial practice for teachers and scholars who aspire to pass Christian wisdom on to others. Dominic was an itinerant preacher, and he used the long walks between towns as opportunities to meditate upon the mysteries he was to preach to the people he would next encounter. His preparation often took the form of singing hymns and psalms, stopping to kneel in the churches he passed along the way, and moving his hands in front of his face as if to physically shoo away any thoughts distracting him from his meditation. These physical gestures were the means by which Dominic penetrated more deeply into the Mystery he contemplated.[38] In similar fashion, contemporary Christian scholars might adopt the habit of stopping in the chapel or reciting a prayer as we make our way to a lecture or conference. Since we contemporary scholars tend to spend more time at our desks than on the road, we should aspire to cultivate spiritual practices suitable to this setting.

36. Cited in "Life of Prayer: Memorizing the Word," Community of the Beatitudes, January 10, 2022, https://tinyurl.com/4x4r6cer.

37. Contemporary spiritual guides and teachers such as John Main and Mary Keator have carried on this practice. See Keator, *Lectio Divina as Contemplative Pedagogy: Re-appropriating Monastic Practice for the Humanities* (New York: Routledge, 2018), 99–103, for more suggestions for embodied and performative reading of texts.

38. Paul Philibert, "Roman Catholic Prayer: The *Novum modi orandi sancti Dominici*," in *Contemplative Literature: A Comparative Sourcebook on Meditation and Contemplative Prayer*, ed. Louis Komjathy (Albany: SUNY Press, 2015), 526.

For example, when taking a break, we might physically kneel in prayer in order to enact the humility we strive to embody in our work.

Researching and Writing Contemplatively

These spiritual practices are means of inscribing God's *Logos* on our hearts, minds, and bodies in such a way that, day by day, we become the kind of people in whom our students and readers might recognize God's own wisdom. In this section, we will explore additional Christian contemplative practices that help us not only to incarnate God's wisdom in the world but also to do better research and writing.

Around the time I was beginning work on this book, our family took a trip to Sequoia and Yosemite National Parks. One of the joys of that trip for our family was getting away from all the car headlights, lampposts, and electric signs of the metro New York area and witnessing the stars shining forth in all their glory. Sometimes we need to do something similar in order to access our inner lights: We need mental space, time, and quiet in order to catch a glimpse of the profoundest truths. Learned Christians of ages past retreated to the desert and monastic enclosures in search of such quiet. Sabbaticals and writing retreats offer something similar to contemporary writers and researchers, especially when they take us away from the usual stresses and distractions of campus.[39] School leadership, for their part, can support their faculty's growth in wisdom by scheduling retreats and no-meeting days and providing course releases for research.

It is ideal when schools can give their faculty this gift of time, but the reality is that fewer and fewer Christian institutions have the resources to grant course releases and similar privileges. Even where

39. Research shows that workers are more satisfied with their jobs, are more productive, are more creative, get along better with colleagues, and deal better with challenges when they take adequate time away from work. Alex Soojung-Kim Pang, *Rest: Why You Get More Done When You Work Less* (New York: Basic Books, 2018), 159–75, 221–39.

such opportunities exist, few scholars can afford to wait for a retreat or a sabbatical to do their work. For this reason we need to cultivate good practices in place. "What we have to learn," suggests Wilfrid Stinissen, "is a new *way* of working, a new way that is characterized by peace and calm instead of stress."[40] More specifically, Stinissen advises worrying less about clocks, deadlines, and the opinions of others and paying more attention to our own natural rhythms, which is perhaps the most concrete way God conveys to us God's will for our lives.[41] Psychologist Gloria Mark confirms that people are more effective and productive when they establish work habits that align with their attentional limits and circadian rhythms.[42] Such habits include planning and sticking to a humane work schedule (akin to the monastic *horarium*), strategically engaging in activities that boost our mood (e.g., taking a walk outside) and, conversely, limiting activities that induce negative emotion (e.g., checking email). Mark also recommends creating "friction" against bad habits by setting alarms or timers that will lock us out of social media apps after ten minutes of use. Most basically, we need to recognize that good thinking and good scholarship take time. If we are seriously concerned with growing in wisdom rather than merely building a CV, we scholars need to give our thoughts time to mature and school leaders need to support scholars in taking this time and rewarding quality over quantity.

Stinissen's remarks about the need for a new way of working will for some bring to mind the concept of "flow." Mihaly Csikszentmihalyi, who first introduced this concept, defines flow as complete absorption in an activity that fosters a sense of mastery and enjoyment. It is an experience of activity motivated not by stress or ambition but rather by wonder, curiosity, and passion. Flow state resembles

40. Stinissen, *Eternity in the Midst of Time*, 87.

41. Berg and Seeber offer additional advice for slowing down scholarly time, including walking to the library, broadening the scope of our reading, and following our passions in our research. *The Slow Professor*, 64–70.

42. Gloria Mark, *Attention Span: A Groundbreaking Way to Restore Balance, Happiness, and Productivity* (Toronto: Hanover Square Press, 2023), 276.

mystical experiences in a number of ways, including transcending awareness of time, ourselves, and our surroundings.[43] Csikszentmihalyi characterizes flow as a state of "optimal performance," and, from a Christian perspective, such a state of unself-consciousness, wonder, and prayerfulness is surely an optimal condition in which to work. Although flow (like contemplative prayer) can be elusive, research suggests that certain conditions make it more likely that we enter into a state of flow. The most basic of these include having a clear goal[44] and rules, means of attaining feedback on performance, and match between the level of challenge and the individual's skills.[45]

For many people, the word "flow" evokes the image of someone focusing intensely or getting "in the zone." However, we would be misguided to strive for a constant state of intense focus in our work. Researchers in a variety of disciplines have observed that effective learning and other forms of intellectual work require a balance between focused concentration and open awareness.[46] Both are necessary, just as breathing involves both inhaling and exhaling. On one hand is the kind of focused attention we typically associate with intel-

43. In fact, Csikszentmihalyi notes that flow and religious experience are intimately connected. See Mihaly Csikszentmihalyi, ed., *Applications of Flow in Human Development and Education: The Collected Works of Mihaly Csikszentmihalyi* (Dordrecht: Springer Netherlands, 2014), 76.

44. Csikszentmihalyi's findings regarding the importance of goal-setting echo ancient wisdom from the desert fathers. Abba Moses says that when our goal is clear, "our actions and thoughts are ordered to attaining it in the most direct way." Cassian, *Conferences*, 44.

45. Generally speaking, flow is not strongly related to time of day or physical location. See Jennifer A. Schmidt, David J. Shernoff, and Mihaly Csikszentmihalyi, "Individual and Situational Factors Related to the Experience of Flow in Adolescence: A Multilevel Approach," in Csikszentmihalyi, *Applications of Flow in Human Development and Education*, 379–405.

46. I take these particular terms from Arthur Zajonc (*Meditation as Contemplative Inquiry*, 39). Martin Laird similarly describes "deepening concentration and expanding awareness" as the two dynamics characterizing contemplative practice. *A Sunlit Absence: Silence, Awareness, and Contemplation* (Oxford: Oxford University Press, 2011), 19.

lectual work—seeking answers, conceptualizing, reasoning, working ideas through. In this mode, our minds fixate on a goal (an answer, a proof, a completed article) and we drive toward that goal, necessarily blocking out distractions and irrelevant thoughts. On the other hand is open attention, in which we are alert and receptive to whatever might emerge from deep within or from beyond us without grasping or imposing our own expectations or concepts.

Although we tend to associate productive work with focused attention, open attention is important for a number of reasons. For one thing, we can know more when we practice open awareness. Focused attention can only operate upon what is immediately before us or readily accessible in our minds. When we move into a more receptive mode (for instance, by meditating slowly on a text or patiently beholding natural phenomena), we open ourselves up to an infinite source of new information and ideas. As countless thinkers, artists, and inventors testify, it is often during or after periods of mental relaxation that breakthroughs occur.[47] (Think of Archimedes's eureka moment in the public baths.) In addition to yielding new ideas, opening our awareness expands and grows our mental capacities. This is what Goethe meant when he wrote, "Every object well contemplated creates an organ of perception in us."[48] Contemporary neuroscience confirms Goethe's insight. According to the research of psychologist Lisa Miller, people who embody an "awakened awareness" have healthier brains than more closed-minded people and can even process more visual stimuli simultaneously.[49] They literally see more.

Despite these benefits of open awareness, modern education tends to neglect its cultivation in favor of more active, focused forms of attention. As Jesuit theologian Walter Burghardt has observed, "All

47. In his study of ninety-six creative artists, scientists, and inventors, Mihaly Csikszentmihalyi observes that moments of creative insight are typically preceded by periods of "preparation" and "incubation." *Creativity: Flow and the Psychology of Discovery and Invention* (New York: Harper, 1996), 80–81.

48. Quoted in Zajonc, *Meditation as Contemplative Inquiry*, 182–83.

49. Lisa Miller, *The Awakened Brain: The New Science of Spirituality and Our Quest for an Inspired Life* (New York: Random House, 2021), 170, 172.

the way through school we are taught to abstract; we are not taught loving awareness."[50] We are trained to be "critical thinkers," but we must ask how well we can really know anything or anyone if we are not prepared to attend to them patiently, attentively, lovingly and to receive what they would offer us. A spirit of receptivity is essential to the Christian life. Jesus tells us that it is when we empty ourselves that we are filled (Luke 1:53) and when we humble ourselves that we are exalted (Luke 18:14). As created, contingent beings, we know more and become more when we open ourselves up to our Creator. We see this attitude modeled preeminently by Mary, whose humility and openness to God's will allowed God's Word to enter the world.[51]

Simone Weil was an educator after Mary's own heart. According to Weil, a twentieth-century philosopher and mystic, Christian educators' first duty toward their students is to teach them to set their hearts upon the truth and wait upon it patiently and attentively. Contemplative practices train us to do precisely this—to wait patiently for the gaps to be filled in, as Richard Rohr says.[52] As such, they have the potential to make us not only better disciples but also better researchers. For example, *visio divina* and other forms of contemplative beholding enhance the powers of attention and observation that are essential to the work of empirical and qualitative research.[53] Deep listening in prayer and in conversation with others can make ethnographic researchers better interviewers.[54] Although not Christian

50. Walter Burghardt, "Contemplation: A Long Loving Look at the Real," in *An Ignatian Spirituality Reader*, ed. G. W. Traub (Chicago: Loyola Press, 2008), 3.

51. Another model is the twelfth-century Benedictine Hildegaard of Bingen. Hildegaard was accomplished in the diverse areas of natural medicine, theology, rhetoric, and musical composition and was able to accomplish all that she did precisely because she cultivated an open disposition in her prayer.

52. Richard Rohr, *The Universal Christ: How a Forgotten Reality Can Change Everything We See, Hope for, and Believe* (New York: Convergent Books, 2019), 8.

53. The meditation on the images from the Webb Telescope earlier in this chapter is an example of contemplative beholding.

54. Valeria Janesick similarly draws out the benefits of Buddhist practices

himself, Arthur Zajonc presents a general model of contemplative inquiry built on an "epistemology of love" that is very much in keeping with Christian theological principles.[55] Zajonc's inquiry process progresses through the stages of studying an object, forming a mental image of that object, and acting upon the image mentally, which gives rise to a new creation or knowledge.[56] The transition between each stage is achieved through "cognitive breathing" or alternating between focused concentration and open awareness. As Christian scholars, we do not work solely on our own strength. When we pray through our work and incorporate contemplative practices such as these into our research, we create space for Mystery to enter in and transform our humble offerings into something that can truly benefit others.

Contemplative practices can enhance our writing as well. In chapter 3, I presented writing as a contemplative practice that helps students reflect more deeply on what they are learning. This practice is no less beneficial for professional scholars. However, it requires a change of mind-set. Quantitative researchers especially often perceive writing as an unpleasant but necessary final step in the research process. We do it begrudgingly in order to get our research published and to share our findings with others. But approached more contemplatively, writing provides an opportunity to reflect more deeply upon what we have learned from our experiments, studies, inter-

---

for qualitative research in her book *Contemplative Qualitative Inquiry: Practicing the Zen of Research* (New York: Routledge, 2015). Although Christian scholars would not accept many of Janesick's Buddhist assumptions, her book offers rich food for thought that can inspire ideas for how analogous Christian contemplative practices might enhance various aspects of qualitative research, including observation, interviews, data analysis, and writing.

55. Zajonc, *Meditation as Contemplative Inquiry*, 179. Zajonc does, however, explicitly note that for many people prayer is a helpful entry point into contemplative inquiry. See 59.

56. Zajonc, *Meditation as Contemplative Inquiry*, 193. There is an interesting parallel between Zajonc's method and the four movements of *lectio divina*.

views, or archival research. The act of writing forces us to slow down and process the information we have gathered. Christian scholars and authors can find a model for this kind of writing in Saint Augustine, for whom writing was a form of prayer. This is most explicit in his *Confessions,* in which Augustine reflects on his life experiences and learning in the context of an extended conversation with God. Writing involves a certain discipline, even for geniuses like Augustine. Research on highly productive writers reveals that good writing is typically the result of disciplined work habits, specifically rising early and working in a focused way for three to four hours before breaking for lunch and then turning to less demanding tasks.[57] In this way, the routines of the most productive authors (and scientists, artists, and entrepreneurs) resemble a sort of neo-monastic *horarium.*

Even though scholarship inevitably involves time alone in our offices, labs, and libraries, no scholarship is truly solitary. We have been reflecting on how deliberately opening ourselves to God's inspiration can enrich our scholarly work. Being open to collaboration with other scholars can similarly benefit our work. Unfortunately, modern academia often discourages collaboration. Scholars in the same field view each other as competitors for positions, grants, and prestige, and tenure and promotion processes reward solo scholarship over collaborative work. Such a competitive approach to research and learning is sadly limiting. It stifles the expansion of knowledge and impedes developments that could improve humanity's lot.

Our Christian faith tells us that there is nothing more essential to our humanity than our relationships. Our knowing, too, is fundamentally relational, as we saw in chapter 3.[58] We see this wisdom encapsulated in the Benedictine vow of *conversatio morum.* This vexing

57. Pang, *Rest,* 78.

58. Writing from a scientific perspective, Zajonc asserts that understanding the full range of phenomena we encounter in the universe requires the "capacity for seeing constant relationships in the flux of experience." *Meditation as Contemplative Inquiry,* 161.

phrase from the Rule of Benedict is normally translated "conversion of life." However, it is interesting that Benedict deliberately chose the word *conversatio*, which can also be translated "conversation," rather than the more straightforward *conversio*. Perhaps Benedict wanted to convey that conversion of life involves an ongoing conversation with God, a conversation that runs through our daily conversations and interactions with the people in our lives. As relational beings, we are always in conversation with our God, our community, and our tradition, whether we acknowledge our conversation partners or not. We Christian scholars have the opportunity to undergo this *conversatio morum* in a practical way by seeking out collaborators and sharing our work generously when it has the potential to help more people. For their part, administrators at Christian institutions can make such collaboration more feasible by rewarding scholars for working collaboratively rather than penalizing them when it comes to tenure and promotion.

Reading Contemplatively

For students and researchers alike, reading is at the heart of the work of education. It is concerning, therefore, that reading seems to be becoming a lost art. Students increasingly struggle with reading even short articles and chapters, much less full books and technical texts.[59] Few students complete the assigned reading, and, of those few, fewer still read with comprehension. Even we scholars, who actually desire to read, often feel it is a luxury we cannot afford. We know that the tenure review board does not care how many books we read, only

59. The rewiring of neural circuitry through constant consumption of bit-sized digital content in rapid succession is one major contributing factor to students' difficulties with reading, as noted in Beth McMurtie, "Is This the End of Reading?," *Chronicle of Higher Education*, May 9, 2024, https://tinyurl.com/3e7tkmpe. However, there may be other reasons, including religious assumptions, which Jessica Hooten Wilson addresses in her book *Reading for the Love of God: How to Read as a Spiritual Practice* (Grand Rapids: Brazos, 2023).

how many we write. Reading therefore becomes yet another act of utility rather than an activity for edifying our souls. In this regard, too, we are like people who have become hypnotized by the flashing screens and lights of the city. Rarely do we look up to behold the wonder of the stars shining in the night sky.

Besides the general distractedness of our culture, reading may also be devalued by how we teach our students to read. Too seldom in our schools do we take up a book with the expectation of being challenged, delighted, or transformed. Far more commonly we train and praise our students for being able to critique the author (and their peers). When our students do not read, we threaten them with quizzes, which only succeeds in further instrumentalizing reading; they read only to extract the information needed to pass the quiz. This is precisely the sort of approach Theophan the Recluse (1815–1894) warned about: "If you read without applying what is read to yourself, nothing good will come of it, and even harm may result. Theories will accumulate in the head, leading you to criticize others instead of improving your own life."[60] Sadly, many of our students never really learn to read a text for understanding or edification. The text is for them an obstacle to get over or a stepping stool for their own self-advancement. Rarely if ever do they enter into genuine conversation with the author and allow the text to touch them.

How can we rediscover the joy of reading? We might look again to the desert fathers, who understood reading Scripture as an endeavor requiring significant personal investment. Abba Isaac, for example, says that Scripture's "inmost organs" are only revealed when we experience what the text describes and have the same disposition in our hearts that was in the authors' hearts when they wrote the text.[61] The desert father's words reflect an understanding that we only truly know something through intimate contact, not critical distance. We

60. Quoted in Igumen Chariton of Valamo, ed., *The Art of Prayer: An Orthodox Anthology* (London: Faber & Faber, 1997), 130.

61. Cassian, *Conferences*, 384.

see a similar spirit animating the reading of monks in the Benedictine tradition. In contrast with the hurried manner of today's students, the Benedictine monk did not rapidly skim the text before him but would often lean back, close his eyes, and reflect or pray over the verse he had just read. The monk's aim is not simply to get the reading done nor to critique it or rip something useful out of it. The monk reads in order to be nourished by the text, to let its meaning "spread through his blood."[62] Just as we savor and digest a healthy meal, so too should we meditate and reflect on the text in order to internalize it.

It was with this intention that the Benedictines developed the practice of *lectio divina. Lectio* is a method of reading Scripture in four steps that facilitates a movement from the head to the heart and "from text to divine wisdom."[63] First, we slowly and attentively read and then reread a selected text.[64] Second, we meditate on a particular word, phrase, or image from the text, turning it over in our mind and pondering its meaning. In the final two steps, we enter into a prayerful conversation with the divine Author about the text and, finally, cease from all mental effort, simply resting in God's love. Other educators have provided helpful guidance for doing *lectio divina* in the classroom with both scriptural and nonscriptural texts.[65] I would merely highlight here how the slow, receptive approach of *lectio* differs from the more analytical, even aggressive ways we often engage texts in academic settings. Although critique surely has its place in Christian education, meditating upon the text moves us into a differ-

62. Charles Cummings, OCSO, *Monastic Practices*, Cistercian Studies Series, no. 75 (Kalamazoo, MI: Cistercian Publications, 1986), 9.

63. André Gushurst-Moore, *Glory in All Things: Saint Benedict and Catholic Education Today* (New York: Angelico, 2020), 88.

64. This first step can be done in various ways. Some read the text twice, others three or four times. Having a different person read the text aloud each time can help those listening to hear the same text in a different way.

65. See Gushurst-Moore, *Glory in All Things*, 89–92; Keator, *Lectio Divina as Contemplative Pedagogy*; Maria Lichtmann, *The Teacher's Way: Teaching and the Contemplative Life* (Mahwah, NJ: Paulist, 2005).

ent mode of thinking and being that engages the fullness of who we are. When our reading culminates in silent contemplation, we open ourselves to receive something more than the ideas and assumptions we bring to the text.

This is not to suggest that we have to do *lectio divina* every time we take up a text in class. The bigger point is that, at least occasionally, we need to take some extra time to help our students enter into the reading. It is becoming more common practice for teachers to read aloud with their students—even at the college level—because students are struggling to complete and understand the material on their own. Such slow reading together may involve reading short passages and then pausing for discussion or reflective writing. Besides *lectio divina*, imaginative reading in the Ignatian style also helps students enter more deeply into Scripture in another way. In this practice, someone reads a passage aloud while pausing periodically and inviting listeners to imagine what it looks, sounds, and feels like to be in the scene.[66] *Visio divina* (see chapter 3) and similar forms of beholding suggest additional possibilities for engaging different media—art, architecture, images, videos—in a way that similarly invites deep reflection and a heartful response.

I have witnessed firsthand how these contemplative practices improve students' engagement with class material. Their understanding is deeper and their comments in class richer. What is more, research shows that practices of slow reading and beholding increase students' interest in the subject matter, help them to make more and deeper connections among the subjects they study, and promote a greater sense of meaning.[67]

We teachers and researchers can enjoy these benefits as well. Admittedly, we often find it harder to make time for ourselves than to

66. See the Creighton Online Ministries website for guidance on this form of imaginative reading and prayer: https://tinyurl.com/mt9m9mw3.

67. See Young Kyung Min, "Slow Looking: Powerful Tool of Mindfulness to Facilitate Transfer," *Journal of Contemplative Inquiry* 9, no. 2 (2022): 6.

do good for our students. However, even busy teachers can create time for spiritual and intellectual enrichment with a little forethought and discipline. Maybe our responsibilities do not permit us to lose ourselves in a good book for hours at a time, but surely we can allow ourselves once or twice a day to lean back and meditate on a beautiful or thought-provoking passage. Likewise, can we not carve out fifteen minutes in the morning or evening for some spiritual readings or, at very least, put on an audiobook or a guided Scripture meditation during our commute?[68]

Contemplating at Home

Practices of contemplative reading can lead to more meaningful learning experiences in the classroom, but what about when students return to their homes, with all the distractions they encounter there? Is it even realistic in today's world to hope that our students might engage their homework attentively and reflectively? Consider high school students' perspective: After being woken up far earlier than they would like, they spend most of the day sitting in classes trying to take in material, most of which is probably not very interesting to them. They have a few blessed respites—for lunch, in between classes, and after school—and then it is on to practice or another extracurricular activity. After practice and dinner, they may sit down to start on homework at seven or eight o'clock, when they have little energy left. Once they do, they must resist the constant pull of incoming text messages and a limitless supply of entertainment that is far more interesting than a set of math problems or an early modern poem.

When we enter into the experience of our students in this way, we can appreciate why they might arrive at class with their homework incomplete or poorly done. Rather than berating them, we might ask what *would* motivate our students. What kind of homework would be more helpful and meaningful? Or should we just do away with home-

68. See the Hallow and Pray as You Go phone apps for such guided meditations.

work altogether? This latter question might strike most as a shocking proposition. Homework seems as immutable a feature of life as death and taxes. A hearty daily serving of homework is baked into our notions of what constitutes a rigorous education, but actual research on homework reveals that more is not necessarily better. The impact of homework on learning outcomes varies widely, depending on how it is used.[69] Some research finds little if any connection between time spent on homework and achievement for elementary students.[70] Although this research does show that homework promotes learning (more so for older students than for elementary students), many schools are probably assigning too much. One to two hours a night is optimal for high school students.[71] Much more important than the amount of homework is the quality of the homework assigned. Education researchers Glenn Whitman and Ian Kelleher identify the following research-based practices for high-impact homework:

- Homework facilitates learning best when it targets and develops specific skills introduced in class. The benefits diminish when homework is assigned indiscriminately or as a matter of routine.
- Effective uses of homework include inviting reflection and metacognitive thinking (e.g., reflecting on the purpose of learning a particular skill, a personal or learning experience, or the students' effort and struggles in the class). Effective assignments may also involve authentic challenge, self-expression, interpersonal relationships, problem solving, competition, and experiences of flow. Meaningful and personalized assignments also decrease the likelihood that students will plagiarize or outsource their assignments to ChatGPT.

69. "Homework," Education Endowment Foundation, accessed October 30, 2024, https://tinyurl.com/ywxzfser.

70. See Glenn Whitman and Ian Kelleher, *Neuroteach: Brain Science and the Future of Education* (Lanham, MD: Rowman & Littlefield, 2016), 116, 119.

71. Whitman and Kelleher, *Neuroteach*, 122. Guidelines for time spent on homework are more fluid for college students, but Whitman and Kelleher's recommended practices apply to this age group as well.

- Homework should challenge students to practice with content and skills at increasing levels of difficulty, which will likely involve making some mistakes that serve as learning opportunities. Providing scaffolded feedback and opportunities to redo homework helps students to progress.
- Grading homework based on effort rather than accuracy encourages growth mind-set rather than achievement mind-set (completing the assignment just for the grade). Feedback should be meaningful and timely.[72] The fact that providing meaningful feedback is time consuming is another reason to assign homework more selectively.

Traditional Christian practices and current research also highlight the influence of environmental factors on how we work at home. In the monastery, each task has its designated space—a chapel for prayer, a scriptorium for copying manuscripts, cells for sleeping, etc. Of course, the average home does not have a chapel, so spiritual directors recommend creating a prayer space or at least designating a chair to be used only for prayer. Sitting in that chair triggers an automatic somatic response that tells our bodies it is time to pray. Likewise, few families have a separate library in their home, but a clean desk or table can serve as an adequate study space. Keeping distracting noise to a minimum and providing adequate lighting and temperature regulation also help students to focus on their work. Gloria Mark offers numerous additional suggestions for self-regulating and focusing attention by modifying environmental structures. For example, we can remove from view things that might distract us (especially phones). If our work requires a computer, we can close unnecessary windows and organize distracting apps so that we will be less tempted to open them (by putting them in a folder, for instance). Simple as they are, these are strategies that young

72. For suggestions regarding mindful assessment of student work, see Eileen Kogl Camfield Leslie Bayers, "Mindful Assessment in Support of Student Learning," *Journal of Contemplative Inquiry* 6, no. 1 (2019): 121–44.

people need to be taught. Therefore, it is helpful for teachers to discuss these strategies with their students and their parents.

The above research points us toward an approach to homework that is more consistent with a Christian understanding of the aims of education. Rather than being guided by a vague, unscientific notion of academic rigor, we should be more concerned to see that time spent on homework is bearing fruit in students' intellectual, social, and spiritual lives. We might take as our model an instance when Jesus once gave a homework assignment. When some Pharisees criticized Jesus for eating with sinners and tax collectors, he responded, "Go and learn what this means, 'I desire mercy, not sacrifice'" (Matt. 9:13). Surely these revered teachers of Torah already had this passage memorized. What Jesus suggests is that they had not yet allowed its meaning to touch their hearts. In order to avoid making Pharisees of our students, we need to be thoughtful about the homework we give them. Memorization and basic knowledge acquisition constitute an indispensable foundation for learning, and a certain amount of skill practice will always be necessary. But such knowledge and skills alone fall well short of the holistic formation aspired to in an authentically Christian education. Following the model of *lectio divina*, homework should facilitate a movement from the head into the heart. It should provide opportunities for learners to extend their thinking, nurture creative insights, apply their learning to their own lives, grow in self-understanding, and wonder at the world into which their Creator has brought them.

Lifting Up Our Work

Research, reading, writing, homework—these are routine activities for those who work and study in school settings. How we go about these activities, however, determines the fruit they bear in our lives. We miss the mark by aiming too low at some times and by acting with too much hubris at others. Distracted by lesser lights and missing the bigger picture, our students often feel they are merely digging holes or jumping through hoops in exchange for a reward. For our part, we professors at times aspire to build intellectual edifices that will elevate us to god-like heights and at other times are reduced to jumping through hoops of our own. In either case, we are called to much more. God beckons us to raise our sights up from the letter grades and journal impact ratings to contemplate the mystery of the world around us. God calls us not just to knowledge but to wisdom, not just to advance our own careers but to love and serve others, not just to make a living but to live a life that is fully human and even divine. In this chapter, we have explored numerous practices that can help us to open ourselves to what is beyond us and allow God to bless and elevate our work. I summarize those practices here.

Contemplative Practices for Research and Study

For starters: Sustain a sense of wonder by taking time to pause before the beauty and complexity of the things you study, if only for one or two minutes a day, rather than always "powering through" and trying to be more productive. Wonder instills gratitude and humility, which attitudes make our work more honest and enjoyable.

Research and writing: Observing the following practices makes our intellectual work more likely to connect us with and serve God and other people as opposed to merely advancing our personal agendas.

- Create a work schedule/*horarium* that aligns with your attentional limits and circadian rhythms. Schedule breaks (e.g., for short walks) and periods when you will refrain from checking email, texts, and social media.
- Create conditions conducive to contemplation and flow in your research and writing: Set clear goals that are attainable, given your abilities and constraints, and seek feedback on your work. Design your work environment to be as orderly, structured, and distraction-free as possible.

- While researching, writing, or working on a project, alternate periods of focused attention (questioning, memorizing, reasoning, analyzing, writing) with periods of open attention (meditating, pondering, praying). Listen for the promptings of the Holy Spirit and allow the time required for mature insights to emerge.
- Seek collaborators. Make time for conversation with colleagues and share your work so you can elevate each other's scholarship and better serve the world.
- School leaders: Support contemplative research and study in your institution by hosting retreats and rewarding collaboration and quality over quantity of scholarship.

Reading: Although we need not read everything according to the process of *lectio divina*, the four steps of *lectio* encapsulate many practices for fruitful, contemplative reading.

- *Lectio*: Read the text slowly, carefully, and in an undistracted manner. Turn off music and close screens so you can give the text your full attention.
- *Meditatio*: Read with the expectation that you will learn something from the text. Try to understand the author's meaning rather than criticizing or imposing your own ideas. When you come to a difficult or profound passage, linger over it and come back to it later.
- *Oratio*: Read in conversation with God and with the author whether the text is Scripture or something else. Praise God for what you are learning about the world God has created. Offer the labor of your reading to God.
- *Contemplatio*: Sit back in silence from time to time or after completing a reading. Allow time for the meaning to sink in and for insights to emerge before moving on to the next assignment or task.

Homework: The following practices can help make homework an opportunity for contemplation and personal reflection rather than a chore.

- Assign homework with specific learning outcomes in mind rather than out of habit. If there is not a clear goal or benefit, do not assign homework.
- Meaningful, effective forms of homework involve reflection, metacognitive thinking, authentic challenge, self-expression, interpersonal relationships, problem solving, projects, competition, and experiences of flow. For example, invite students to reflect on their intellectual and spiritual growth or a personal experience in light of what they learned in class.
- Assigning less homework (one to two hours for high school students) enables students to give their work more thought and teachers to give richer feedback. When homework is approached this way, feedback promotes students' holistic growth, for example, by engaging in shared reflection on students' progress in learning and growth in prayer, virtue, and other areas.
- Talk with students and parents about creating a study environment at home that is orderly and free of distractions (at least a clutter-free desk or table).

6

Recreation, Rest, and Leisure

Resting in the Lord

These days I am privileged to teach at a Catholic university, but I got my start as a high school teacher, and I will never forget what those first couple of years of teaching were like. If I close my eyes, I can picture myself walking to the parking lot after a long day at school, and all the feelings come flooding back . . .

When I reach my car, I slump wearily into the driver's seat and just sit there for a minute. I have been rushing from one thing to the next all day up until now. I lost a planning period because I had to cover a class for a sick colleague. Most of lunch was taken up by a student who needed to talk. When school was out, I moved to the gym to coach basketball practice. With all that now behind me, I can finally breathe for a minute. Eventually I muster the energy to turn the key in the ignition and begin the thirty-minute drive home. Those thirty minutes provide an oasis of solitude and a much-needed opportunity to decompress, but they also give all the thoughts and anxieties I had been pushing out of my mind a chance to catch up with me: *What am I going to do about Melanie? She hasn't turned in any homework for weeks. Jasmine has been really quiet lately. I wonder if everything is okay at home. Did I do the right thing when Henry started talking back in class? Was I too harsh? The department chair is coming to observe me on Thursday. I really hope Henry doesn't pull anything like that then.* Suddenly I am home. At some point during the drive the final rays of light faded from the sky. It was probably a pretty sunset. I wish I had noticed.

Walking in the door, I drop my bags, grab a frozen dinner from the freezer, and pop it in the microwave. I zone out while it is cooking and then am brought back to reality with a start when the microwave dings. I take my sad little dinner into the living room, sit down in the recliner, and automatically click on the TV. I flip through channels for a while (this was before Netflix) and eventually settle on some sitcom. After a few minutes, I have finished my dinner, but I cannot motivate myself to get up out of the recliner. One TV episode rolls into the next, and I meekly acquiesce.

Eventually a sense of urgency takes over. I cannot put off work any longer. I get up, throw away the packaging of my dinner (which now seems even sadder), sit down at the table, and take out my computer and a stack of student papers. I settle into the work of grading and preparing tomorrow's lessons, feeling no more refreshed for having spent an hour in front of the TV. I work as long as I can stand it. At some point I realize I have read the same sentence three times without comprehending it. Clearly, this is not productive. I just need to go to bed. But before I do, I check my in-box one last time. I respond to a few emails and then finally shut down the computer.

I brush my teeth and collapse into bed. I am beyond tired, but I cannot fall asleep. My mind is still racing with thoughts of all the things I have to do tomorrow. Before I know it, my alarm is going off and sunlight is slipping in through the window. I feel as if I hardly slept, but it is time to get up and start it all over again.

Our Stubborn Refusal to Rest

After those two years of teaching high school, I returned to graduate school and transitioned to a career in higher education. Teaching at the college level is, in my opinion, far easier than teaching younger students. My colleagues at the university and I have the luxury of spending less energy managing students' behavior, not to mention being able to go to the bathroom whenever we want. Nevertheless, if I originally had any illusions about living a life of leisure as a college professor, that bubble was quickly burst. Despite teaching fewer classes each day, my schedule somehow seems just as full now as it did when I was teaching high school. At day's end, I am still racing to send a few last emails or grade one more assignment. Many days I still collapse into bed exhausted. And this seems to be the norm among my colleagues. Everyone is tired. Why can we not let ourselves rest?

It seems to me there are multiple reasons. One is that teaching is an inherently demanding profession. Teachers have a lot to do between writing lessons, creating assignments and exams, grading, talking with students, corresponding with parents, attending faculty meetings, and so on. Our sense of responsibility (bordering on guilt) is compounded by living in a society that does not know how to rest and even disparages it. "Sleep is for the weak," they say. Today's elite business class has fully embraced this mind-set, working longer hours now than ever before and setting the pace for everyone who works under them.[1] When we do allow ourselves rest, we justify it as a necessary means to the end of productivity. We must rest in order to do more work.[2] Even when we leave work, we are still always on—on social media, on email, on call.[3] Most people seem to recognize that things have become unbalanced in our society. We work too much,

1. See Jonathan Gershuny, "Busyness as the Badge of Honor for the New Superordinate Working Class," *Social Research* 72 (2005–2009), https://doi.org/10.1353/sor.2005.0018. There are notable exceptions to this trend, as we will see below.

2. The ancients would have regarded this rationalization as completely backward. According to Aristotle, we work (literally are not-at-leisure) so we can be at leisure. *Nicomachean Ethics* 10.7 (1177b4–6), cited in Josef Pieper, *Leisure: The Basis of Culture*, trans. Gerald Malsbary (South Bend, IN: St. Augustine's Press, 1998), 4.

3. According to one survey, one-third of teens report being on social media "almost constantly." Monica Anderson, Michelle Faverio, and Jeffrey Gottfried, "Teens, Social Media and Technology 2023," Pew Research Center, December 11, 2023, https://tinyurl.com/bdv4nmur.

have too little time for the people and things that matter most, and feel tired and stretched thin. In light of these circumstances, John Perry Barlow poses a provocative question: "How thin can I spread myself before I am no longer 'there'?"[4]

Still, we cannot lay the blame solely on the culture "out there." The roots of our resistance to rest lie deep within each one of us. On the neurological level, we are wired to worry. Whenever we are not devoting our mental energy to some specific task, our minds default to thinking about ourselves, our to-do lists, and perceived threats. No sooner do we finish our to-do list than this "default mode network" kicks in and our minds start scanning for something else to do or worry about. Buddhism refers to this kind of thinking as "monkey mind." Christians might call it "Martha mind."

If not addressed, this psychological tendency can metastasize into spiritual maladies. Virtually every meditative tradition sees the quieting of the monkey mind as key to growth in peace and interior freedom. Our production-driven culture, by contrast, goads on the monkey mind, telling us that happiness lies in status, achievement, and material comfort. To acquire these things, it says, we must achieve something—attend a prestigious college, make partner, amass a fortune, etc. There is little place for rest or stillness in this worldview. On this point, Andrew Sullivan offers an astute observation: "The reason we live in a culture increasingly without faith is not because science has somehow disproved the unprovable, but because the white noise of secularism has removed the very stillness in which it might endure or be reborn."[5]

From consumer culture we imbibe these ideas that acquisitiveness and constant self-exertion are the way to happiness, but what does actual scientific research tell us? The conclusions could not be more different or more clear: When work-life balance becomes blurred, overall

4. John Perry Barlow, cited in Nigel Thrift, *Knowing Capitalism* (London: Sage, 2005), 152.

5. Andrew Sullivan, "I Used to Be a Human Being," *New York*, September 19, 2016, https://tinyurl.com/4yp237c2.

life satisfaction diminishes and stress increases.[6] This stress is extremely harmful to us. It puts us at higher risk of many health problems, including depression, digestive problems, heart disease, heart attack, high blood pressure, stroke, sleep problems, and weight gain.[7] Regarding the brain specifically, stress shrinks the regions involved in memory and grows the region associated with fear and anxiety.[8] In short, writes Nathan Stucky of Princeton University, "Our refusal to rest is killing us."[9] We have been told a story about how more work will lead to a better life, but this story is fiction. Instead of yielding greater rewards, more work has created more problems. Instead of achieving a worry-free life and "financial freedom," we have become slaves to our work.

Although these ways of thinking dominate our contemporary culture, many contemplative traditions, including Christianity, propose a different way. I invite you now into another meditation that might help us to see our way out of the endless labor and into rest.

A Meditation on Handing Over the Work of Our Hands

Throughout the biblical narrative we see a pattern repeated: human beings, anxious for their livelihood, try to reassure themselves by taking matters into their own hands. They inevitably mess things up, and God has to intervene to save them from themselves. This is what happened with Adam and Eve, the people of Babel, and the Israelites during their desert wandering. Even after God has delivered the Israelites from slavery in dramatic fashion, they repeatedly fall back

6. Krystin Arneson, "How 'Feierabend' Helps Germans Disconnect from the Workday," BBC, October 7, 2020, https://tinyurl.com/y48dz93d.

7. "Chronic Stress Puts Your Health at Risk," Mayo Clinic, accessed October 30, 2024, https://tinyurl.com/4j9bt77n.

8. Armita Golkar et al., "The Influence of Work-Related Chronic Stress on the Regulation of Emotion and on Functional Connectivity in the Brain," *PLoS One* 9, no. 9 (2014): e104550, https://doi: 10.1371/journal.pone.0104550.

9. Nathan T. Stucky, *Wrestling with Rest: Inviting Youth to Discover the Gift of Sabbath* (Grand Rapids: Eerdmans, 2019), 176.

into worrying about what they will eat, what they will drink, and how they will protect themselves from their enemies. We can better understand God's command to honor the Sabbath in this context. This commandment comes with an admonition to remember the reason for the Sabbath: "Remember that you were a slave in the land of Egypt, and the LORD your God brought you out from there with a mighty hand" (Deut. 5:15). If the Israelites are no longer slaves to Pharaoh or to work, it is because God has delivered them. The day of rest is a reminder that God has made possible this life of freedom—not we ourselves. For this reason the Sabbath is a day of worship and celebration (Exod. 5:1).

When Jesus came, he spoke to these same anxieties and reiterated God's instructions to the people in the Old Testament: "You cannot serve God and wealth. Therefore I tell you, do not worry about your life, what you will eat or what you will drink, or about your body, what you will wear" (Matt. 6:24–25). Before entering into his passion, Jesus established a new passover and a new Sabbath. At the Last Supper, he told his disciples, "You are my friends if you do what I command you. I do not call you servants any longer, because the servant does not know what the master is doing; but I have called you friends" (John 15:14–15). And what does Jesus command? Giving them the bread and the wine, he says, "Do this in remembrance of me" (Luke 22:19). To be Jesus's friends, to enjoy a life free from anxiety, we must celebrate his death and resurrection each Sunday and remember that he has set us free.

The Eucharist thus becomes the template for the Christian life. We see this in a particular way in the prayer following the presentation of the gifts in the Catholic liturgy: "Blessed are you, Lord God of all creation, for through your goodness we have received the bread we offer you: fruit of the earth and work of human hands, it will become for us the bread of life." When the people respond, "Blessed be God forever," we acknowledge that we depend upon God for our livelihood. We put our own efforts in proper perspective, recognizing that the work of our hands only becomes truly life-giving when we hand it over to God. We acknowledge the same in the act of receiving communion. By opening our hands (or mouths) to receive the bread of life week after week, we are inscribing a habit of receptivity in our bodies and on our hearts. For us as contingent creatures, this is our proper stance in life. We stand before the Lord, hands open to receive what we need.[10] Adopting this posture is the heart of what it means to enter into the Sabbath. We only experience true rest when we find our place in the order of creation and entrust ourselves to our Creator's loving care.

I invite you to assume this posture now and to enter into prayer. If you have access to a church or chapel, you might move there for this meditation. Wherever you decide to pray, sit in a comfortable but alert position. Rest your hands in your lap palms up, with one cupped inside the other as if you were receiving communion. Close your eyes or let them relax into a soft focus. Begin your prayer by taking several deep breaths. Inhale deeply through the nose and slowly through the mouth. With each breath be aware that you are breathing in God's gift of life. Be aware of God's presence here with you. Then allow your breathing to return to its normal rhythm and simply rest in God's loving presence. Try to do this for fifteen or twenty minutes. Just rest. There is nothing you have to do right now. You have nothing to prove. God delights in you simply because you are. Bask in this gratuitous love for a while.

When you are ready, open your eyes and offer God a word of thanks for this time of rest. Remember this experience when you return to church and perhaps whenever you have a moment to pause throughout the day.

After completing this exercise, reflect on the following:

- What was this prayer experience like for you?
- Did you find it restful, or did you find it hard to sit and do "nothing"? If it was difficult, why do you think that is?

10. The anti-image of this gesture is Adam and Eve grasping at the fruit God had forbidden them from eating (Gen. 3:6).

- How do you react to Jesus's words about not worrying and not serving two masters? When you reflect honestly on your life, who seems to be your master—God or wealth (or reputation, achievement, etc.)?

Creating Space for Leisure

God calls us to a life of purpose that includes work but is not consumed with work. A Christian vision for a full, well-integrated life also includes rest, recreation, prayer, and community. Because we are embodied beings who are sensitive to our surroundings, such integration requires ordering not only our schedules but also the spaces we inhabit. The world is a busy, often chaotic place, and that chaos is reproduced inside us. (As it happens, my progress on this chapter was stalled because my house was filled with screaming children home for snow days.) In order to still our minds and souls, it is helpful to move to a still place. God instructed the Israelites to go a three-days' journey into the wilderness to worship. Jesus sought "lonely" places to pray. Early monastics retreated to the desert and established monasteries—sometimes in remote places but also in bustling cities. Today few people make their way into the desert and the number of monasteries has dwindled, but students still need to go to school. Christian schools may therefore provide the spaces best suited to helping us relearn what it looks like to live a well-ordered life in contemporary society.[11]

The etymology of the word "school" is a hint that schools were once thought of in precisely this way. "School" comes from the Greek word *scholē*, which means "leisure" or "rest." Inherent in the name is a recognition that learning requires some measure of leisure. As we saw

11. D. Graham Burnett and Stevie Knauss have similarly suggested that universities might provide the "attentional sanctuaries" we need to resist exploitation of our attentional resources. *Twelve Theses on Attention* (Princeton: Princeton University Press, 2022).

in chapter 3, we cannot rush meaningful learning any more than we can rush the growth of a plant. These things simply take time. They also require certain favorable conditions. Earlier we explored some of these conditions as they pertain to the classroom. In the present chapter, we move beyond the classroom to consider other spaces in the school that contribute to a leisurely, contemplative environment.

Before diving into the details, I need to clarify what I mean when I describe the school as a place of leisure. I do not mean that a school is a place lacking in activity. A school is not a museum and certainly not a place for idleness. Josef Pieper, following Thomas Aquinas, notes that idleness (*acedia*) is quite contrary to genuine leisure, which is characterized by a disposition of receptivity to "superhuman, life-giving forces"[12] and an acceptance of "not-being-able-to-grasp" reality in its mysteriousness and transcendence.[13] Leisure is the disposition proper to contemplation. The stillness and silence of the contemplative are not inactivity, though they appear so from the outside. There is great activity in this stillness in that the contemplative is channeling an infinite source of power, an energy that is inaccessible to those closed in upon their own plans and projects. It is in this sense that leisure is opposed to mundane work.[14] Students playing on their phone under the desk during class are acting in an idle manner. By contrast, those absorbing the class conversation about a text and pondering its meaning are in a state of leisure.

What features of the school environment might dispose students to the latter state rather than the former? Like a chapel or a church, a school is a place set apart. When we are at worship, we experience a cell phone ringing as discordant because the church is supposed to be a sacred space free from mundane objects and activities. Such distractions likewise disrupt the atmosphere of contemplation proper

12. Pieper, *Leisure*, 36. Regarding idleness versus leisure, see Pieper, *Leisure*, 30, and Aquinas, *Summa Theologica* II-II, qu. 35, 3, ad 1um.

13. Pieper, *Leisure*, 31.

14. Pieper, *Leisure*, 31.

to a Christian school. Maintaining this atmosphere therefore requires regulating and possibly excluding objects and images that might pull us back into the world of the mundane, for example, advertisements, digital entertainment, and cell phones. More positively, beautiful architecture, artwork, and decorations create an environment that is generally conducive to contemplation. Banners, plaques, statues, and memorials subtly influence the mind-set of members of the community in ways that are more fine-tuned to the school's particular mission and heritage. Maintaining the orderliness and cleanliness of the school reinforces the sense that this is a place of purposeful work and therefore deserving of respect and care.

An atmosphere of leisure is most effectively maintained when these conditions pervade the entire school or campus. That being said, different activities (learning, art, athletics, etc.) require different kinds of spaces.[15] This specialization of space is more than a matter of mere utility.[16] Ideally in a Christian school, as in the monastery, a Christian vision of what constitutes a full, well-integrated life governs the allocation of space just as it governs the allocation of time in the daily *horarium*. Many contemporary college campuses still retain some vestiges of their monastic heredity, including the campus green or quad. Amid the more functional spaces like classrooms, offices, and dining halls, the green stands out as a symbol of the leisure that traditionally characterized scholastic life and harkens back to the cloister gardens typically found at the center of monasteries. Chapels and prayer/meditation rooms are other examples of traditional contemplative

15. See John Skillen, *Making Schools Beautiful: Restoring the Harmony of Place* (Camp Hill, PA: Classical Academic Press, 2020), 138.

16. Even as modern campus plans have prioritized utility over beauty, many schools have installed meditation and wellness rooms as a way of addressing the mental health needs of students. Although better than nothing, installing these rooms reflects a highly compartmentalized way of thinking. Fortunately, there are some signs of a renaissance of contemplative principles in campus design. See, for example, the new "Contemplative Commons" at the University of Virginia: https://tinyurl.com/5n7983x8.

spaces still found on most Christian campuses. Although not explicitly religious in nature, art galleries and quiet study areas in libraries serve as "attention sanctuaries," spaces where students and faculty can find respite from the din outside, think deeply, and gaze undistracted into the depths of something beautiful.[17] Thoughtfully designed hallways, walking paths, and colonnades encourage us to sustain a contemplative mind-set as we make our way from one place to the next.[18]

Thus far I have been speaking of human-made beauty, but of course some of the most beautiful elements of school campuses showcase natural beauty. Thomas Merton goes so far as to describe nature as the one "irreplaceable thing" for cultivating interior silence. In his words, "The effect of sun on the stones and light and shadow, these are things that you don't pay too much attention to, but they're healthy and they create a certain atmosphere of silence."[19] Merton's assertion that spending time in nature is healthy for us is not an idle claim. Some of the many well-documented health benefits include promoting positive affect and reducing anxiety, fatigue, and depression.[20] Merton's more central point, however, is that no environment is more conducive to contemplation than God's own creation, even with all the meditation apps and wellness rooms offered on campuses today. The truth of Merton's assertion is reflected in the testimonies of many modern people who identify nature as the place they are most likely to encounter the sacred.[21] Of course, not every school

17. Underprivileged young people may be particularly challenged in this regard as they are often afforded fewer opportunities to think for extended periods of time. Christina Brown et al., "Cognitive Endurance as Human Capital," accessed October 30, 2024, https://tinyurl.com/38xyty2e.

18. Skillen, *Making Schools Beautiful*, 120–21.

19. Thomas Merton, quoted in Kim Haines-Eitzen, *Sonorous Desert: What Deep Listening Taught Early Christian Monks—and What It Can Teach Us* (Princeton: Princeton University Press, 2022).

20. Terry Hartig et al., "Nature and Health," *Annual Review of Public Health* 35 (2014): 207–28.

21. *The State of Religion and Young People 2023: Exploring the Sacred*, Springtide Research Institute (Winona, MN: Springtide Research Institute, 2023), 25.

is blessed with beautiful gardens, trails, lakes, and the like. But any school can endeavor to be a good steward and cultivator of whatever natural beauty its particular location and resources afford, even if that is only a small garden or a few trees. Alternatively, going off campus for wilderness retreats and nature walks can provide opportunities for contemplation for students and teachers in urban schools.

The Blessings of Breaks

Breaks are both a religious imperative and a biological necessity, but we seem determined to ignore both. In schools we have the benefit of numerous natural breaks (between classes, for example), yet so often we deprive ourselves of the benefits of those breaks by using them to send a quick email, run copies, or make a phone call. We imagine that doing so makes us more productive, but current research reveals that such habits are actually counterproductive, especially when it comes to intellectual labor. Powering through without regard for our natural limits deprives the brain of the "negative space" it needs to replenish attention, decrease stress, and increase creativity.[22] (Again, recall Archimedes's eureka moment in the bath.) Even more harmful in the long run, constantly utilizing the parts of the brain needed for task completion prevents the activation of the parts involved in processing autobiographical memory, generating a coherent sense of self, and empathizing with others.[23]

Concerned with employee retention and potential burnout, even profit-driven corporations are increasingly providing resources and implementing policies to encourage workers to rest and otherwise practice healthy lifestyles.[24] As Christians who are obligated to rest on religious grounds, how much greater motivation do we have for

22. Gloria Mark, *Attention Span: A Groundbreaking Way to Restore Balance, Happiness, and Productivity* (Toronto: Hanover Square Press, 2023), 20, 23, 274, 277.

23. Felicia Wu Song, *Restless Devices: Recovering Personhood, Presence, and Place in the Digital Age* (Downers Grove, IL: IVP Academic, 2021), 158.

24. For examples, see Mark, *Attention Span*, 286–90, and Daniel H. Pink,

observing these kinds of practices in our schools? God commands us to rest. Even still, because most of us have internalized the "total work" mentality, we need to reassure one another that it is okay to take a break from time to time and that our worth is not determined by our productivity.[25] School leaders in particular have an opportunity and a responsibility to create a school culture where rest is valued. No matter how many colleagues encourage us to take breaks, it is difficult to heed their advice if the boss is sending a different message.[26] Practically speaking, school leaders can make personal well-being and integration an explicit goal for students, faculty, and staff; regularly emphasize this goal in meetings and communications; embed it into school practices and policies for evaluation and promotion; and model healthy habits themselves.[27]

Students, too, need encouragement to take healthy breaks. I emphasize the word "healthy." The practice of taking "brain breaks" during class time is now common in elementary schools. A brain break might include physical exercise, playing a short game, or engaging in a mindfulness activity that gives students a mental reset.[28] Structured breaks such as these are beneficial for older students too because, left to their own devices (pun intended), most will immediately take out their phones to get caught up on texts and social media posts. Although watching videos and playing video games can offer some relaxation, social media just as often generates anxiety. Young people know this but nevertheless struggle to change their habits. Recognizing this difficulty again highlights the opportunity schools

---

When: The Scientific Secrets of Perfect Timing (New York: Riverhead Books, 2018), 71.

25. Pieper, *Leisure*, 4. Workplace studies confirm that setting such boundaries at work is only effective when done collectively. Mark, *Attention Span*, 287.

26. For research on this phenomenon, see Pink, *When*, 184.

27. For additional suggestions, see Mark, *Attention Span*, 274, 279–81.

28. See more on brain breaks here: "60 Engaging Brain Breaks for Elementary Students," Success by Design, accessed November 12, 2024, https://tinyurl.com/5n7n24te.

have to serve as attention sanctuaries where students can experience the reprieve from technology they need but struggle to give themselves. Without a doubt, some students initially resent being deprived of their phones, but most eventually get used to it and even appreciate it.[29] Teachers can encourage students to extend these habits outside of school hours by giving them challenges or even assignments such as a "tech fast," a personal technology audit,[30] or making a technology pact with their friends.[31]

Distilling the findings of numerous studies, Daniel Pink offers five principles for a restorative break:[32]

1. Frequent—Short (five to fifteen minutes), frequent (every thirty to sixty minutes) breaks keep us energized and mentally sharp better than longer, infrequent breaks. This rhythm syncs well with many high school class schedules. Those teaching at the university level or on block schedules can build breaks into class time. When working outside of class, consider setting a timer to chime every thirty minutes as a prompt to take a break.
2. Active—Walking or simply moving in some way boosts energy levels, sharpens focus, improves mood, enhances creativity, and reduces fatigue. Activity is built into the monastic *horarium* in the form of periods of physical labor throughout the day. For teach-

29. One recent study of 1,000 college students found that on average participants were actually willing to pay money to have their and others' social media accounts deactivated. Leonardo Bursztyn et al., "When Product Markets Become Collective Traps: The Case of Social Media," Becker Friedman Institute for Economics at the University of Chicago, October 2023, https://tinyurl.com/mvmr7fjn.

30. Song's book *Restless Devices* includes numerous examples of such assignments and prompts.

31. Song points out that the biggest obstacle to young people getting off social media is their very realistic fear that they will miss out on experiences with friends or otherwise be out of the loop. Encouraging pacts among students and their friends can help to mitigate this pressure.

32. Pink, *When*, 60–63.

ers this might require getting up from our desk and taking a lap around the building or climbing some stairs.

3. Social—Talking with coworkers about something other than work reduces stress and improves mood and workplace retention, so invite a colleague to join you for your walk.
4. Outdoors—Getting outside or at least looking out a window provides more of a mood boost than taking a break indoors.
5. Detached—Thinking and talking about things other than work make breaks more restorative and reduces stress.

While regular breaks are ideal, the reality is that a busy teacher's day involves many demands and interruptions that sometimes make such regular breaks impossible. The good news is that even "microbreaks" that require very little time (e.g., having a snack, drinking a caffeinated beverage, listening to music) have been found to counteract fatigue and boost vitality.[33] Pausing briefly to take a few deep breaths[34] or reground ourselves in our bodies can be similarly beneficial.[35] "There are lots of mini-Sabbaths around if you know where to look for them," says educator Mary Rose O'Reilly—a kind word from a colleague, a student finally understanding a concept, the sunlight streaming through the classroom window.[36] It is a matter of cultivating an awareness open to whatever gifts the day might bring.

33. Hannes Zacher, Holly A. Brailsford, and Stacey L. Parker, "Micro-Breaks Matter: A Diary Study on the Effects of Energy Management Strategies on Occupational Well-Being," *Journal of Vocational Behavior* 85, no. 3 (2014): 287–97.

34. We typically breathe in a shallow way that hinders our ability to concentrate and leads to the buildup of carbon dioxide in our systems, which can create anxiety and disorientation. Deep breathing dispels toxins, calms our parasympathetic nervous system, lowers blood pressure, and increases mental alertness and cognitive processing.

35. Resmaa Menakem suggests massaging one's hands with oil or lotion. *My Grandmother's Hands: Racialized Trauma and the Pathway to Mending Our Hearts and Bodies* (Las Vegas: Central Recovery Press, 2017), 159. This is something we can do every time we wash our hands, making each trip to the bathroom a mini-spa retreat.

36. Mary Rose O'Reilly, *Radical Presence: Teaching as Contemplative Prac-*

Lest we busy teachers idealize the *vita contemplativa* of the monk, we can find ample affirmation for our vocation to the active life in the Christian contemplative tradition. For most of us, being a contemplative means being a "contemplative in action," to use a popular Jesuit phrase. We live in a world that does not stop just because we need a break, but it need not do so in order for us to sink into God's loving presence. Saint Paul invites us to abide in the presence of the divine Mystery at all times and whatever we are doing (1 Thess. 5:17). We find a model of this spirituality of active contemplation in Brother Lawrence's "practice of the presence of God," doing all things for God and maintaining an awareness of God's presence at all times, whether washing dishes or sweeping the floor (or in teachers' case, making copies or putting the classroom in order).[37]

All this being said, there are limits to how much we should accommodate our culture of busyness. Sometimes we as a school community must simply insist on time for rest. God commanded the Sabbath observance to be just such a reminder to us that there are more important things than work. Father Stinissen assures us, "You do not need to have scruples and feel that you are neglecting your duty when you stop every hour and devote five minutes to allow time to be refilled with eternity."[38] Indeed, there is no more valuable use of our time. Setting limits to work has become particularly important in the era of virtual meetings. Since virtual meetings eliminate the need to walk from one place to another, it is now possible to schedule one meeting after another with no intervening breaks. This is a perfect recipe for increased stress and decreased attentiveness to other peo-

---

tice (Portsmouth, NH: Boynton/Cook Publishers, 1998), 44. Brother David Steindl-Rast has similarly said, "Leisure is not the privilege of those who have time, but rather the virtue of those who give to each instant of life the time it deserves." Quoted in Ronald Rolheiser, *Domestic Monastery: Creating Spiritual Life at Home* (Brewster, MA: Paraclete, 2022), 77.

37. Brother Lawrence, *Practice of the Presence of God*, Christian Classics Ethereal Library, accessed October 30, 2024, https://tinyurl.com/2nrvbhbh.

38. Wilfrid Stinissen, *Eternity in the Midst of Time*, trans. Sister Clare Marie (San Francisco: Ignatius, 2018), 83.

ple and therefore demands greater intentionality on our part when scheduling meetings. Even if we enjoy a humane meeting schedule, each of us needs to be attentive to our own limits. Stinissen again offers valuable advice: As soon as we notice we have become tense and have lost contact with God, we should stop our work and return to an inner disposition of peace.[39] Otherwise we risk doing more harm than good by pushing through.

Nourishing Our Bodies

We human beings are a unity of body and spirit, and each depends on the other. Sadly, our embodiedness is one more aspect of our humanity that we tend to neglect on account of our totalizing work habits. The "sad desk lunch" has become all too common. Prioritizing productivity over care for ourselves, we often mindlessly scarf down food as we continue working, if we eat anything at all.

Our Christian tradition offers us a source of resistance to such dehumanizing and devitalizing habits. It is no coincidence that Jesus spent so much time in table fellowship with his followers nor that he established a meal as the central symbol of his enduring presence with us. In the Eucharist, Jesus offers bread to a hungry world. If so many in modern society remain spiritually and physically hungry, that is partly because we do not allow ourselves to be fed. Like Adam and Eve, we grasp at seductive but deadly fruit (money, possessions, achievements) while spurning the life-giving food God is offering us. As we saw in the opening meditation, the rites of the eucharistic celebration invite us to symbolically and literally lay our work down before the Lord. When we receive communion, we extend our empty hands so that we may receive.

Recent studies affirm the benefits of the mind-set this practice inculcates. Daniel Pink cites research findings that taking a lunch break away from your desk and detaching mentally from work (especially if

39. Stinissen, *Eternity in the Midst of Time*, 78.

you have some autonomy over when and how) reduce workplace stress and exhaustion and enhance performance.[40] Pink emphasizes that detachment is key to receiving the salutary benefits. We need to lay our work down for a time in order to be renewed. We see this practice of detachment embedded in the monastic *horarium*. The monk does not eat while working but rather, when the bell rings, sets down his work and goes to the refectory to eat. Interestingly, some companies, informed by the above-cited research, are implementing similar practices in order to encourage their employees to enjoy a more restorative lunch break.[41] As Christians, we bless our food when we eat, recognizing with gratitude that this food is a gift God has given us for our nourishment. We can increase our sense of gratitude as well as our enjoyment by intentionally savoring the meal. Rather than automatically pulling out our phones, we can make a practice of noticing and enjoying the appearance, smell, taste, and texture of each bite we take.

Another reason Jesus chose a meal as the sacrament of salvation is its communal nature. The Eucharist not only nourishes us individually; it also forms us into a community, into the one body of Christ. Even in the case of common meals, there is just something about eating together that breaks down barriers and forges bonds. Studies have even found that eating together enhances team performance.[42] Both contemporary research and Christian tradition, then, underscore the importance of communal meals and suggest that lunchtime ought to be protected for the good of the community. Some Jesuit institutions, for example, block out three hours on one afternoon each week for a "repast" when members of the community gather to celebrate the Eucharist and enjoy a communal meal. If your school sees every week as too ambitious, consider hosting special lunches on liturgical feast days or designated community days. Sharing meals outside of the school day can be impactful in other ways. Some schools and de-

40. Pink, *When*, 65.
41. Pink, *When*, 66.
42. Pink, *When*, 65.

partments have the custom of professors inviting their classes to their homes for dinner. School leaders might do the same for their faculty and staff. For example, the former president of Spelman College in Atlanta hosted monthly dinners with faculty members in order to build relationships, foster trust, and encourage open dialogue.[43]

Exercise and Play

Despite the success of the US fitness industry, which generates $33 billion in revenue annually, many Americans are as quick to cut out exercise as they are to skip meals when things are busy at work. We know we should exercise. All work and no play makes Jack susceptible to cardiovascular diseases, diabetes, and obesity. Furthermore, if knowing the health benefits were not reason enough, for Christians there are also spiritual reasons to make time for exercise and play in our lives.

Even God plays, after all. As proof, Thomas Aquinas points to Proverbs 8:30, which says the divine Wisdom "plays all the time, plays throughout the world."[44] Aquinas goes on to remark that we experience something like this divine playfulness in contemplation: "For just as the activities of play are not desired for the sake of something else, but possess their delight within their very selves, so too is the contemplation of wisdom."[45] Play, like contemplation, is its own good. In this sense, play serves as a kind of preparation for contemplation, which is our highest calling as human beings. We are created to delight in God, to participate in the playfulness of the Trinity.

The words Aquinas quotes from Proverbs come in the context of a description of Wisdom's role in creating the world. The preceding

43. See Parker Palmer and Arthur Zajonc, eds., *The Heart of Higher Education: Transforming the Academy Through Collegial Conversations* (San Francisco: Jossey-Bass, 2010), 200–204.

44. Josef Pieper's translation of a quotation from Aquinas's *Commentary on the Sentences* I, d. 2 (expositio textus), in Pieper, *Leisure*, 18.

45. Thomas Aquinas, *Commentary on the Sentences* I, d. 2 (expositio textus), Aquinas Institute, 2020, https://tinyurl.com/a77jzmdv.

line reads, "then I was beside him [the LORD], like a master worker" (Prov. 8:30). This passage suggests that, in the divine Wisdom, work and play are united. We finite beings, however, struggle to reconcile what is united perfectly in God.[46] Yet at the height of the contemplative life, these two things are reconciled. An experienced contemplative like Brother Lawrence can be resting in God even while working or engaging in other activity. Father Stinissen suggests that contemplatives, when concluding a time of prayer, do not simply jump back into the rush of mundane affairs. "When we rise from our prayer," he writes, "it means, not that we finish it, but that we let it flow out into our work."[47] Short of that attainment, however, most of us do the best we can to find a balance by alternating between the two.

Certainly the classroom can be a playful space,[48] but play tends to happen more naturally in other contexts.[49] For many young people, those contexts are the athletic field and the gym. Because young people are typically more passionate about sports than they are about their academic studies, these are also the places where they are most open to growth—most coachable, we might say. Sports therefore

46. There are exceptions, however. Stuart Brown, MD, the founder of the National Institute for Play, notes that for experts work, too, is like play. *Play: How It Shapes the Brain, Opens the Imagination, and Invigorates the Soul* (New York: Avery Books, 2010), 63–64.

47. Stinissen, *Eternity in the Midst of Time*, 75.

48. For examples of playful approaches to learning, see Maria Montessori, *The Montessori Method* (Mineola, NY: Dover Publications, 2002); Jerome Berryman, *Godly Play: An Imaginative Approach to Religious Education* (Minneapolis: Augsburg, 1995); and Courtney Goto, *The Grace of Playing: Pedagogies for Leaning into God's New Creation* (Eugene, OR: Pickwick, 2016).

49. Research shows that adolescents are most likely to experience flow in active leisure activities such as those afforded by after-school programs. Jennifer A. Schmidt, David J. Shernoff, and Mihaly Csikszentmihalyi, "Individual and Situational Factors Related to the Experience of Flow in Adolescence: A Multilevel Approach," in *Applications of Flow in Human Development and Education: The Collected Works of Mihaly Csikszentmihalyi* (Dordrecht: Springer Netherlands, 2014).

present a distinct opportunity for spiritual and moral development. The disciplined training required for achieving athletic excellence develops habits that can translate into spiritual training (*askēsis*) and builds confidence that generalizes into other areas of life. Team sports provide opportunities for growth in leadership and working with others. Pregame chapel talks and rituals such as blessings of cleats, paddles, etc., provide natural opportunities to invite athletes into prayer. Injuries, losses, and roster cuts provide opportunities for discernment, growth in maturity and resilience, and reflection on suffering. Still, every moment need not be a lesson. There is a good simply in enjoying the game itself and in comradery with teammates.

While sports are perhaps the most popular form of organized play, other student activities also present opportunities for growth. We discussed several of these in chapter 4. Most schools sponsor a variety of student clubs and activities related to music, art, drama, games, ethnic groups, and so on. "Affinity courses" such as those offered at Welsh Academy in Cleveland encourage students to nurture passions and learn skills related to mechanics, cooking, creative writing, martial arts, wilderness survival, and other student interests. Service clubs and activities help to break students out of the bubble of their personal concerns, develop compassion, and challenge assumptions. Residential halls provide exceptionally fertile ground for fostering a culture of social play (including praying, serving, and eating together) on account of how this living arrangement creates shared time and space.[50] This is especially true of living learning communities, in which groups of students live together and attend classes and other activities together.

The benefits of play are numerous. Play has a key role in neural development from an early age and is necessary for healthy socialization.[51] Psychiatrist Daniel Siegel includes playtime and physical time among seven key practices for promoting adolescent integration

50. For more on this point, see James K. A. Smith, *Desiring the Kingdom: Worship, Worldview, and Cultural Formation* (Grand Rapids: Baker Academic, 2009), 226–27.

51. Stuart Brown, *Play*, 41, 32.

and well-being.[52] In light of this research, it seems highly regrettable that modern education leaves so little time for play in the schedules of older students. Jonathan Haidt has recently presented research connecting the loss of a play-based childhood and its opportunities for physical, psychological, and social development with the dramatic increase in mental health problems among young people.[53] Even if the adults responsible for their education do not always recognize the value of play, many students do. In one national study, 40 percent of young people said activating the imagination and engaging in play are very important for their growth.[54]

Fortunately, some school leaders are paying attention to this emerging research. Certain high schools, recognizing the manifold benefits of play and recreation, require students to participate in at least one extracurricular activity. As with the monastic *horarium*, this sort of requirement provides a structure (a trellis) to ensure balance in the lives of the students that they might not maintain if left to their own initiative. This practice is in line with research showing that youth with balanced schedules show fewer symptoms of stress then peers who are either overscheduled or uninvolved.[55] Encouraging or requiring students to engage in extracurriculars also increases the likelihood that they will develop a network of supportive adults (teachers, coaches, moderators, campus ministers), which translates into reduced stress and feelings of isolation.[56]

52. Daniel Siegel, *Brainstorm: The Power and Purpose of the Teenage Brain* (New York: Penguin Books, 2013), 281–93. The other five are time-in, sleep time, focus time, downtime, and connecting time.

53. Jonathan Haidt, *The Anxious Generation: How the Great Rewiring of Childhood Is Causing an Epidemic of Mental Illness* (New York: Penguin Books, 2024).

54. Josh Packard et al., *Meaning-Making: 8 Values That Drive America's Newest Generations* (Bloomington, MN: Springtide Research Institute, 2020), 108.

55. Sandra L. Hofferth, David Kinney, and Janet Dunn, "The Hurried Child: Myth vs. Reality," in *Life Balance: Multidisciplinary Theories and Research*, ed. Kathleen Matuska and Charles Christiansen (N.p.: AOTA Press, 2009), 183–206.

56. Josh Packard et al., *Belonging: Reconnecting America's Loneliest Generation* (Bloomington, MN: Springtide Research Institute, 2020), 46–47.

Of course, play is not just for children. Adults need to play too, though we easily forget or downplay this need. Contrary to what we might expect, the highest achievers in a variety of fields make rest and recreation a priority. Lower achievers, by contrast, commonly see themselves as too busy for recreation.[57] Take the example of Albert Einstein, whose breakthrough theory of relativity germinated over years of hiking and talking philosophy with friends. Winston Churchill was an avid painter. Jack Kelley, the inventor of the mouse pad and the modern cubicle, spent his weekends racing sailboats on Lake Michigan. Analyzing research on the habits of such successful individuals, Alex Soojung-Kim Pang explains that play provides an invaluable means of recovery for driven individuals thanks to the combination of absorption and satisfaction, opportunity to apply skills in new contexts, and personal connection. "Creative people don't engage in deep play despite their high levels of activity and productivity," concludes Pang; "they're active and productive because of deep play."[58] In light of this research, it is clearly in the best interest of faculty and the institutions that support them to make time for play. Most faculty have access to exercise classes, adult intramural leagues, and pickup games at their university recreation center. Reading groups, affinity groups, and lunchtime walks provide other opportunities for those who cannot make it to the gym or are more inclined to alternative forms of play.

Resting in God in Prayer

Our bodies need rest and nourishment in order to maintain their health and energy. Still, it is possible to be physically well rested and

57. Robert Root-Bernstein, Maurine Bernstein, and Helen Garnier, "Correlations Between Avocations, Scientific Style, Work Habits, and Professional Impact of Scientists," *Creativity Research Journal* 8, no. 2 (1995): 115–37.

58. Alex Soojung-Kim Pang, *Rest: Why You Get More Done When You Work Less* (New York: Basic Books, 2018), 202.

nevertheless beset with restlessness. We inhabit not only bodies but also minds, and our minds are wearied by many things—work, relationships, bills, discrimination, politics, the economy. Our default ways of dealing with these worries tend to be escape and distraction. When we need a break from it all, we reach instinctively for our phones or turn on Netflix. We go to spas and take vacations. We do these things hoping that taking our mind off our worries will give us some relief, but the relief is temporary at best and often these distractions only stir up more anxious thoughts and disordered desires. If these escapes fail to give us the lasting peace we seek, Thomas Merton suggests, that is because "a 'peace' that is guaranteed only by getting out of the traffic, turning off the radio, and forgetting the world—is not by itself the real thing."[59]

If the peace we seek on our phones and vacations is not the "real thing," then what is? Merton's statement points to a truth of vital importance for us as Christians, educators, and human beings. More than temporary relief from worry or the momentary satisfaction we get from created things, we yearn for interior peace, freedom, and fulfillment. Only something infinite and transcendent can satisfy these deepest yearnings of the human heart. Only God can give us true rest (Matt. 11:28). This is what Augustine meant when he penned those famous words, "you have made us for yourself, and our heart is restless until it rests in you."[60] This central truth of our Christian faith puts into perspective everything else we do in our schools. To put it bluntly, we are failing our students today to the extent that we train them merely to fulfill future job responsibilities and achieve lives of material comfort while neglecting to lead them to the one thing actually necessary for their peace and fulfillment.

We can each confirm this truth in our own experience. We are incapable of giving ourselves lasting peace. Even when we manage

59. Thomas Merton, "Learning to Live," in *Love and Living*, ed. Naomi Burton Stone and Brother Patrick Hart (San Diego: Harcourt, 1985), 10–11.

60. Augustine, *Confessions* 1.1.5.

to escape the stress and noise around us, we still have to contend with the noise inside us—our anxious thoughts, feelings of anger and sadness, disordered desires to gratify our impulses and our egos. No less than the great saint Teresa of Ávila struggled to escape such a "turmoil of thoughts."[61] The solution she found did not lie in distraction or entertainment. To the contrary, she would advise us that these are useless substitutes for what we truly seek. She would affirm the wisdom of the desert fathers: "Pray attentively and you will soon straighten out your thoughts."[62]

Only by abiding in Christ in prayer can we experience true peace and inner freedom in this life because a discipline of prayer keeps our minds and hearts trained on that one necessary thing. This is why prayer ought to be central to the formation students receive in Christian schools rather than a tack-on to the school day. The Christian tradition offers numerous practices to help school communities cultivate a habit of prayer in their members. The Liturgy of the Hours, for instance, has for centuries served as the backbone of the lives of countless clergy, religious, and even laypeople.[63] Praying prime and vespers ensures that our workday begins and ends with prayer. Pausing at midday for sext (or the Angelus or the Ignatian examen) draws our thoughts back to God at the time of day when they are most likely to have been pulled elsewhere.

Silent prayer such as we experienced in this chapter's opening meditation can be equally transformative, if not more so. As with the Liturgy of the Hours, contemplative prayer is most fruitful in our lives when it becomes an ingrained habit. Spiritual guides like Martin Laird

61. Teresa of Ávila, *The Interior Castle*, trans. Mirabai Starr (New York: Riverhead Books, 2003), 91.

62. Thomas Merton, *The Wisdom of the Desert: Sayings from the Desert Fathers of the Fourth Century* (Boston: Shambhala Publications, 2004), 181.

63. The daily prayers of the Liturgy of the Hours can be accessed at https://divineoffice.org/ as well as on prayer apps like iBreviary. Daily prayers from the Book of Common Prayer can be found at https://www.bcponline.org/ and on the Book of Common Prayer app.

and Thomas Keating recommend two prayer periods of at least twenty-five minutes every day.[64] Early in the morning and before dinner tend to be the times when we are most alert, least distracted, and therefore disposed to pray best. Even just a few minutes of silence can be restorative. Those who have access to a church or chapel might make a practice of stopping in to rest in Jesus's presence for a moment on the way into school, in between class periods, or before leaving for the day. With time and practice, we find that we are better able to carry an abiding awareness of God's presence from these moments of dedicated prayer into the rest of the day. Utilizing a prayer word like the Jesus Prayer as we go about our work can be very helpful in this regard.

These various practices of prayer provide a means of resting in God's peace all throughout the day. However, we should not make the mistake of reducing prayer to a relaxation technique. While certain breathing techniques and other mindfulness practices have been demonstrated to slow the heart rate and reduce stress and anxiety, the peace Jesus speaks of is even more profound.[65] This peace operates on a level deeper than our thoughts and feelings. It endures even when we are suffering or experiencing provocations. It is the peace Jesus himself possesses, as evidenced in his ability to sleep peacefully in a boat even as a storm raged all around him (Mark 4:38–40). When we pray, we open ourselves to receive this peace that God is always offering us. Anything more is beyond our control. We cannot manufacture a specific effect or compel God by our prayers.

Because perfect union with God is only possible in eternal life, we all have to endure some restlessness in this life. However, we ex-

64. See Martin Laird, *Into the Silent Land: A Guide to the Christian Practice of Contemplation* (Oxford: Oxford University Press, 2006), for a good introduction to the practice of contemplative prayer.

65. In this regard, contemplative prayer offers the best of all worlds. Studies on centering prayer have found that the neurological effects of this practice are nearly identical to those of mindfulness meditation. Andrew Newberg and Mark Robert Waldman, *How God Changes Your Brain: Breakthrough Findings from a Leading Neuroscientist* (New York: Ballantine Books, 2009), 193.

perience in contemplation a foretaste of that perfect union and so too the rest that only God can offer. This is the peace we all yearn for. Contemplative prayer can be a particular gift for teachers and other people who, by virtue of their intellectual work, are constantly consumed by thoughts. In prayer, writes Father Stinissen, "all the scattered thoughts and feelings can disappear, while I, who am infinitely more than my thoughts and feelings—only rest, stretched out on the firm and eternal rock who is my Creator and God."[66] In contrast with the claustrophobic feelings we experience when beset with anxious thoughts, Teresa of Ávila describes the soul as she has come to know it in prayer as "vast, spacious, plentiful."[67] Martin Laird similarly describes meeting God in contemplative prayer as an encounter "brimming over with the flow of vast, open emptiness that is the ground of all."[68] This experience of a tranquil vastness in contemplation, promises the author of *The Cloud of Unknowing*, will have a favorable effect not only on the soul but also on the body of anybody who practices it.[69]

On this point, too, current research confirms the experience and wisdom of the Christian contemplative tradition. According to brain scans, experienced meditators not only exhibit elevated levels of gamma activation during meditation (which corresponds to the experience of inner spaciousness described above) but are also able to maintain a state of equilibrium and open presence even when they are not meditating.[70] Other studies suggest that Christian practices

66. Stinissen, *Eternity in the Midst of Time*, 65.

67. Teresa of Ávila, *The Interior Castle*, 45.

68. Laird, *Into the Silent Land*, 14.

69. *The Cloud of Unknowing*, Christian Classics Ethereal Library, accessed October 30, 2024, https://tinyurl.com/2p82xvff, chapter 54.

70. Daniel Goleman and Richard Davidson, *Altered Traits: Science Reveals How Meditation Changes Your Mind, Brain, and Body* (New York: Avery Books, 2018), 235–36. While the subjects of these tests have been mostly yogis, their accounts mirror those found in the writings of Christian contemplatives like Saint Augustine, Teresa of Ávila, and Martin Laird.

such as centering prayer and the rosary may help to decrease anxiety and promote cardiovascular health.[71] There is growing evidence that prayer helps to mitigate depression,[72] which finding is consistent with research on the protective benefits of spirituality more generally.[73] Other research has found connections between prayer and health benefits for hypertension, pain, anxiety, and posttraumatic stress.[74]

To conclude this section with the wise words of Evagrius Ponticus, "We are not commanded to work the whole time . . . but there is a law that we should pray ceaselessly."[75] The reason for this command should be clearer after reading the preceding pages. We human beings

71. Jane K. Ferguson, Eleanor W. Willemsen, and MayLynn V. Castañeto, "Centering Prayer as a Healing Response to Everyday Stress: A Psychological and Spiritual Process," *Pastoral Psychology* 59, no. 3 (2010): 305–29, https://doi:10.1007/s11089-009-0225-7; P. Gregg Blanton, "The Other Mindful Practice: Centering Prayer and Psychotherapy," *Pastoral Psychology* 60 (2011): 133–47; Matthew W. Anastasi and Andrew B. Newberg, "A Preliminary Study of the Acute Effects of Religious Ritual on Anxiety," *Journal of Alternative and Complementary Medicine* 14, no. 2 (2008): 163–65; and Luciano Bernardi et al., "Effect of Rosary Prayer and Yoga Mantras on Autonomic Cardiovascular Rhythms: Comparative Study," *British Medical Journal* 323, no. 7327 (2001): 1446–49.

72. Harold G. Koenig, *Medicine, Religion, and Health: Where Science and Spirituality Meet*, Templeton Science and Religion Series (West Conshohocken, PA: Templeton Foundation Press, 2008), 72. It is also noteworthy that Christian contemplative authors write at length about difficulties in prayer, including depressive periods, whereas the literature around mindfulness is more reticent regarding such difficulties. See Tomas Rocha, "The Dark Knight of the Soul," *Atlantic*, June 25, 2014, https://tinyurl.com/cjnaszaj. For firsthand accounts of how contemplation helps people with chronic depression, see Martin Laird, *An Ocean of Light: Contemplation, Transformation, and Liberation* (Oxford: Oxford University Press, 2019), 185–218.

73. Lisa Miller, *The Awakened Brain: The New Science of Spirituality and Our Quest for an Inspired Life* (New York: Random House, 2021), 57, 61.

74. Koenig, *Medicine, Religion, and Health*; Newberg and Waldman, *How God Changes Your Brain*, 159.

75. Evagrius Ponticus, *Praktikos and Chapters on Prayer*, trans. John Eudes Bamberger (Kalamazoo, MI: Cistercian Publications, 1981), #49.

need physical and spiritual rest. Many things in the world promise rest and relaxation, but only one can offer us true peace. So when we are in need of a recharge in between classes, while completing or grading assignments, or at the end of the day, we should not be so quick to reach for our phones. In these moments, the Lord of Peace is beckoning us to close the door and enter the inner room of our souls where he awaits us in the stillness.

Sabbath Rest

A discipline of prayer is essential for the life of a Christian. Returning to the Lord in prayer throughout the day, we are able to access a fathomless reservoir of peace and renewal whatever may arise. And yet God invites us into a still more radical gesture of resignation and rest in the Sabbath. When we look honestly at how we live and work today, it is clear that we desperately need a real practice of rest. We have accepted the lie that our worth and fulfillment depend on what we accomplish and acquire. No matter what we do, there is always something more to do or get—a newer phone, a better job, a bigger grant. This mind-set traps us in a system devoid of rest and grace. For teachers, this mind-set manifests less as a fixation on maximizing material gain and more as an obsession with maximizing time. Time always seems to be in short supply, so we steal more time for work in the evenings and on the weekends. We squirm for the hour or two we spend in church on Sunday, which feels uncomfortably unproductive. Ironically, research shows that our refusal to rest, rather than making us more productive, leads to declining job performance, poor decision making, and higher rates of error, not to mention emotional exhaustion and decreased empathy for others.[76] Rather than adding to our lives, these extra hours of work leave us feeling depleted.

The disappointing results of our overwork again confront us with a fundamental truth of human existence: Try as we might, we

76. Pang, *Rest*, 161.

can never fulfill ourselves. In order to receive life in its fullness, we need to cease from activity from time to time and open ourselves to a Source outside ourselves. This is what Rowan Williams is getting at when he says that good liturgy is about silence.[77] When we enter into silence and stillness, as the Sabbath invites us to do, "we are letting God be God, and in the process we're letting ourselves become more fully human, because," Williams explains, "we are human by being human for God; and all joy and fulfillment opens up once we recognize this."[78] In other words, we fully realize our humanity and our highest calling, not by producing or consuming, but by offering praise and worship to our Creator. Herein lies the wellspring of life in abundance, the "source and summit of the Christian life," as the *Catechism of the Catholic Church* refers to Eucharist.[79]

Essential though silence and stillness are to our humanity, our impulses rebel against them. To us this stillness looks like a kind of death, and in a sense it is. As Nathan Stucky puts it, "If Sabbath is going to live and thrive in our lives, something else will have to die."[80] Honoring the Sabbath will likely mean leaving some lesson plans unperfected, some emails and texts unanswered for a time.[81] It may even demand the more radical measure of reevaluating our life priorities and considering how our work habits and ambitions align with the kind of life to which God calls us. It will certainly mean relinquishing control. That is what is really hard about the Sabbath, but that is also precisely the point. Honoring the Sabbath reminds us that there are limits to what we can achieve by our work, that salvation comes

77. Rowan Williams, *Being Human: Bodies, Minds, Persons* (Grand Rapids: Eerdmans, 2018), 98.

78. Williams, *Being Human*, 104–5.

79. *Catechism of the Catholic Church*, 2nd ed. (Washington, DC: United States Conference of Catholic Bishops, 2019), #1324, https://tinyurl.com/54unjbfr.

80. Stucky, *Wrestling with Rest*, 100.

81. For more practical suggestions on how to practice Sabbath rest, see Dorothy Bass, "Keeping Sabbath," in *Practicing Our Faith: A Way of Life for a Searching People*, ed. Dorothy Bass (San Francisco: Jossey-Bass, 2010), 75–88.

from elsewhere: "Six days you shall labor and do all your work. But the seventh day is a sabbath to the LORD your God" (Deut. 5:13–14). God surely understands our difficulty with relinquishing control, and perhaps that is why God *commands* us to honor the Sabbath.

When we do finally let go and accept God's invitation to rest, we come to appreciate what a gift it is. Entering into the Sabbath, like sinking into contemplative prayer, creates a sense of abundance. In contrast with the rest of the week when every minute must be accounted for, on the Sabbath we can stop counting the minutes and simply be. Receiving this gift inspires gratitude, and this giving thanks is an essential part of Sabbath celebration. (The word "Eucharist" literally means "thanksgiving.") This weekly act of thanksgiving forms us in the attitude of gratitude that is proper to us as created, graced, and redeemed beings and, it turns out, is very good for our mental and physical health.[82]

Christian schools can and should be places where faculty, students, and staff experience this life of grace and abundance. Recognizing that many people struggle to take time for rest on their own, even when encouraged (or commanded!) to do so, school leaders can incorporate moments of celebration and rest in the school schedule. Special feast days in the liturgical calendar provide natural opportunities for schools to pause from normal activities to worship together, enjoy a special meal, go on retreat, engage in service or play, and otherwise be reminded of what is most important. Following scriptural precedent (e.g., Lev. 25:3–5), our school communities might also consider how they can promote rest and renewal of the natural world as part of their practices of Sabbath keeping.[83]

82. People who cultivate a practice of gratitude are happier, more empathetic and forgiving, healthier, and less depressed, anxious, and neurotic. Because of these many benefits, researcher Sonja Lyubomirsky describes gratitude as a "metastrategy" for achieving happiness. *The How of Happiness: A Scientific Approach to Getting the Life You Want* (New York: Penguin Press, 2007), 89.

83. For example, schools can implement programs for recycling, composting, and conserving water and electricity. See Francis, *Laudato Si'*, Vatican, 2015, https://tinyurl.com/3j9xsbjx, #71.

School leaders who worry that taking away from academic instruction time will impugn the reputation of the school might be encouraged to learn that similar changes are becoming more common in workplaces around the world. Recognizing that overwork has become a public health issue, the governments of France, Italy, Ireland, the Philippines, and the Canadian province of Ontario have recently enshrined the right to disconnect from work as a human right worthy of legal protections.[84] Some of these new laws protect employees' right not to answer work email outside of normal work hours. Leaders in Christian schools might consider similar policies regarding email and weekend homework assignments that encourage students, faculty, and staff to honor the Sabbath. By taking the Sabbath seriously in these ways, our Christian schools can become communities where members flourish and God's sovereignty over creation is honored.

Sleep

Teaching can be exhausting. Many teachers return home after a long day at school feeling utterly depleted. And yet, even then, we can find it difficult to rest. Rather than gearing down, our minds are still racing with thoughts about everything we did not get done that day and everything we have to do the next day. In an effort to alleviate our anxiety, we put off sleep in order to finish lesson plans, work on committee reports, or send emails.

We have seen throughout this chapter how we benefit from breaks and rest in various forms, but sleep is one form of rest without which we simply cannot survive. During sleep, our brains purge toxins, process experiences, and consolidate memories. Our bodies store energy, fix or replace damaged cells, and grow new ones. When we do not get enough sleep, it has immediate effects on our ability to

84. Mark, *Attention Span*, 288. Regarding the health benefits of detaching from work and the negative effects on those who struggle to detach, see Pang, *Rest*, 170–71.

focus, make good judgments, cope with stress, and think creatively. Long-term sleep deprivation inhibits immune function, contributes to cardiovascular disease and cancer, and can lead to impaired memory, dementia, and psychosis.[85] Despite these harmful consequences, we seem determined to deprive ourselves of this most basic necessity. The problem is particularly acute among our students. According to recent surveys, 73 percent of high school students are sleep-deprived and 60 percent of college students report poor sleep quality.[86] Their lack of sleep is linked to lower grades, compromised attention, mood disorders, substance abuse, violence, poor school attendance, inability to self-regulate, and increased behavior problems.[87]

We rationalize our poor habits by telling ourselves that we cannot afford to sleep. We have too much to do. However, current research exposes the fallacy of this thinking. The scientific fact is that getting enough rest enables us to perform better at the things we skip sleep to do. Take students' habit of staying up late to cram for tests, for example. Research shows that this behavior is counterproductive because sleep is necessary for consolidating learning and that students who go to bed earlier tend to get better grades.[88] Of course, late-night studying is not the only problem. Just as often it is students' overly full extracurricular schedules that crowd out sleep. However, student-athletes might reconsider their habits if they understood the important role of sleep in growing and repairing cells and producing

85. Pang, *Rest*, 145–52.

86. Melissa Janco, "Study: 73% of High School Students Not Getting Enough Sleep," AAP News, January 25, 2018, https://tinyurl.com/yfunjkuv; Angelika Anita Schlarb, Anja Friedrich, Merle Claßen, "Sleep Problems in University Students—an Intervention," *Neuropsychiatric Disease and Treatment* 13 (2017): 1989–2001, https://doi.org/10.2147/NDT.S142067.

87. Mary A. Carskadon, ed., *Adolescent Sleep Patterns: Biological, Social, and Psychological Influences* (Cambridge: Cambridge University Press, 2002).

88. Kana Okano et al., "Sleep Quality, Duration, and Consistency Are Associated with Better Academic Performance in College Students," *NPJ Science of Learning* 4, no. 16 (2019), https://doi.org/10.1038/s41539-019-0055-z.

testosterone, giving well-rested athletes an edge in performance and resistance to injury.[89] The American Academy of Pediatrics recommends that middle schools and high schools start no earlier than 8:30 a.m. based on numerous studies citing benefits for physical and mental health, safety, academic performance, and quality of life.[90] Logistical challenges around transportation and extracurricular schedules cause many communities to balk at later start times. However, new research on the importance of setting bounds on extracurriculars for nurturing faith might cause some Christian parents to reconsider.[91]

We educators might think that we have better reasons for shortchanging ourselves on sleep. We lose sleep thinking about how to motivate struggling students, fix problems plaguing the department, or advance research that will lead to a cure for disease. But, again, sleep research suggests that we are usually better served by just going to bed. Though we are not aware of it, our brains remain highly active while we sleep. As we lie unconscious, our brains are busy dreaming, processing the day's events, and encoding memories and new skills. These unconscious processes account for the well-documented phenomenon of people waking up with creative breakthroughs that had eluded them in their waking hours.[92] If we just went to bed at a reasonable hour, we might find the solution we were seeking when we open our eyes in the morning. While there is no substitute for a good night's rest,

89. Kenneth C. Vitale et al., "Sleep Hygiene for Optimizing Recovery in Athletes: Review and Recommendations," *International Journal of Sports Medicine* 40, no. 8 (2019): 535–43.

90. Adolescent Sleep Working Group, Committee on Adolescence, Council on School Health, "School Start Times for Adolescents," *Pediatrics* 134, no. 3 (2014): 642–49, 10.1542/peds.2014-1697.

91. Mark Gray and Greg Popcak, *Future Faithful Families Project: Successfully Raising Catholic Children to Be Active Catholics as Adults* (Washington, DC: CARA, 2023), 17.

92. One famous example is Friedrich August Kekulé's dream about dancing snakes that revealed to him the structure of the chemical compound benzene. For more examples, see Pang, *Rest*, 152–54.

even short naps of ten to twenty minutes can improve accuracy and cognitive performance, reaction time, and problem-solving ability, in addition to strengthening the immune system and reducing blood pressure and the risk of heart disease.[93] These findings are so compelling that companies such as Zappos, Ben and Jerry's, Uber, and Nike all now provide napping spaces for employees in their offices.[94]

Sleep is also an important part of a healthy spiritual life, novel though this suggestion might seem at first blush. It might even be considered a spiritual practice in its own right, a daily practice of letting go, as pastor and author A. J. Sherrill suggests.[95] Pope John XXIII is a good model in this regard. When offering God his evening prayers, he would say, "Well, I did my best. It's your Church, so I'm going to bed now." If we struggle to let go at day's end, we need to ask ourselves, *Do I think myself so important that the world will collapse if I do not finish this task right now? Can I not trust God to take care of the world while I sleep?* If the man responsible for the entire Catholic Church could entrust it to God and rest in peace, certainly those of us responsible for a school or a classroom can do likewise. If we need assurance, we can look to the many instances in Scripture of God working wonders while human beings slept.[96]

One way we can habituate ourselves to this attitude of trust and surrender is by praying the traditional Night Prayer from the Catholic Liturgy of the Hours or the Anglican Book of Common Prayer, which includes the Canticle of Simeon (a.k.a. Nunc Dimittis). This

93. Pink, *When*, 66–67. Pink offers the following guidelines for taking the perfect nap: Schedule your nap for your afternoon trough time, create a peaceful environment, set a timer for twenty-five minutes, drink a cup of coffee immediately beforehand (the caffeine will kick in when the timer goes off), repeat consistently.

94. Pink, *When*, 71.

95. A. J. Sherrill, *Being with God: The Absurdity, Necessity, and Neurology of Contemplative Prayer* (Grand Rapids: Brazos, 2021), 144.

96. For example, the creation of the first woman (Gen. 2:21–22) and revelations to Jacob (Gen. 28:10–17), his son Joseph (Gen. 37), the prophet Daniel (Dan. 7), and Joseph, husband of Mary (Matt. 1:20–21; 2:13; 2:19–20; 2:22), in their dreams.

prayer includes the words, "Lord, now you let your servant go in peace. Your word has been fulfilled. My eyes have seen your salvation, which you have prepared in the sight of all peoples." Praying these words at day's end has brought peace to generations of Christians. The Ignatian examen can serve the same purpose. When we pray the examen, we both acknowledge our failings and give thanks for what God has done that day. As part of a regular practice of gratitude, this ritual can yield many benefits, including higher levels of happiness and positive mood, increased empathy and prosocial behavior, life satisfaction, satisfaction with one's job or school, and enhanced sense of meaning and connection.[97]

A Day and a Place Unlike Others

God told the Israelites that, for them, the seventh day should not be like other days. Their observance of the Sabbath was to be one important way that Israel would distinguish itself from other peoples and serve as a light to the nations. The same might be said for Christian schools in our day. Although formal Sabbath observance occurs on the weekend when most teachers and students are at home, the spirit of surrender, receptivity, and gratitude that the Sabbath represents should pervade our Christian schools every day of the week. Were this spirit of Sabbath observance to pervade our schools, they would surely stand out on account of their respect for the needs and dignity of the human person, the balance they maintain between work and rest, and, above all, the deference they show to God's initiative over human efforts. Schools that embrace the Sabbath and other practices of rest not only honor God's commands but also act in accord with the research findings cited throughout this chapter on the benefits of rest for our work and well-being. I summarize below some of these practices recommended by this research and by Christianity's contemplative tradition.

97. Giacomo Bono, Taylor Duffy, and Selena Moreno, "Gratitude in School: Benefits to Students and Schools," in *Handbook of Positive Psychology in Schools*, ed. Kelly-Ann Allen et al. (New York: Routledge, 2022), 118–34.

Contemplative Practices for Rest and Recreation

For starters: Incorporate "micro-breaks" into your day such as pausing for moments of prayer, massaging your hands when going to the bathroom, or simply doing certain actions more slowly and deliberately.

Restful spaces: Consider the following suggestions for creating contemplative spaces in schools that help students and teachers to think deeply and maintain an awareness of God's presence:

- Engage people's aesthetic senses by decorating the school with beautiful decor, artwork, and greenery. Maintain the orderliness and cleanliness of the school as much as possible.
- Populate the school and classrooms with visual reminders of the school's mission and of God's presence (banners, signs, plaques, statues, memorials, etc.). Minimize the visibility of things that will divert attention away from the proper work of the school and into the world of the mundane (e.g., advertisements, digital entertainment, cell phones).
- Where possible, cultivate the natural beauty of the school property, including gardens, pathways, malls, ponds, and the like.
- Create spaces dedicated to contemplation such as chapels, prayer rooms, meditation gardens, walking labyrinths, and reading rooms.

Breaks: Balancing periods of work and rest both boosts productivity and keeps us focused on the one necessary thing. Some practices for rejuvenating breaks include:

- Set a timer to ring every twenty-five minutes as a reminder to pause, pray, breathe deeply, and stretch.
- Incorporate movement into your day whenever possible. Take a walk around the building every hour or a walk around the campus on your lunch break. Get outside if possible or at least look out a window.

- Recharge by spending break time with others. Talk about something other than work.
- Eat a real meal, ideally away from your desk and in the company of others. Savor your food.
- Schedule longer passing periods (eight to ten minutes) so students are less rushed and have time to visit with friends.

Recreation: Finding time in our day for play not only improves physical health and enhances cognitive function but serves as preparation for contemplation.

- Students more readily experience genuine play outside the classroom. Take advantage of the opportunities presented by their passion for sports, clubs, and service to deepen spirituality, for example, by praying together in moments of loss and adversity. Encourage and perhaps even require student participation in extracurriculars.
- Nurture healthy relationships through living learning communities and other small communities in residence halls.
- Faculty and staff: Build play into your weekly schedule by participating in exercise classes, adult intramural leagues, pickup games, reading groups, or affinity groups.
- School leaders: Support teachers and staff in this in your communications and by creating concrete structures and opportunities for play (e.g., designated "no meeting" times).

Prayer: Jesus offers us a peace that even the best nap or vacation cannot give. Some ways of receiving this peace include:

- Observing two twenty-five-minute periods of silent prayer each day, ideally early in the morning and again in the evening.
- Committing to set times of prayer (e.g., during lunch and planning periods) as a way of returning to Christ throughout the school day and keeping the concerns of work in perspective.

- Praying through the day, for example, using the Jesus Prayer, whenever you have a spare moment or when engaged in tasks that do not require much mental engagement.
- Praying Night Prayer or the Ignatian examen as a gesture of handing over the day's work and worries to God.

Sabbath rest and worship: Observing a day of Sabbath rest reminds us that the world rests in God's hands, not ours, and provides a weekly opportunity for us to be rejuvenated through celebration and thanksgiving.

- Attend Sunday worship and otherwise celebrate God's gifts of life and salvation by doing something special (e.g., gathering with friends and family, cooking a nice meal, doing an activity you enjoy).
- Take a break from work, chores, and anything that feels like toil.
- School leaders: Institute policies about emailing and homework that encourage students and teachers to honor the Sabbath and rest during the weekend.
- In the spirit of Sabbath rest, celebrate feast days as a school community by pausing normal activities, worshiping together, having a retreat day, engaging in service or play, or enjoying a communal meal.

Sleep: Besides serving as a spiritual gesture of surrender, sleep in adequate quantities is essential for academic, work, and athletic performance as well as physical and mental health.

- Get a good night's rest every night (eight to ten hours for high school students, seven to nine for college students and adults).
- Take naps if/when your schedule permits, especially when you do not sleep well at night. Schedule your nap for your afternoon trough time, create a peaceful environment, and set a timer for twenty-five minutes so you wake up rested but not drowsy.
- High school leaders: Consider pushing back the school's start time to give students extra sleep.

Epilogue

In my final weeks of working on this book, my life became exceptionally busy . . . or shall I say, full. Classes needed to be prepared, unanticipated administrative tasks were dumped on me, publication deadlines threatened, and my home was occupied by children caught between the end of summer camps and the start of school. These circumstances again put to the test the things I had written in this book about abiding in the present moment, entrusting our work to God, and balancing labor and rest. Rather than causing me to question the practicality of a contemplative approach to education, these intensifying pressures only reinforced my conviction of its value and necessity. It became even more important to stay grounded in prayer so I did not become overwhelmed by my to-do list and to practice an inner watchfulness so I did not transmit the stress I was experiencing to my family and colleagues.

That is not to say it was an easy time. Nor do I harbor any illusions that incorporating Christian contemplative practices and wisdom into the life of our schools will be easy. We never work in ideal circumstances, but neither did those from whom we inherit these practices. Recall that the desert fathers and mothers retreated into the desert because Christianity had become too easily aligned with political agendas following the Edict of Milan. The Benedictines founded their first monasteries, which sparked a renewal of learning and culture, at a time when society was in social and moral decay. Saint Ignatius fathered a spirituality that has proved life-giving for millions over the centuries precisely in response to the challenge of remaining contemplative in a world that is anything but. Far from requiring ideal circumstances, the practices and wisdom of these Christian contemplative traditions are most helpful when we find ourselves in the midst of imperfect circumstances and imperfect people.

The bottom line is that we do not need to wait for our schools to be perfect to take up these practices. Neither should we expect perfection after we have taken them up. I have attempted to share a vision of what our schools might be like if we embraced our contemplative heritage. This vision is more of a guiding light than a template schools should aim to replicate point by point. The great contemplatives would tell us the same. In the words of Abba Moses:

> To cling to God unceasingly and to remain inseparably united to him in contemplation is indeed . . . impossible for the person who is enclosed and perishable flesh. But we ought to know where we should fix our mind's attention and to what goal we should always recall our soul's gaze.[1]

As we live into this vision, our day-to-day experience in our schools will likely be a mix of moments of serene contemplation and the kinds of scenes I describe at the beginning of each chapter—a rushed class, a maddening meeting, a race against deadlines. The goal is not to eliminate all stress and conflict in our lives. This will never happen this side of eternity. The goal, rather, is to bring an abiding awareness of God's loving presence to the stress and conflict (and joy) we experience each day.

There is no doubt that maintaining this awareness is a great challenge. So much in our current culture conspires against contempla-

1. John Cassian, *The Conferences*, trans. Boniface Ramsey, OP (Mahwah, NJ: Paulist, 1997), 50.

tion—the corporatization of our schools, attention-hijacking technologies, the erosion of community, the forgetfulness of religious tradition. Overcoming these challenges is probably impossible for any individual teacher, student, or even school. These circumstances demand a collective response, which is all the more reason to return to our heritage of contemplation now. Contemplation is above all about communion—communion with God and with one another. This communion is the one necessary thing, the cornerstone around which everything else falls into place. When we embrace and prioritize our call to loving communion in how we work and learn together, we see improved academic outcomes, mental health, relationships, and spirituality in our school communities. This is the testimony not only of the Christian tradition but also of the contemporary research we have examined throughout this book. Based on this testimony as well as my own experience and that of fellow educators, I have come to believe that Christian schools are our greatest hope for renewing our communities and restoring our culture today. I sincerely believe that, if we live into this vision for contemplative education, people will flock to our Christian schools as they once did to the desert communities of Egypt and Syria and the medieval monasteries.

Of course, the desert did not become a city overnight. People like Anthony and Benedict had to take the first bold step into what was then the wilderness. In time others followed. My hope is that this book represents a step in the right direction. I do not imagine it is more than that. Herein I have shared a number of time- and research-tested contemplative practices. Others need to be studied more. There remain many questions to be answered and problems to be solved. I hope others will join those of us who are working toward solutions and take their own first steps in their respective school communities. I do not expect any school to implement everything proposed in this book all at once. To attempt to do so is neither practical nor prudent. I am merely inviting Christian educators to consider these gifts of our contemplative traditions and discern and adopt those that make sense for your school community, beginning perhaps with just one or a few simple practices. What is most important—and potentially most transformative—is that we resolve to abide in prayer and mutual love in all that we do. If we can do this much, we will see our schools growing into more contemplative, loving communities just as the seed ever so gradually pushes forth from the soil and reaches toward the light.

Gratitudes

As a parent, I can affirm the truth of the saying that it takes a village to raise a child. As an author, I feel that something similar is true of writing a book, or at least any book worth reading. I am grateful to be enmeshed in a supportive community and to stand within a long tradition of saints (and sinners), contemplatives, scholars, artists, and humble Christians doing their best to seek the Lord day by day. I am very conscious of the fact that without them my life would not be what it is and this book would not be at all. A book—as you saw in one of the meditations above—is like a berry growing upon a vine. The fruit appears only after a long period of slow growth. It is the privilege of an author to witness this process of development and to facilitate its fruition. It is also an author's happy obligation to acknowledge the people who were part of this development—the branches that support the fruit—when a book finally comes into public view.

Among those helping most directly to bring this book to fruition were the good people at Eerdmans Publishing: James Ernest, who initially encouraged and received this project at Eerdmans; Andrew Knapp, who guided it through the review process; and Kimberly Benedict, who ushered it into the production phase. I am grateful to Tom Raabe for making me sound like a better writer and to Jenny Hoffman for coordinating all the moving parts in the production process. I offer my thanks also to all the other members of the Eerdmans team who transformed the Word document I gave them into a beautiful book that people can hold and annotate and loan to friends.

In addition to the assistance of these professionals, I benefited from the generosity of friends and colleagues who read and offered feedback on various portions of the manuscript, including Peter Corrigan, Joe Betz, Grace May, Jac Mullen, David Smith, and Susan Felch. These last two deserve special thanks. David has been a generous conversation partner and arranged introductions with Eerdmans. Susan not only provided feedback in the intermediate stages of writing but also offered invaluable guidance when the idea for this book was still incubating.

To mention Susan is to tug at a thread interwoven with many others. I met Susan through the Lilly Faculty Fellows Program, which operates under the wise direction of Joe Creech and the highly competent coordination of Jenna Van Sickle. I am grateful to Joe, Jenna, and Susan, as I am to Stephanie Schlacter and the other faculty fellows for the time, conversations, and excellent meals we shared during the two years of the fellowship. It was a most formative and rejuvenating experience that nurtured many of the ideas found in this book and drew me into the Lilly network. I continue to be nourished and inspired by this group of generous, faithful people.

I owe much to my colleagues at Seton Hall University. It was thanks to Jon Radwan and K. C. Choi that I had the opportunity to participate in the Lilly Faculty Fellowship. And it was thanks to the support of the University and Immaculate Conception Seminary School of Theology that I had the gift of a year to contemplate these matters more deeply and to share the fruits of my contemplation in this book. I offer special thanks to my colleagues at the seminary, who picked up the slack for me in myriad ways while I was on leave.

While their support made it possible for me to be away, others welcomed me in. Primary among these were Fr. Ray Guiao, Anthony Fior, Augie Pacetti, and the generous and talented people of Saint Ignatius High School. Saint Ignatius provided me not only invaluable opportunities to learn from their faculty, staff, and students but also financial support for this project. I owe special thanks to the Theology Department, with whom I worked most closely, particularly the chair, Joe Betz, and Peter Corrigan, who has long been an advocate of my work. I also want to extend profuse thanks to Mary Ann Vogel, Erin Conway, and Ryan Hough at Welsh Academy for their hospitality, insights, and abundant inspiration.

Several other communities opened their doors to me throughout the course of this project. Thank you to Fr. Tim Christy, Jay Locquiao, and the faculty of Saint Francis Cathedral School for the opportunity to work with and learn from you. Thanks to Aileen Baker, Kale Zelden, Daniel Caplin, Lauren Revay, Chris Fisher, Darryl De Marzio, Abbot Michael Brunner, and the Benedictine community of Portsmouth Abbey School. To the faculty, staff, students, and Benedictine community at Saint Benedict's Prep I want to express my sincere thanks and esteem. Nowhere have I encountered such a strong school community. A few individuals were largely responsible for my introduction (I am tempted to say initiation) to this community—Br. Bruno Mello, Fr. Edwin Leahy, Fr. Albert Holtz—but my heart overflows with admiration for all the individuals who give of themselves to make Saint Benedict's the family that it is.

Besides these school communities that welcomed me in, there were many individuals who shared insights, experiences, research, hopes, and dreams that shaped this book. Jamie Smith, Jessica Hooten Wilson, Rodger Narloch, Gretchen Rumohr, Fr. Bob Keller, Ken Parker, Dori Baker, Michael Rubbelke, Jonathan Heaps, and Margarita Mooney are some of these kind souls. I am also grateful to friends who have offered encouragement and various forms of help along the way—to Christian and Katherine Clark, Patty Rodriguez, Joanne DePasquale-Parent, Stephen Audobato, Marianne Lloyd, and many others.

I reserve for my final and most heartfelt thanks for my wife, Margaret. I am grateful to Margaret for blessings and helps beyond number but especially for her support during my sabbatical. All that year (she would probably say every year), she played the Martha to my Mary, driving the kids to school and cooking most dinners so I could carve out the time, space, and quiet in our chaotic, beautiful shared life to read, pray, converse, and write. A few words printed on a page are surely inadequate thanks, but, Margaret, I hope you feel you gained a more attentive and loving husband in exchange for all your sacrifices.

Bibliography

Adobato, Stephen. "Ascetics in the City." *American Benedictine Review* 69, no. 4 (2018): 366–74.

Adolescent Sleep Working Group, Committee on Adolescence, Council on School Health. "School Start Times for Adolescents." *Pediatrics* 134, no. 3 (2014): 642–49. https://doi:10.1542/peds.2014-1697.

Allen, Kelly-Ann, Michael J. Furlong, Dianne Vella-Brodrick, and Shannon Suldo, eds. *Handbook of Positive Psychology in Schools.* New York: Routledge, 2022.

American Psychological Association. "Episode 225: Why Our Attention Spans Are Shrinking, with Gloria Mark, PhD." *Speaking of Psychology Podcast.* Accessed October 30, 2024. https://tinyurl.com/ypf4behe.

Amstutz, Lorraine Stutzman, and Judy H. Mullet. *The Little Book of Restorative Discipline for Schools: Teaching Responsibility; Creating Caring Climates.* New York: Good Books, 2005.

Anderson, Monica, Michelle Faverio, and Jeffrey Gottfried. "Teens, Social Media and Technology 2023." Pew Research Center, December 11, 2023. https://tinyurl.com/bdv4nmur.

Antonovsky, Aaron. *Unraveling the Mystery of Health: How People Manage Stress and Stay Well.* San Francisco: Jossey-Bass, 2010.

Aphrahat. "Demonstration IV, on Prayer." In *The Syriac Fathers on Prayer and the Spiritual Life,* translated by Sebastian Brock, 1–28. Kalamazoo, MI: Cistercian Publications, 1987.

Aquinas, Thomas. *Commentary on the Sentences.* Aquinas Institute, 2020. Accessed October 30, 2024. https://tinyurl.com/a77jzmdv.

Aranda, Julie H., and Safia Baig. "Toward 'JOMO': The Joy of Missing Out and the Freedom of Disconnecting." *MobileHCI '18: Proceedings of the 20th*

International Conference on Human Computer Interaction with Mobile Devices and Services. September 2018. https://doi:10.1145/3229434.

Aristotle. *Nicomachean Ethics.* Translated by D. P. Chase. Project Gutenberg, 2021. https://tinyurl.com/mv9av9vb.

Arneson, Krystin. "How 'Feierabend' Helps Germans Disconnect from the Workday." BBC, October 7, 2020. https://tinyurl.com/y48dz93d.

Augustine. *Confessions.* Translated by Henry Chadwick. Oxford: Oxford University Press, 1998.

Bailey, Chris. "How to Get Your Brain to Focus." TEDxManchester. Accessed October 30, 2024. https://tinyurl.com/ymjh5mms.

Barbezat, Daniel P., and Mirabai Bush. *Contemplative Practices in Higher Education: Powerful Methods to Transform Teaching and Learning.* San Francisco: Jossey-Bass, 2014.

Bass, Dorothy. "Keeping Sabbath." In *Practicing Our Faith: A Way of Life for a Searching People*, edited by Dorothy Bass, 75–88. San Francisco: Jossey-Bass, 2010.

———, ed. *Practicing Our Faith: A Way of Life for a Searching People.* Minneapolis: Fortress, 2019.

Bass, Dorothy, Kathleen Cahalan, Bonnie Miller-McLemore, and Christian Scharen. *Christian Practical Wisdom: What It Is, Why It Matters.* Grand Rapids: Eerdmans, 2016.

Bass, Dorothy, and Miroslav Volf, eds. *Practicing Theology: Beliefs and Practices in Christian Life.* Grand Rapids: Eerdmans, 2001.

Baumeister, Roy F., Kathleen D. Vohs, and Wilhelm Hofmann. "What People Desire, Feel Conflicted About, and Try to Resist in Everyday Life." *Psychological Science* 23, no. 6 (2012).

Benedict, Saint. *The Rule of Benedict.* Translated by Leonard Doyle. Order of Saint Benedict, 2014. https://tinyurl.com/yc7p48nr.

Benedict XVI. *Deus Caritas Est.* Vatican, 2005. https://tinyurl.com/2xbdw9j3.

———. "General Audience." Castel Gandolfo, August 31, 2011. https://tinyurl.com/ffrcdw4m.

Benne, Robert. *Quality with Soul: How Six Premier Colleges and Universities Keep Faith with Their Religious Traditions.* Grand Rapids: Eerdmans, 2001.

Berg, Maggie, and Barbara K. Seeber. *The Slow Professor: Challenging the Culture of Speed in the Academy.* Toronto: University of Toronto Press, 2016.

Bernard, Abbot of Clairvaux. "Sermon on the Song of Songs." In *The Steps to Humility*, translated by George Bosworth Birch. Notre Dame: University of Notre Dame Press, 1963.

Berryman, Jerome. *Godly Play: An Imaginative Approach to Religious Education.* Minneapolis: Augsburg, 1995.

Bloom, Susan D., ed. *Ungrading: Why Rating Students Undermines Learning (and What to Do Instead).* Morgantown: West Virginia University Press, 2020.

Bonet, Giselle, and Barbara R. Walters. "High Impact Practices: Student Engagement and Retention." *College Student Journal* 50, no. 2 (2016): 224–35.

Bono, Giacomo, Taylor Duffy, and Selena Moreno. "Gratitude in School: Benefits to Students and Schools." In *Handbook of Positive Psychology in Schools,* edited by Kelly-Ann Allen, Michael J. Furlong, Dianne Vella-Brodrick, and Shannon Suldo, 118–34. New York: Routledge, 2022.

Bottaro, Gregory. *The Mindful Catholic: Finding God One Moment at a Time.* North Palm Beach, FL: Beacon Publishing, 2018.

boyd, danah. *It's Complicated: The Social Lives of Networked Teens.* New Haven: Yale University Press, 2014.

Boyer, Ernest. *Scholarship Reconsidered: Priorities of the Professoriate.* San Francisco: Jossey-Bass, 1997.

Brigham, Erin. *See, Judge, Act: Catholic Social Teaching and Service Learning.* Winona, MN: Anselm Academic, 2013.

Brother Lawrence. *Practice of the Presence of God.* Christian Classics Ethereal Library. Accessed October 30, 2024. https://tinyurl.com/2nrvbhbh.

Brown, Brené. *Daring Greatly: How the Courage to Be Vulnerable Transforms the Way We Live, Love, Parent, and Lead.* New York: Avery Books, 2015.

Brown, Christina, Supreet Kaur, Geeta Kingdon, Heather Schofield. "Cognitive Endurance as Human Capital." Accessed October 30, 2024. https://tinyurl.com/38xyty2e.

Brown, Stuart. *Play: How It Shapes the Brain, Opens the Imagination, and Invigorates the Soul.* New York: Avery Books, 2010.

Bruff, Derek. *Intentional Tech: Principles to Guide the Use of Educational Technology in College Teaching.* Morgantown: West Virginia University Press, 2019.

Burdick, Alan. *Why Time Flies: A Mostly Scientific Investigation.* New York: Simon & Schuster, 2017.

Burghardt, Walter. "Contemplation: A Long Loving Look at the Real." In *An Ignatian Spirituality Reader,* edited by G. W. Traub, 187–202. Chicago: Loyola Press, 2008.

Burnett, D. Graham, Alyssa Loh, and Peter Schmidt. "Powerful Forces Are Fracking Our Attention. We Can Fight Back." *New York Times,* November 24, 2023. https://tinyurl.com/4vz8afas.

Burnett, D. Graham, and Stevie Knauss. *Twelve Theses on Attention.* Princeton: Princeton University Press, 2022.

Bursztyn, Leonardo, Benjamin Handel, Rafael Jiménez-Durán, and Christopher Roth. "When Product Markets Become Collective Traps: The Case of Social Media." Becker Friedman Institute for Economics at the University of Chicago, October 2023. https://tinyurl.com/mvmr7fjn.

Cahalan, Kathleen. "Unknowing: Spiritual Practices and the Search for a Wisdom Epistemology." In *Christian Practical Wisdom: What It Is, Why It Matters*, edited by Dorothy Bass et al., 275–321. Grand Rapids: Eerdmans, 2016.

Camfield, Eileen Kogl, and Leslie Bayers. "Mindful Assessment in Support of Student Learning." *Journal of Contemplative Inquiry* 6, no. 1 (2019): 121–44.

Carskadon, Mary A., ed. *Adolescent Sleep Patterns: Biological, Social, and Psychological Influences.* Cambridge: Cambridge University Press, 2002.

Casey, Michael. *Sacred Reading: The Ancient Art of Lectio Divina.* Liguori, MO: Liguori/Triumph, 1996.

Cassian, John. *The Conferences.* Translated by Boniface Ramsey, OP. Mahwah, NJ: Paulist, 1997.

Catechism of the Catholic Church. 2nd ed. Washington, DC: United States Conference of Catholic Bishops, 2019. https://tinyurl.com/54unjbfr.

Caussade, Jean-Pierre de. *The Sacrament of the Present Moment.* Translated by Kitty Muggeridge. San Francisco: Harper & Row, 1989.

Cavalletti, Sofia. *The Religious Potential of the Child: Experiencing Scripture and Liturgy with Young Children.* Translated by Patricia M. Coulter and Julie M. Coulter. Edited by Rebekah Rojcewicz. 3rd ed. Chicago: Catechesis of the Good Shepherd Publications, 2020.

"Characteristics of Jesuit Education." Jesuit Resource. Accessed October 30, 2024. https://tinyurl.com/4xc28xxu.

"Chronic Stress Puts Your Health at Risk." Mayo Clinic. Accessed October 30, 2024. https://tinyurl.com/4j9bt77n.

Chryssavgis, John. *In the Heart of the Desert: The Spirituality of the Desert Fathers and Mothers.* Rev. ed. Bloomington, IN: World Wisdom, 2008.

Clement, Joe, and Matt Miles. *Screen Schooled: Two Veteran Teachers Expose How Technology Overuse Is Making Our Kids Dumber.* Chicago: Chicago Review Press, 2017.

The Cloud of Unknowing. Christian Classics Ethereal Library. Accessed October 30, 2024. https://tinyurl.com/2p82xvff.

Coniaris, Anthony M. *Philokalia: The Bible of Orthodox Spirituality.* Minneapolis: Light and Life Publishing, 1998.

Crawford, Matthew. *The World Beyond Your Head: How to Flourish in an Age of Distraction.* New York: Penguin Books, 2015.

Creating a Successful Urban School Culture: A Summary of the Principles, Programs, and Practices of Saint Benedict's Preparatory School. Newark, NJ: Benedictine Abbey of Newark, 2014.

Croteau, Jeanne. "What Is Restorative Justice in Schools? Everything Educators Need to Know." We Are Teachers, July 29, 2024. https://tinyurl.com/52p23hny.

Csikszentmihalyi, Mihaly, ed. *Applications of Flow in Human Development and Education: The Collected Works of Mihaly Csikszentmihalyi.* Dordrecht: Springer Netherlands, 2014.

———. *Creativity: Flow and the Psychology of Discovery and Invention.* New York: Harper, 1996.

———. *Flow: The Psychology of Optimal Experience.* New York: Harper & Row, 1990.

Cummings, Charles, OCSO. *Monastic Practices.* Cistercian Studies Series, no. 75. Kalamazoo, MI: Cistercian Publications, 1986.

Dante Alighieri. *The Divine Comedy.* Digital Dante Edition. Columbia University, 2020. https://tinyurl.com/mpdnn2jm.

Day, Dorothy. *The Long Loneliness.* San Francisco: HarperCollins, 1997.

Dockrell, Julie E., and Bridget M. Shield. "Acoustical Barriers in Classrooms: The Impact of Noise on Performance in the Classroom." *British Educational Research Journal* 32, no. 3 (2006): 509–25.

Doherty, Catherine. *Poustinia: Encountering God in Silence, Solitude, and Prayer.* Combermere, ON: Madonna House Publications, 2000.

Donald, James N., Paul W. B. Atkins, Philip D. Parker, Alison M. Christie, and Richard M. Ryan. "Daily Stress and the Benefits of Mindfulness: Examining the Daily and Longitudinal Relations Between Present-Moment Awareness and Stress Responses." *Journal of Research in Personality* 65 (2016): 30–37.

"Education within the Benedictine Wisdom Tradition." Association of Benedictine Colleges and Universities. Accessed October 30, 2024. https://tinyurl.com/ahf2vv7e.

Eliot, T. S. "Choruses from 'The Rock.'" In *The Complete Poems and Plays of T. S. Eliot.* London: Faber & Faber, 1969.

Ellwood, Sophie, et al. "The Incubation Effect: Hatching a Solution?" *Creativity Research Journal* 21, no. 1 (2009): 6–14.

Ergas, Oren. "Attention Please: Positioning Attention at the Center of Curriculum and Pedagogy." *Journal of Curriculum Theorizing* 31, no. 2 (2016): 66–81.

Escrivá, Josemaría. *The Way.* New York: Image Books, 2006.

Fanelli, Daniele. "How Many Scientists Fabricate and Falsify Research? A Systematic Review and Meta-analysis of Survey Data." *PloS One* 4, no. 5 (2009): e5738.

Francis. *Christus Vivit.* Vatican, 2019. https://tinyurl.com/3vpetjcp.

———. *Evangelii Gaudium.* Vatican, 2013. https://tinyurl.com/bdd6926h.

———. *Laudato Si'.* Vatican, 2015. https://tinyurl.com/3j9xsbjx.

———. "Morning Meditation in the Chapel of Domus Sanctae Marthae: For a Culture of Encounter." *L'Osservatore Romano*, September 23, 2016. https://tinyurl.com/55ny9mrh.

Frankl, Viktor E. *Man's Search for Meaning.* Boston: Beacon, 2006.

Frerking, Abbot Thomas. "Saint John Henry Newman on Benedictine Life and on Benedictine Schools." In *A Benedictine Education*, edited by Christopher Fisher, 175–210. Providence: Cluny Media, 2020.

Fritson, Krista K., Krista D. Forrest, and Mackenzie L. Bohl. "Using Reflective Journaling in the College Course." In *Promoting Student Engagement*, edited by Richard Miller et al., 1:157–61. N.p.: Society for the Teaching of Psychology, 2011.

Gershuny, Jonathan. "Busyness as the Badge of Honor for the New Superordinate Working Class." *Social Research* 72 (2005–2009). https://doi.org/10.1353/sor.2005.0018.

Giussani, Luigi. *The Risk of Education: Discovering Our Ultimate Destiny.* New York: Crossroad, 1996.

Goleman, Daniel, and Richard Davidson. *Altered Traits: Science Reveals How Meditation Changes Your Mind, Brain, and Body.* New York: Avery Books, 2018.

Golkar, Armita, Emilia Johansson, Maki Kasahara, Walter Osika, Aleksander Perski, and Ivanka Savic. "The Influence of Work-Related Chronic Stress on the Regulation of Emotion and on Functional Connectivity in the Brain." *PloS One* 9, no. 9 (2014): e104550. https://doi:10.1371/journal.pone.0104550.

Goto, Courtney. *The Grace of Playing: Pedagogies for Leaning into God's New Creation.* Eugene, OR: Pickwick, 2016.

Gray, Mark, and Greg Popcak. *Future Faithful Families Project: Successfully Raising Catholic Children to Be Active Catholics as Adults.* Washington, DC: CARA, 2023.

"Guidelines for Using Groups Effectively." Center for Research on Learning and Teaching, University of Michigan. Accessed October 30, 2024. https://tinyurl.com/mvzan8ze.

Guigo II. *The Ladder of Monks: A Letter on the Contemplative Life and Twelve Meditations.* Translated by Edmund Colledge and James Walsh. Kalamazoo, MI: Cistercian Publications, 1981.

Guillaumont, Antoine. "The Jesus Prayer among the Monks of Egypt." *Eastern Churches Review* 6 (1974): 66–71.

Gunn, Charlotte, Maria Vahdati, and Mehdi Shahrestani. "Green Walls in Schools: The Potential Well-Being Benefits." *Building and Environment* 224 (2022): 109560. https://doi.org/10.1016/j.buildenv.2022.109560.

Gushurst-Moore, André. *Glory in All Things: Saint Benedict and Catholic Education Today*. New York: Angelico, 2020.

Haidt, Jonathan. *The Anxious Generation: How the Great Rewiring of Childhood Is Causing an Epidemic of Mental Illness*. New York: Penguin Books, 2024.

Haidt, Jonathan, and Zach Rausch. "The Effects of Phone-Free Schools: A Collaborative Review." Unpublished manuscript. New York University (ongoing). https://tinyurl.com/mj6sph2v.

Haines-Eitzen, Kim. *Sonorous Desert: What Deep Listening Taught Early Christian Monks—and What It Can Teach Us*. Princeton: Princeton University Press, 2022.

Hartig, Terry, Richard Mitchell, Sjerp De Vries, and Howard Frumkin. "Nature and Health." *Annual Review of Public Health* 35 (2014): 207–28.

Hathaway, W. E. "Non-visual Effects of Classroom Lighting on Children." *Educational Facility Planner* 32, no. 3 (1994): 12–16.

Heschong, Lisa, and Carey Knecht. "Daylighting Makes a Difference." *Educational Facility Planner* 37, no. 2 (2002): 5–14.

Himes, Michael. *Doing the Truth in Love: Conversations about God, Relationships, and Service*. Mahwah, NJ: Paulist, 2014.

Hofferth, Sandra L., David Kinney, and Janet Dunn. "The Hurried Child: Myth vs. Reality." In *Life Balance: Multidisciplinary Theories and Research*, edited by Kathleen Matuska and Charles Christiansen, 183–206. N.p.: AOTA Press, 2009.

"Homework." Education Endowment Foundation. Accessed October 30, 2024. https://tinyurl.com/ywxzfser.

Hooten Wilson, Jessica. *Reading for the Love of God*. Grand Rapids: Brazos, 2023.

Huberman, Andrew. "Dr. Jonathan Haidt: How Smartphones & Social Media Impact Mental Health & the Realistic Solutions." *Huberman Lab Podcast*, June 10, 2024. https://tinyurl.com/bdeytmpj.

Ignatian Pedagogy: A Practical Approach. Society of Jesus. Accessed October 30, 2024. https://tinyurl.com/47avdk2p.

Ignatius of Loyola. "On Dealing with Others." Woodstock Theological Library at Georgetown University, 1546. https://tinyurl.com/5xe5p92f.

———. *The Spiritual Exercises of St. Ignatius*. Edited by Louis J. Puhl. Chicago: Loyola Press, 1951.

Igumen Chariton of Valamo, ed. *The Art of Prayer: An Orthodox Anthology*. London: Faber & Faber, 1997.

Irenaeus of Lyons. *Against Heresies*. In *Ante-Nicene Fathers*, vol. 1, edited by Alexander Roberts, James Donaldson, and A. Cleveland Coxe. Buffalo: Christian Literature Publishing Co., 1885.

"Is Your Child Overscheduled? Kids Need 'Down Time.'" Cleveland Clinic, July 16, 2018. https://tinyurl.com/52p5u35t.

James, William. *The Principles of Psychology*. Vol. 1. New York: Holt, 1890.

Janco, Melissa. "Study: 73% of High School Students Not Getting Enough Sleep." AAP News, January 25, 2018. https://tinyurl.com/yfunjkuv.

Janesick, Valeria. *Contemplative Qualitative Inquiry: Practicing the Zen of Research*. New York: Routledge, 2015.

Jennings, Willie James. *After Whiteness: An Education in Belonging*. Grand Rapids: Eerdmans, 2020.

———. *The Christian Imagination: Theology and the Origins of Race*. New Haven: Yale University Press, 2010.

John of the Cross. *The Living Flame of Love*. In *The Collected Works of St. John of the Cross*, translated by K. Kavanaugh and O. Rodriguez. Washington, DC: Institute of Carmelite Studies Publications, 1979.

John Paul II. *Ex Corde Ecclesiae*. Vatican, 1990. https://tinyurl.com/258cvtt6.

———. *Fides et Ratio*. Vatican, 1998. https://tinyurl.com/d876ybdk.

Junco, Reynol. "In-Class Multitasking and Academic Performance." *Computers in Human Behavior* 28, no. 6 (2012): 2236–43.

Keating, Thomas. *Open Mind, Open Heart*. Twentieth anniversary ed. New York: Bloomsbury, 2006.

Keator, Mary. *Lectio Divina as Contemplative Pedagogy: Re-appropriating Monastic Practice for the Humanities*. New York: Routledge, 2018.

Kegan, Robert. *In Over Our Heads: The Mental Demands of Modern Life*. Cambridge, MA: Harvard University Press, 1996.

Kennedy, Margaret E., et al. "Contemplative/Emotion Training Reduces Negative Emotional Behavior and Promotes Pro-social Responses." *Emotion* 1, no. 2 (2012): 338–50.

Keynes, John Maynard. "Economic Possibilities for Our Grandchildren." In *Essays in Persuasion*, 358–73. New York: Norton, 1963.

King, Martin Luther, Jr. "'The Birth of a New Age,' Address Delivered on 11 August 1956 at the Fiftieth Anniversary of Alpha Phi Alpha in Buffalo." Stanford University. Accessed October 30, 2024. https://tinyurl.com/2s3rkc7a.

Kraus, Michael W., Cassy Huang, and Dacher Keltner. "Tactile Communication, Cooperation, and Performance: An Ethological Study of the NBA." *Emotion* 10, no. 5 (2010): 745–49.

Laal, Marjan, and Seyed Mohammad Ghodsi. "Benefits of Collaborative Learning." *Procedia-social and Behavioral Sciences* 31 (2012): 486–90.

Laird, Martin. *Into the Silent Land: A Guide to the Christian Practice of Contemplation.* Oxford: Oxford University Press, 2006.

———. *An Ocean of Light: Contemplation, Transformation, and Liberation.* Oxford: Oxford University Press, 2019.

———. *A Sunlit Absence: Silence, Awareness, and Contemplation.* Oxford: Oxford University Press, 2011.

Lang, James. *Distracted: Why Students Can't Focus and What You Can Do About It.* New York: Basic Books, 2020.

Leclercq, Jean. *The Love of Learning and the Desire for God: A Study of Monastic Culture.* Translated by Catharine Misrahi. New York: Fordham University Press, 1961.

Levy, David M., Jacob O. Wobbrock, Alfred W. Kaszniak, and Marilyn Ostergren. "The Effects of Mindfulness Meditation Training on Multitasking in a High-Stress Information Environment." *Proceedings of Graphics Interface 2012*, 45–52. Toronto.

Lichtmann, Maria. *The Teacher's Way: Teaching and the Contemplative Life.* Mahwah, NJ: Paulist, 2005.

"Life of Prayer: Memorizing the Word." Community of the Beatitudes, January 10, 2022. https://tinyurl.com/4x4r6cer.

Mark, Gloria. *Attention Span: A Groundbreaking Way to Restore Balance, Happiness, and Productivity.* Toronto: Hanover Square Press, 2023.

Marsden, George. *The Soul of the American University: From Protestant Establishment to Established Nonbelief.* Oxford: Oxford University Press, 1994.

Maslow, Abraham H. "A Theory of Human Motivation." *Psychological Review* 50, no. 4 (1943): 370–96. https://doi:10.1037/h0054346.

Mason, Charlotte. *A Philosophy of Education: Charlotte Mason's Original Home Schooling Series.* Vol. 6. Lawrenceville, GA: Simply Charlotte Mason, 2017.

Massingale, Brian. *Racial Justice and the Catholic Church.* Maryknoll, NY: Orbis Books, 2010.

McGilchrist, Iain. *The Master and His Emissary: The Divided Brain and the Making of the Western World.* New Haven: Yale University Press, 2019.

McMurtrie, Beth. "Is This the End of Reading?" *Chronicle of Higher Education*, May 9, 2024. https://tinyurl.com/3e7tkmpe.

Menakem, Resmaa. *My Grandmother's Hands: Racialized Trauma and the Pathway to Mending Our Hearts and Bodies.* Las Vegas: Central Recovery Press, 2017.

Merton, Thomas. *Contemplative Prayer.* New York: Image Books, 1996.

———. "Learning to Live." In *Love and Living,* edited by Naomi Burton Stone and Brother Patrick Hart, 3–14. San Diego: Harcourt, 1985.

———. "The Need for a New Education." In *Contemplation in a World of Action.* Garden City, NY: Doubleday, 1971.

———. *The Seven Storey Mountain.* Fiftieth anniversary ed. San Diego: Harcourt Brace & Co., 1998.

———. *The Wisdom of the Desert: Sayings from the Desert Fathers of the Fourth Century.* 1st Shambhala Library ed. Boston: Shambhala Library, 2004.

Mills, Kim. "Episode 225: Why Our Attention Spans Are Shrinking, with Gloria Mark, PhD." *Speaking of Psychology Podcast.* Accessed August 17, 2024. https://tinyurl.com/ypf4behe.

Mitchell, David, and Dean Sutherland. *What Really Works in Special and Inclusive Education: Using Evidence-Based Teaching Strategies.* New York: Routledge, 2020.

Molina-Markham, Elizabeth. "Finding the 'Sense of the Meeting': Decision Making Through Silence Among Quakers." *Western Journal of Communication* 78, no. 2 (2014): 155–74. https://doi.org/10.1080/10570314.2013.809474.

Montessori, Maria. *The Montessori Method.* Mineola, NY: Dover Publications, 2002.

Mowreader, Ashley. "Residential Spaces Combine Living and Learning in New Ways." *Inside Higher Ed,* February 19, 2023. https://tinyurl.com/yzyt44c7.

Mulkey, Sarah B., Cynthia F. Bearer, and Eleanor J. Molloy. "Indirect Effects of the COVID-19 Pandemic on Children Relate to the Child's Age and Experience." *Pediatric Research* 94, no. 5 (2023): 1586–87. https://doi:10.1038/s41390-023-02681-4.

Mullen, Jac. "The Use of 'Attention Capture' Technologies in Our Classrooms Has Created a Crisis." *Nation,* April 22, 2024. https://tinyurl.com/yzm7nxsb.

Murphy-Shigematzu, Stephen. *From Mindfulness to Heartfulness: Transforming Self and Society with Compassion.* Oakland: Berret-Koehler, 2018.

Nash, Jonathan. "Practicing Benedictine Values to Create an Inclusive Learning Environment." *Headwaters* 30 (2017): 223–41. https://tinyurl.com/yn438anw.

Newberg, Andrew, and Mark Robert Waldman. *How God Changes Your Brain:*

Breakthrough Findings from a Leading Neuroscientist. New York: Ballantine Books, 2009.

Newman, John Henry. "The Benedictine Schools." In *A Benedictine Education*, edited by Christopher Fisher, 57–104. Providence: Cluny Media, 2020.

———. *The Idea of a University*. Notre Dame: University of Notre Dame Press, 1982.

———. "The Mission of Saint Benedict." In *A Benedictine Education*, edited by Christopher Fisher, 1–56. Providence: Cluny Media, 2020.

Nolen-Hoeksema, Susan, Blair E. Wisco, and Sonja Lyubomirsky. "Rethinking Rumination." *Association for Psychological Science* 3, no. 5 (2008): 400–424.

Nucci, Larry, and Elliot Turiel. "Capturing the Complexity of Moral Development and Education." *Mind, Brain, and Education* 3, no. 3 (2009): 151–59. https://doi.org/10.1111/j.1751-228X.2009.01065.x.

Okano, K., J. R. Kaczmarzyk, N. Dave, J. D. E. Gabrieli, and J. C. Grossman. "Sleep Quality, Duration, and Consistency Are Associated with Better Academic Performance in College Students." *NPJ Science of Learning* 4, no. 16 (2019). https://doi.org/10.1038/s41539-019-0055-z.

O'Reilly, Mary Rose. *Radical Presence: Teaching as Contemplative Practice*. Portsmouth, NH: Boynton/Cook Publishers, 1998.

"Our Epidemic of Loneliness and Isolation: U.S. Surgeon General's Advisory on the Healing Effects of Social Connection and Community." Office of the U.S. Surgeon General, 2023. https://tinyurl.com/46j626r3.

Packard, Josh, et al. *Belonging: Reconnecting America's Loneliest Generation*. Bloomington, MN: Springtide Research Institute, 2020.

———. *Meaning-Making: 8 Values That Drive America's Newest Generations*. Bloomington, MN: Springtide Research Institute, 2020.

Palalas, Agnieszka, et al. "Mindfulness Practices in Online Learning: Supporting Learner Self-Regulation." *Journal of Contemplative Inquiry* 7, no. 1 (2020): 247–78.

Palmer, Parker, and Arthur Zajonc, eds. *The Heart of Higher Education: Transforming the Academy Through Collegial Conversations*. San Francisco: Jossey-Bass, 2010.

Pang, Alex Soojung-Kim. *Rest: Why You Get More Done When You Work Less*. New York: Basic Books, 2018.

Papadatou, Aphrodite. "Phone Fear Affects over Half of UK Office Workers." *HR Review*, May 17, 2019. https://tinyurl.com/4cd4wd9t.

Pariser, Eli. *The Filter Bubble: How the New Personalized Web Is Changing What We Read and How We Think*. New York: Penguin Books, 2011.

Paul VI. *Apostolic Actuositatem*. Vatican, 1965. https://tinyurl.com/3unmhpfx.

———. *Gaudium et Spes*. Vatican, 1965. https://tinyurl.com/yeyvvycn.

Pérez, Pauline, et al. "Conscious Processing of Narrative Stimuli Synchronizes Heart Rate Between Individuals." *Cell Reports* 36, no. 11 (2021). https://doi.org/10.1016/j.celrep.2021.109692.

Philibert, Paul. "Roman Catholic Prayer: The *Novum modi orandi sancti Dominici*." In *Contemplative Literature: A Comparative Sourcebook on Meditation and Contemplative Prayer*, edited by Louis Komjathy, 503–45. Albany: SUNY Press, 2015.

Pieper, Josef. *Leisure: The Basis of Culture*. Translated by Gerald Malsbary. South Bend, IN: St. Augustine's Press, 1998.

Pink, Daniel H. *When: The Scientific Secrets of Perfect Timing*. New York: Riverhead Books, 2018.

Ponticus, Evagrius. *Praktikos and Chapters on Prayer*. Translated by John Eudes Bamberger. Kalamazoo, MI: Cistercian Publications, 1981.

Putnam, Robert D. *Bowling Alone: The Collapse and Revival of American Community*. New York: Simon & Schuster, 2000.

Radcliffe, Timothy. *Listening Together: Meditations on Synodality*. Collegeville, MN: Liturgical Press, 2024.

Rocha, Tomas. "The Dark Knight of the Soul." *Atlantic*, June 25, 2014. https://tinyurl.com/cjnaszaj.

Rohr, Richard. *Dancing Standing Still: Healing the World from a Place of Prayer*. Mahwah, NJ: Paulist, 2014.

———. *The Universal Christ: How a Forgotten Reality Can Change Everything We See, Hope for, and Believe*. New York: Convergent Books, 2019.

Rolheiser, Ronald. *Domestic Monastery: Creating Spiritual Life at Home*. Brewster, MA: Paraclete, 2022.

Root-Bernstein, Robert, Maurine Bernstein, and Helen Garnier. "Correlations Between Avocations, Scientific Style, Work Habits, and Professional Impact of Scientists." *Creativity Research Journal* 8, no. 2 (1995): 115–37.

Rowe, Mary Budd. "Wait Time: Slowing Down May Be a Way of Speeding Up!" *Journal of Teacher Education* 37, no. 1 (1986): 43–50.

Rudd, Melanie, Kathleen D. Vohs, and Jennifer Aaker. "Awe Expands People's Perception of Time, Alters Decision Making, and Enhances Well-Being." *Psychological Science* 23, no. 10 (2012): 1130–36.

Schlarb, Angelika A., Anja Friedrich, and Merle Claßen. "Sleep Problems in University Students—an Intervention." *Neuropsychiatric Disease and Treatment* 13 (2017): 1989–2001. https://doi.org/10.2147/NDT.S142067.

Schmidt, Jennifer A., David J. Shernoff, and Mihaly Csikszentmihalyi. "Individual and Situational Factors Related to the Experience of Flow in Adolescence: A Multilevel Approach." In *Applications of Flow in Human Development and Education: The Collected Works of Mihaly Csikszentmihalyi*, 379–405. Dordrecht: Springer Netherlands, 2014.

Schwehn, Mark R. *Exiles from Eden: Religion and the Academic Vocation in America.* New York: Oxford University Press, 1993.

Scripp, Larry. "An Overview of Research on Music and Learning." In *Critical Links: Learning in the Arts and Student Academic and Social Development*, edited by Richard Deasy, 132–36. Washington, DC: Arts Education Partnership, 2002.

Sherrill, A. J. *Being with God: The Absurdity, Necessity, and Neurology of Contemplative Prayer.* Grand Rapids: Brazos, 2021.

Siegel, Daniel. *Brainstorm: The Power and Purpose of the Teenage Brain.* New York: Penguin Books, 2013.

Sievertsen, Hans Henrik, Francesca Gino, and Marco Piovesan. "Cognitive Fatigue Influences Students' Performance on Standardized Tests." *Proceedings of the National Academy of Sciences* 113, no. 10 (2016): 2621–24.

Silverman, Sarah, Kimberly Swan, Scott Ziolko, and Boróka Bó. "Time for Change: Findings from a Survey of Time Use in Schools." *Unlocking Time*, 2020. https://tinyurl.com/6s7s7726.

Skillen, John. *Making Schools Beautiful: Restoring the Harmony of Place.* Camp Hill, PA: Classical Academic Press, 2020.

Small, Gary, and Gigi Vorgan. *iBrain: Surviving the Technological Alteration of the Modern Mind.* New York: Collins, 2008.

Smith, James K. A. *Desiring the Kingdom: Worship, Worldview, and Cultural Formation.* Grand Rapids: Baker Academic, 2009.

———. *You Are What You Love: The Spiritual Power of Habit.* Grand Rapids: Brazos, 2016.

The State of Religion and Young People 2023: Exploring the Sacred. Springtide Research Institute. Winona, MN: Springtide Research Institute, 2023.

Stinissen, Wilfrid. *Eternity in the Midst of Time.* Translated by Sister Clare Marie. San Francisco: Ignatius, 2018.

Stucky, Nathan T. *Wrestling with Rest: Inviting Youth to Discover the Gift of Sabbath.* Grand Rapids: Eerdmans, 2019.

Sullivan, Andrew. "I Used to Be a Human Being." *New York*, September 19, 2016. https://tinyurl.com/4yp237c2.

Symeon the New Theologian. "The Three Methods of Prayer." In *The Philokalia: The Complete Text*, translated by G. E. H. Palmer, Philip Sherrard, and Kallistos Ware, 4:74–75. London: Faber & Faber, 1998.

Taylor, Charles. *A Secular Age*. Cambridge, MA: Belknap Press of Harvard University Press, 2007.

Teresa of Ávila. *The Interior Castle*. Translated by Mirabai Starr. New York: Riverhead Books, 2003.

Thayer, Paul B. "Retention of Students from First Generation and Low Income Backgrounds." *Opportunity Outlook*, May 2000, 2–8.

Thompson, Derek. "America's Fever of Workaholism Is Finally Breaking." *Atlantic*, January 31, 2023. https://tinyurl.com/yeyjr8f2.

Thralls, Chad. *Deep Calls to Deep: Mysticism, Scripture, and Contemplation*. Maryknoll, NY: Orbis Books, 2020.

Thrift, Nigel. *Knowing Capitalism*. London: Sage, 2005.

Thurman, Howard. *Disciplines of the Spirit*. San Francisco: Harper & Row, 1963.

Treleaven, David. *Trauma-Sensitive Mindfulness: Practices for Safe and Transformative Healing*. New York: Norton, 2018.

Twenge, Jean. *iGen: Why Today's Super-Connected Kids Are Growing Up Less Rebellious, More Tolerant, Less Happy—and Completely Unprepared for Adulthood*. New York: Atria Books, 2017.

Twenge, Jean M., Brian H. Spitzberg, and W. Keith Campbell. "Less In-Person Social Interaction with Peers among US Adolescents in the 21st Century and Links to Loneliness." *Journal of Social and Personal Relationships* 36, no. 6 (2019): 1892–1913.

Vickhoff, Björn, et al. "Music Structure Determines Heart Rate Variability of Singers." *Frontiers in Psychology* 4 (2013): 334.

Vitale, Kenneth C., Roberts Owens, Susan R. Hopkins, and Atul Malhotra. "Sleep Hygiene for Optimizing Recovery in Athletes: Review and Recommendations." *International Journal of Sports Medicine* 40, no. 8 (2019): 535–43.

Waldinger, Robert, and Marc Schulz. *The Good Life: Lessons from the World's Longest Scientific Study of Happiness*. New York: Simon & Schuster, 2023.

Walton, Gregory M., and Geoffrey L. Cohen. "A Brief Social-Belonging Intervention Improves Academic and Health Outcomes of Minority Students." *Science* 331, no. 6023 (2011): 1447–51.

Watson, Andrew. "The Best Length of Time for a Class." Learning & the Brain, October 7, 2018. https://tinyurl.com/3atwntnf.

Weber, Max. *The Protestant Ethic and the "Spirit" of Capitalism and Other Writings*. New York: Penguin Books, 2002.

Weil, Simone. "Reflections on the Right Use of School Studies with a View to the Love of God." In *Waiting on God*. New York: Fontana Books, 1959.

"What the VU Block Model Means for the Future of Education." Victoria University. Accessed October 30, 2024. https://tinyurl.com/5b4w7bkc.

Whitehead, Alfred North. *The Aims of Education and Other Essays*. New York: Free Press, 1967.

Whitfield, Joshua. "The Spiritual Place and Moment of Listening." *Church Life Journal*, June 27, 2023. https://tinyurl.com/3ajerav9.

Whitman, Glenn, and Ian Kelleher. *Neuroteach: Brain Science and the Future of Education*. Lanham, MD: Rowman & Littlefield, 2016.

Whitt, J. D. "Teaching Attentiveness in the Classroom and Learning to Attend to Persons with Disabilities." *International Journal of Christianity and Education* 19, no. 3 (2015): 215–28. https://doi.org/10.1177/2056997115588869.

Williams, Rowan. *Being Christian: Baptism, Bible, Eucharist, Prayer*. Grand Rapids: Eerdmans, 2014.

———. *Being Human: Bodies, Minds, Persons*. Grand Rapids: Eerdmans, 2018.

———. *A Century of Poetry: 100 Poems for Searching the Heart*. London: SPCK, 2022.

Winterbottom, Mark, and Arnold Wilkins. "Lighting and Discomfort in the Classroom." *Journal of Environmental Psychology* 29, no. 1 (2009): 63–75.

Worthen, Molly. "Why Universities Should Be More like Monasteries." *New York Times*, May 25, 2023. https://tinyurl.com/59yjht48.

Zacher, Hannes, Holly A. Brailsford, and Stacey L. Parker. "Micro-Breaks Matter: A Diary Study on the Effects of Energy Management Strategies on Occupational Well-Being." *Journal of Vocational Behavior* 85, no. 3 (2014): 287–97.

Zirschy, Andrew. *Beyond the Screen: Youth Ministry for the Connected but Alone Generation*. Nashville: Abingdon, 2015.

Index

«Casi todos los días oro que el Señor cree en mí mayor hambre por su Palabra y sus caminos. Aunque, para que eso ocurra, mis apetitos deben reorientarse. En *Ayuda para el alma hambrienta*, Kristen Wetherell revela nuestros profundos retorcijones de hambre al señalarnos la única fuente verdadera de satisfacción. Por lo tanto, toma este libro y podrás probar y ver que el Señor es bueno».

COURTNEY DOCTOR, Directora de Womens's Initiatives (Iniciativas Femeninas), Coalición por el evangelio; Profesora de Biblia; autora de *From Garden to Glory* (Del jardín a la gloria) y *In View of God's Mercies* (Viendo las misericordias de Dios)

«En *Ayuda para el alma hambrienta*, Kristen Wetherell ha encontrado una manera de defender el hábito de la lectura de la Biblia sin caer en los frecuentes efectos secundarios de la culpa o el legalismo. Nos invita a adentrarnos más profundamente en la preciosa Palabra de Dios y, al mismo tiempo, nos libera de la "hora silenciosa" obligatoria. Este libro es un estímulo lleno de esperanza para aquellos que anhelan más de Dios y que, sin embargo, constantemente se sienten incapaces de encontrar el tiempo o la energía para seguir adelante en busca de él».

KELLY NEEDHAM, Esposa; madre de cinco hijos; autora de *Friendish* (Amigable) y *Purposefooled* (Engañada en mi propósito)

«Este libro es más que una buena lectura. Es un agente transformador de vida que aumentará tu hambre por la Palabra de Dios. Las historias personales y honestas de personas reales te permitirán identificarte con sus luchas por crecer en su Palabra. Las ideas perceptivas de Kristen Wetherell aumentan mi compromiso de orar que cada uno de mis veintiún nietos se enamoren de la Palabra de Dios (Salmo 119:105)».

SUSAN ALEXANDER YATES, Oradora; bloguera, SusanAlexanderYates.com; autora de *Risky faith* (Fe arriesgada) y *One Devotional* (Un devocional)

«“Recoge la porción para cada día”. Esta es una verdad que me encanta repetir por la mañana cuando abro la Biblia y pido la ayuda de Dios. Es un recordatorio de que no tengo que hacer demasiado en el devocional matutino y que solo necesito asegurarme de hacer lo más importante. También es una imagen de la alimentación: una imagen del hambre, la comida y la satisfacción. De las muchas y buenas formas en las que podemos abordar la lectura, el estudio y la meditación de la Palabra de Dios, la figura de la alimentación es tan importante —y tan útil— como cualquier otra. Por eso me encanta la visión de este libro: hacer que crezca el apetito de tu alma por Dios a través de su Palabra. Kristen Wetherell es una guía hábil y confiable. Así que comienza, lee hasta que sientas mayor hambre y aliméntate de nuevo, del único que en verdad satisface».

DAVID MATHIS, Profesor titular y Editor ejecutivo de desiringGod.org; Pastor de Cities Church, Saint Paul, en Minnesota; autor de *Hábitos de Gracia*